The Politics of Violence in Latin America

Latin American and Caribbean Series
Hendrik Kraay, General Editor
ISSN 1498-2366 (Print), ISSN 1925-9638 (Online)

This series sheds light on historical and cultural topics in Latin America and the Caribbean by publishing works that challenge the canon in history, literature, and postcolonial studies. It seeks to print cutting-edge studies and research that redefine our understanding of historical and current issues in Latin America and the Caribbean.

No. 1 · **Waking the Dictator: Veracruz, the Struggle for Federalism and the Mexican Revolution** Karl B. Koth

No. 2 · **The Spirit of Hidalgo: The Mexican Revolution in Coahuila** Suzanne B. Pasztor · Copublished with Michigan State University Press

No. 3 · **Clerical Ideology in a Revolutionary Age: The Guadalajara Church and the Idea of the Mexican Nation, 1788–1853** Brian F. Connaughton, translated by Mark Allan Healey · Copublished with University Press of Colorado

No. 4 · **Monuments of Progress: Modernization and Public Health in Mexico City, 1876–1910** Claudia Agostoni · Copublished with University Press of Colorado

No. 5 · **Madness in Buenos Aires: Patients, Psychiatrists and the Argentine State, 1880–1983** Jonathan Ablard · Copublished with Ohio University Press

No. 6 · **Patrons, Partisans, and Palace Intrigues: The Court Society of Colonial Mexico, 1702–1710** Christoph Rosenmüller

No. 7 · **From Many, One: Indians, Peasants, Borders, and Education in Callista Mexico, 1924–1935** Andrae Marak

No. 8 · **Violence in Argentine Literature and Film (1989–2005)** Edited by Carolina Rocha and Elizabeth Montes Garcés

No. 9 · **Latin American Cinemas: Local Views and Transnational Connections** Edited by Nayibe Bermúdez Barrios

No. 10 · **Creativity and Science in Contemporary Argentine Literature: Between Romanticism and Formalism** Joanna Page

No. 11 · **Textual Exposures: Photography in Twentieth Century Spanish American Narrative Fiction** Dan Russek

No. 12 · **Whose Man in Havana? Adventures from the Far Side of Diplomacy** John W. Graham

No. 13 · **Journalism in a Small Place: Making Caribbean News Relevant, Comprehensive, and Independent** Juliette Storr

No. 14 · **The Road to Armageddon: Paraguay versus the Triple Alliance, 1866–70** Thomas L. Whigham

No. 15 · **The Politics of Violence in Latin America** Edited by Pablo Policzer

 UNIVERSITY OF CALGARY
Press

The Politics of Violence in Latin America

EDITED BY **Pablo Policzer**

Latin American and
Caribbean Series
ISSN 1498-2366 (Print)
ISSN 1925-9638 (Online)

 **UNIVERSITY OF CALGARY**
FACULTY OF ARTS
Latin American Research Centre

© 2019 Pablo Policzer

University of Calgary Press
2500 University Drive NW
Calgary, Alberta
Canada T2N 1N4
press.ucalgary.ca

This book is available as an ebook which is licensed under a Creative Commons license. The publisher should be contacted for any commercial use which falls outside the terms of that license.

LIBRARY AND ARCHIVES CANADA CATALOGUING IN PUBLICATION

Title: The politics of violence in Latin America / edited by Pablo Policzer.
Names: Policzer, Pablo, editor.
Series: Latin American and Caribbean series ; no. 15.
Description: Series statement: Latin American and Caribbean series, 1498-2366 ; no. 15 | Includes bibliographical references and index.
Identifiers: Canadiana (print) 20190053372 | Canadiana (ebook) 20190053402 | ISBN 9781552389065 (softcover) | ISBN 9781552389072 (Open Access PDF) | ISBN 9781552389089 (PDF) | ISBN 9781552389096 (EPUB) | ISBN 9781552389102 (Kindle)
Subjects: LCSH: Violence—Political aspects—Latin America.
Classification: LCC HN110.5.Z9 V5 2019 | DDC 303.6/098—dc23

The University of Calgary Press acknowledges the support of the Government of Alberta through the Alberta Media Fund for our publications. We acknowledge the financial support of the Government of Canada. We acknowledge the financial support of the Canada Council for the Arts for our publishing program.

   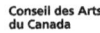

Copyediting by Ryan Perks
Cover image: Colourbox 1940330 and 15737146
Cover design, page design, and typesetting by Melina Cusano

CONTENTS

Preface and Acknowledgments	VII
Introduction: Structural vs. Contingent Violence in Latin America	1
Pablo Policzer	

PART I

1	Making Sense of Haiti's State Fragility and Violence: Combining Structure and Contingency?	19
	Andreas E. Feldmann	
2	Operation Condor as an International System of State Violence and Terror: A Historical-Structural Analysis	53
	J. Patrice McSherry	

PART II

3	Written in Black and Red: Murder as a Communicative Act in Mexico	89
	Pablo Piccato	
4	Protest and Police "Excesses" in Chile: The Limits of Social Accountability	113
	Michelle D. Bonner	

5   The Police Ombudsman in Brazil as a Potential   143
    Mechanism to Reduce Violence
       Anthony W. Pereira

6   Democracy, Threat, and Repression: Kidnapping and   171
    Repressive Dynamics during the Colombian Conflict
       Francisco Gutiérrez Sanín

7   To End the War in Colombia: *Conversatorios* among   199
    Security Forces, Ex-Guerrillas, and Political Elites,
    and Ceasefire Seminars-Workshops for the Technical
    Sub-Commission
       Jennifer Schirmer

Contributors   245
Index   249

PREFACE AND ACKNOWLEDGMENTS

The idea for this book emerged from a series of discussions and meetings at the University of Calgary and the Banff Centre in 2008 and 2009. In retrospect, although we didn't know it at the time, this was a period of transition in the way we think about the problem of violence. In the 1990s, ethnic conflict and other forms of violence emerged in many parts of the world, criminal violence related to the drug trade became a serious problem in parts of Latin America, and the seemingly intractable civil war in Colombia grew even more deadly, despite efforts to bring it to an end. While authoritarian rule and later the transition to democracy had preoccupied a previous generation of analysts in Latin America, by the 1990s the focus had begun to shift to the problem of violence and insecurity. The region might have become more democratic than in the recent past, but fear and insecurity related to complex combinations of armed conflict and criminal violence persisted. In addition, the news from places throughout Africa, the Middle East, the Caucasus, the Balkans, and elsewhere contributed to the impression that even though the Cold War had ended, new forms of violent conflict were making the world a more insecure place.

That view began to change by the turn of the millennium. New datasets were beginning to show that, contrary to our popular impressions, all forms of violence—from interstate war to genocide and crime—were in fact declining around the world. I first encountered this research as a postdoctoral fellow at the University of British Columbia, where the Human Security Centre was located at the time. The Centre's *Human Security Report 2005* broke new ground by showing that, notwithstanding the headlines of the 1990s, major wars and other forms of armed conflict had in fact *declined* dramatically. This argument made an impact in mostly academic circles until the publication of Steven Pinker's *The Better Angels of our Nature* in 2011. Pinker's book, which drew on much of the same new evidence contained in the *Human Security Report*, was widely read, and it has substantially changed how we understand and discuss the problem of violence. The common notion that the world is becoming more violent is simply no longer a given.

The discussions at the University of Calgary and the Banff Centre, which included the authors featured in this book as well as other colleagues, aimed to question assumptions around what might be structurally given in different patterns of violence in Latin America. True, rates of criminal violence, especially, have skyrocketed throughout the region, giving it the dubious honor of being the most violent place on the planet. But by contrast to others who sought to make sense of the emergence of violence or of societies driven by fear, we believed it was time to assess the debate over the politics of violence. Violence has not always been a feature of Latin American societies, nor is it evenly distributed. Without underestimating the seriousness of the problem, we shared the conviction that it was important not only to take a broad view on the question of violence, but also to assess it from different angles.

It has been a pleasure and an honor to work with the wonderful and diverse group of authors in this book. They responded to all stages of this project—from the initial invitations to the final edits—with enthusiasm, grace, and generosity. In bringing together this group of academics and practitioners, we benefitted from the generous help and support of a number of people and institutions. The United States Institute of Peace provided funding for a meeting, as did the Latin American Research Centre, the Institute for United States Policy Research, and the Centre for Military and Strategic Studies at the University of Calgary, where Christon Archer and Stephen Randall, especially, encouraged this project from the beginning and provided excellent guidance and support.

Many other people also provided helpful feedback at different stages of the project. I am especially grateful to Hendrik Kraay, the late Ginny Bouvier, Jorge Zaverucha, Jean Daudelin, Graham Denyer Willis, Alex McDougall, Jillian Dowding, Rob Muggah, Raul Molina, Robert Holden, Eric Hershberg, Susan Franceschet, Hal Klepak, Donna Livingstone, Ram Manikkalingam, and Lucía Dammert. To bring this project to a conclusion I benefited from the excellent help and support provided by Monique

Greenwood at the Latin American Research Centre. I'm also grateful to Brian Scrivener at the University of Calgary Press for his enthusiastic encouragement, to Ryan Perks for his sharp copyediting, and to the anonymous reviewers whose feedback helped strengthen the final result.

My deepest debts are personal, to Lara Olson and our three children: André, Nico, and Hanna. A project like this inevitably takes a toll at home, and I'm grateful to have such a loving and supportive family. Lara, in particular, is my sharpest academic critic and my most stubborn and determined supporter. No one could wish for a better partner.

Pablo Policzer
Calgary
November 2018

Introduction:

Structural vs. Contingent Violence in Latin America

Pablo Policzer

Latin America is the most violent region on the planet.[1] The continent has suffered waves of repressive authoritarian rule, organized armed insurgency and civil war, violent protest, and, especially in recent decades, very high rates of criminal violence. Born of the clash between Europe and the New World, violence has been a staple of Latin American history, culture, and politics since the colonial period. It is a recurring theme from Bartolomé de las Casas's *Apologetic History of the Indies* to Fernando Meirelles and Kátia Lund's *City of God*. In recent decades, scholars, policymakers, and advocacy groups have also paid attention to the pervasive problems of violence in the region.[2] Indeed, many analysts who previously ignored violence as a problem—focusing instead on issues such as the collapse of democracy or the transition from authoritarianism to democracy[3]—have turned their attention to the fact that when states are unable to provide basic law and order, democracy suffers as violence becomes endemic.[4]

The problem is real and this attention is welcome, but the time is ripe for a critical assessment of the debate over how to understand the causes of violence in the region, and by extension, the policies by which the problem may be addressed. Is Latin America doomed to violence? The question is deliberately posed somewhat informally, to draw attention to an assumption that bears scrutiny. With few exceptions, scholars and others have approached the problem of violence in Latin America from various types of (sometimes pessimistic) structural perspectives. Whether understood as "enduring social arrangements [that] people take for granted and allow to shape their actions,"[5] or as the "past social relations [that] constrain present social relations,"[6] or as "the basic institutions, arrangements and imaginative preconceptions that circumscribe our routine practical or discursive activities and conflicts,"[7] structural perspectives emphasize the *given*, inherited constraints on social and political life.

In Latin America, violence has been attributed to such diverse factors as Spanish colonialism or American neo-imperialism;[8] socioeconomic inequality and class conflict;[9] entrenched partisan or cultural divisions;[10] illiberal constitutions that give too much power to the region's armed forces to use extraordinary force to suppress dissent;[11] difficult geography;[12] or the region's structurally weak states,[13] which results in what some have called "low-intensity citizenship," whereby states are unable to enforce the rule of law, and citizens lack the tools to make states accountable.[14] Indeed, a number of scholars have expressed deep pessimism regarding the potential for democracy in the region, given its structurally embedded relations of violence. Arias and Goldstein, for example, argue that democracy is less likely in Latin America than "violent pluralism." From this perspective,

> violence [is] critical to the foundation of Latin American democracies, the maintenance of democratic states, and the political behavior of democratic citizens. In contemporary Latin American society violence emerges as much more than a social aberration: violence is a mechanism for keeping in place the very institutions and policies that neoliberal democracies have fashioned over the past several decades, as well as an instrument for coping with the myriad problems that neoliberal democracies have generated.[15]

In a previous work, Goldstein also argues that the existence of mobilized civil-society groups, "rather than serving to promote democratic institutions and values and advance the cause of civil and human rights, instead operates to constrain to limit those rights" and to justify greater state repression.[16] Arias in turn points out that "violence in Rio stems from a particular articulation of state, social and criminal relations which actively deploy state power in the service of criminal interests."[17]

There are important differences among the perspectives highlighted above. Those who focus on institutional failures, for example, argue that violence is rooted in the weak and ineffective states that plague the region, and the consequent absence of the rule of law. Others focus on the way in which powerful interests, especially those rooted in fundamental economic relationships, have used state power to perpetuate domination through violent means. These views echo those of classic thinkers, especially Weber and Marx, and emphasize a wide range of different factors. Nevertheless, they are grounded in a similar set of assumptions—that there is a given, and relatively limited, set of possible or imaginable orders to choose from.

The institutional perspective is grounded in a tradition that certainly encompasses Weber, and dates back to Hobbes's view that life outside a well-ordered state with a clear monopoly on coercion is dangerous (or "nasty, brutish, and short"). With this diagnosis, the solution to the problem of violence is straightforward—namely to reinforce the state, and to guarantee basic rights, liberties, and the rule of law. In other words, an institutional problem requires an institutional solution: something resembling the liberal-democratic state, ideally with a clear monopoly on coercive force. The interest perspective, on the other hand, is grounded in the Marxian idea that powerful economic interests determine fundamental political relationships. They are the basis upon which the structure of politics is built, and which in turn perpetuate the policy failures that result in entrenched patterns of violence. While it points to a different set of factors than the institutional perspective, the interest perspective assumes a similarly narrow and fixed set of given possibilities. Insofar as structures are patterns of social relationships that shape behavior over time,[18] both of these are structural perspectives, even while pointing to different sorts of factors, whether institutions or interests.

Without denying the validity of structural perspectives and explanations in some cases, there are reasons to be skeptical of structural accounts in all cases. For example, much of the current concern with the outbreak of criminal violence in parts of the region stems from the consequences of the drug trade. This is no doubt a difficult problem posed by a complex phenomenon, but the drug trade has a distinct beginning, has evolved over time, and it is at least possible to imagine its end. Like the proliferation of violence associated with Prohibition in the United States, today's "narco violence" in parts of Latin America is also arguably rooted in a historically contingent set of social, economic, and political factors. Some observers have noted that the prohibition of narcotics itself creates the conditions for violence, and that legalization may be a "least bad" type of solution.[19] Without entering into a debate over the merits of legalization versus prohibition, it is worth noting that this is the opposite of a deeply embedded structural factor over which actors have little control.

Put differently, the problem with structural generalizations is not that there is no room for change. (Indeed, some of the best-known structural accounts—such as Marx's—encompass large-scale economic, social, and political change.) The problem—which is arguably why structural accounts are so often pessimistic—is that the possibilities for change are limited by a narrow set of imaginable alternatives. Although less deterministic than Marx, Weber also imagined a limited range of possible institutional arrangements that would serve to preserve political order. By contrast to these perspectives, we can point to the fact that many of the institutions and interests that we might think of as given, fixed, and limited, are in fact the product of a historically diverse and highly contingent set of circumstances: they are not given, or fixed, and they vary over time and space; they were created under particular circumstances, and can therefore be recreated under others.

By contrast to the standard social science distinction between structure and agency, or the capacity of individuals to exercise their free will, in this volume we suggest that contingency is the appropriate, and often overlooked, counterpoint to structure. Contingency certainly encompasses individual agency, but it emphasizes a different point in questioning the "givenness" or necessity of social structures. Instead of being the product of necessary historical processes or relationships, many structures are in fact rooted in more historically contingent arrangements and outcomes, often determined by individual agents. Such outcomes need not have happened, and might have turned out differently. Pointing out the historical, political, and legal contingency of what appear to be structural phenomena is often the first step toward overcoming them. The pessimism of necessity can be replaced with the optimism of possibility.[20]

Another reason to doubt the general applicability of structural accounts of violence in the region is simply that violence has not been a general or uniform phenomenon. Criminal violence has arisen in some places (with parts of Mexico and Central America, for example, the focus of much current concern), but it has decreased in other areas that were previously seriously afflicted. The experience of Colombian cities such as Bogotá and Medellín, where violence has decreased, draws our attention to an ultimately contingent set of political, social, and economic factors causing this drop. Something similar may also be observed in Brazil, where criminal violence is not evenly distributed. The crime rate in Rio de Janeiro is higher than in São Paulo, for example, even though both cities share many of the same underlying structural conditions outlined above.

A brief look at other cases beyond Latin America and other debates beyond the issue of violence also suggests reasons to be skeptical of generalizations based on structural accounts. In Sweden, for example, the often intensely violent struggles between unions and employers until the early part of the twentieth century were replaced by the now well-known Swedish model of a generous welfare state overseeing peaceful corporate bargaining and accommodation. Similar "transitions from mistrust to trust" have also been observed in other countries in Europe and elsewhere.[21] Other debates in political economy suggest that structural perspectives pertaining, for example, to the necessary presence of Fordist modes of mass production have been replaced by those emphasizing the contingency of the forms of economic organization and production.[22]

While some of the pessimism regarding the potential for democracy in Latin America today stems from the prevalence of violence, it is also worth remembering that in a previous generation it stemmed from a different set of seemingly given structural factors, such as those associated with culture. Latin America was thought to be a poor locale for democracy because Latin Americans were not culturally predisposed to the values of self-discipline, honesty, toleration, and respect that modern democracy required. During a time when democracy had an admittedly weak foothold in the region, such structural explanations (e.g., modernization theory) were widely accepted as valid. From today's perspective, and notwithstanding serious challenges to democracy that remain in the region,[23] the notion that Latin Americans are culturally not prepared for democracy is no longer valid. Authoritarian regimes have largely been replaced by democratic ones that, despite their shortcomings, dispel the notion that Latin American culture is structurally incompatible with democracy.[24] Recent alarm over the rise of antidemocratic elements in parts of the world where democracy was previously thought to be consolidated, such as Western Europe and the United States, puts to rest the notion of culture as a structural precondition for democracy.[25]

The shift from structural to contingent perspectives also entails an epistemological shift, from describing a relatively narrow range of fixed underlying structural factors to examining a broader range of mechanisms—understood as discrete processes or actions that causally link inputs and outcomes—that produce more contingent outcomes.[26]

Explanations of violence need to do more than simply assert the relationship between variables such as class conflict or neo-imperialism and violence: they need to examine the precise mechanisms by which such variables are related. The opposite of a mechanism where the role of each part is clear is a "black box," which ignores the precise connections among different factors.[27]

Another consequence of the shift from structural to contingent perspectives is political. As suggested above, structural perspectives can lead to pessimistic assessments of the prospects of democracy, to choose one example. By contrast, a focus on more contingent outcomes—such as the replacement of systems of violence and mistrust by systems of peace and trust—suggests reasons for optimism. Without underestimating the complex challenges faced by Latin Americans in building more peaceful societies, shining a light on the contingent, and not just the structural, opens up new possibilities and solutions. It is not necessary to change everything in order to change some things; and changing some things has clear—and potentially significant—consequences.

With this in mind, this book aims to critically assess of some of the principal accounts of violence in Latin America. Our aim is not an exhaustive account of all manifestations of all types of violence throughout the continent and across different historical periods. Indeed, we include neither the full range of possible case studies nor strict typologies. Instead, through a variety of distinct settings and disciplinary perspectives, we aim to compare and contrast the differences between structural and more contingent accounts of the patterns of violence in the region. We do not reject structural accounts, which are valid in some cases; we aim, rather, to introduce contingent accounts, which are also valid in different cases, and to shed light on the contingencies at the center of even some seemingly deeply embedded structures.

If structural accounts are valid anywhere, they should apply to the first cases we consider: the coordinated operations by authoritarian regimes in the Southern Cone, and the structural determinants of violence in Haiti, the poorest country in the region. In each case, however, we find that although the structures determining violence—whether coordinated authoritarian state repression in the Southern Cone, or widespread civil and political violence in Haiti—are deep, there is also a great deal more contingency and choice than we might at first assume. Even though the structures are real and powerful, they are not set in stone.

Andreas Feldmann's chapter shows that in Haiti we find many of the strongest structural causes of violence: frequent and widespread repression and corruption, a state incapable of maintaining the monopoly on coercion, deep poverty, and massive ecological damage. In recent years, these have been joined by further structural changes brought on by the difficult and incomplete transition to democracy and the entry of organized crime, along with the spread and increasingly easy availability of small arms and light weapons. If ever a place was structurally predisposed to violence of different types, it is Haiti. Feldmann notes that Haiti (along with Colombia) offers probably the strongest proof that violence is structurally embedded. Yet even here, in this critical case, Feldmann argues that "structural conditions do not in and of themselves seem able to provide a full, convincing account for the changes in the nature of violence experienced in Haiti over the last two decades." Once we open up the black box of the structural causes of violence, we find contingent conditions derived from the process of political and economic globalization. In particular, Haiti's difficult transition to democracy and the spread of organized crime and small arms are important—yet historically contingent—mechanisms that have shaped violence in recent years.

None of these factors is easy to change. The forces of globalization are powerful and weak countries like Haiti are more often than not in the position of having to respond to such forces instead of being able to control them. Yet we know from other countries and other examples that even powerful forces are not immutable. Poor countries with weak governments can develop, just as rich countries with strong governments can run aground. Haiti's problems are deep and seem intractable, yet Haiti is also a critical case. It is by far the poorest country in the region, with the weakest institutions. Without minimizing the significance of Haiti's problems, the structural determinants for violence in the rest of the region are less powerful than in Haiti. Various countries have made choices to undertake sometimes radical transformations. The problems of poverty, corruption, repression, crime, and the availability of weapons are experienced beyond Haiti, but the resources to combat these problems are greater in these countries as well.

The armed forces are also the focus of Patrice McSherry's chapter on Operation Condor. Like Feldmann, McSherry tackles a critical case for structural accounts of violence in Latin America: state repression under authoritarian rule in the Southern Cone countries. Building on her previous work on Operation Condor,[28] McSherry explores the structural and contingent factors that shaped this covert "black operations" collaboration between six Latin American countries and the United States. Authoritarian regimes and their operations during this period often appear as powerful monoliths, leading many to see them as confirmation of structural accounts of violence and repression, including as an expression of US hegemony in a strategically important region during the Cold War. In this chapter, like in her previous work on Operation Condor, McSherry provides evidence of the widespread patterns of collaboration that created and perpetuated Condor, making it a fearsome and powerful force. What at the time seemed intractable—authoritarian repression with the full support of a global superpower—nevertheless came to an end, and it rested on what turned out to be a much more contingent set of conditions. To be sure, US Cold War strategic-hegemonic interests and national-security doctrines throughout the region were powerful forces. Yet even these receded as different actors chose to disengage from Condor and authoritarian rule as a whole. In hindsight, what seemed deeply rooted and immovable was in fact based on a complex and powerful yet contingent set of forces. McSherry emphasizes the importance of choice in putting an end to violence and repression. Her chapter does not suggest that change is easy or that everything is contingent. Yet it does belie arguments about violence rooted in timeless and unchanging structures, and it highlights the fundamental importance of choice in changing even deeply rooted structures.

The second part of the book addresses a number of mechanisms that produce and reproduce violence, as well as those that can curb it. Mechanisms are different from structures, insofar as they emphasize the importance of actors over variables.[29] Actors' choices are not unlimited, and they often face very real constraints. But keeping the focus on actors and choices suggests the need to question assumptions based on variables and structures devoid of abstract agents. As the chapters in part I suggest, even deep structures rest on the contingency of choices made or not made. Part II does not provide an exhaustive account of all mechanisms that either perpetuate or curb violence in Latin America. Even if such an account were possible, our aim is more modest: to list some examples of different mechanisms and how they work.

Pablo Piccato's chapter sheds light on such a mechanism. Murder is not simply a crime. Piccato shows that it is also a "communicative act intended to be received and decoded by an audience." The communicative dimension of murder is critical to understanding not only the evolution of patterns of crime over time, but also the public concern about it: concern about crime has risen even though, somewhat surprisingly, crime has in fact decreased in Mexico. Piccato focuses on the development of the *nota roja* sections of Mexican newspapers, the crime stories that are relegated to the back sections of "serious" newspapers or to the more popular tabloid press altogether. These crime stories lend themselves to exquisitely graphic treatment and are widely read. They convey a sense of dramatic urgency even though over time the overall crime rates may have decreased rather than increased. Public concern over rising crime is often driven by the graphic and brutal messages communicated through the *nota roja* sections of the press, instead of the far less graphic and dramatic rise and fall of statistical trends. The press is an important mechanism both for the increase and decrease of violence. By magnifying and distorting the patterns of murder, the *nota roja* shape the public's opinion, and provide a venue for murderers themselves—such as drug traffickers and other criminals—to send messages to potential rivals as well as to the public at large.

Violence has a deliberate public meaning that is used to shape what type of crime is discussed and how, and it can force governments to take particular actions against crime. The *nota roja* display graphic images of crime scenes, reinforcing the message that it is the victim who is likely to be humiliated, and that there is little public respect for their fate. When charges are laid, the police news allows the criminals to tell their story, further robbing the victims of their perspective. Because the newspapers are the medium through which violence is communicated, criminal actors attempt to influence the way in which violence is depicted—including violence and coercion toward journalists—in order to shape the message being sent to the government, the public, and their criminal rivals. Once understood in this way, the element of choice is made clear: the press can but need not act this way. There are other possibilities.

Michelle Bonner's chapter also focuses on the media as a mechanism in the production and perpetuation of violence. Bonner examines the Chilean police's repression of student protests that took place in Chile on 30 May 2006, and how these events were covered by the national media. She focuses in particular on *El Mercurio*, the leading elite newspaper. By contrast to the claims about the media's potential as a mechanism of social accountability,[30] Bonner focuses on the limits of such potential. In Chile, *El Mercurio* framed the 2006 student protests as a law-and-order, rather than a human or civil rights, issue.

Although news coverage of the protests clearly ascribed the greatest responsibility for the excesses to the *Carabineros* (police), Bonner shows that there was very little social accountability following the protests. There was some horizontal accountability when President Bachelet condemned the police's actions and dismissed ten policemen and several officers. Due to legal restrictions against offending or harming the morale of state authorities, however, these criticisms cautiously focused on the excesses of individual members of the police and generally ignored institutional change or larger-scale accountability by the *Carabineros* or its senior leadership. In other words, Bonner argues that "high levels of police repression of social protest are not simply structurally determined; they are in part contingent on media coverage." The media's failure to perform its social-accountability role is an important, though contingent, mechanism in the perpetuation of state violence.

Anthony Pereira's chapter addresses a similar problem as Bonner's—police violence—but from the perspective of a different mechanism to curb it: Brazilian police ombudsmen. These institutions are relatively new, having been introduced in Brazil over the past couple of decades, and Pereira acknowledges that "more is unknown than known about the impact of ombudsmen on levels of police violence in Brazil." Nevertheless, ombudsmen are a potentially significant mechanism by which to curb violence. Pereira compares ombudsmen in São Paulo and Pernambuco and finds that the former has a much higher degree of capacity and autonomy—that is, they are able to gather information about police abuses without interference from the police itself and the secretary of public security. Although it is too early to tell whether and in what way the ombudsmen's offices can contribute to the reduction of violence in Brazil, Pereira's chapter highlights two key issues that run counter to what structural perspectives may suggest: first, that it is possible to create institutions with the potential to curb violence; and second, that societies have a choice about these institutions' design and operation. Social structures are not simply given or predetermined. Societies can choose to create them or not, and can determine how to operate them.

Francisco Gutiérrez Sanín's chapter examines the phenomenon of kidnapping in Colombia, long considered an especially invidious aspect of that country's civil war. The practice of kidnapping for ransom was adopted by the guerrillas, especially, but also by other actors. It was incorporated into the "repertoire of violence" in Colombia and it must be explained as such. Gutiérrez Sanín shows that kidnapping is neither a structural feature of violence, nor a response to a clear rational calculation. Especially puzzling is the fact that kidnapping emerged during a period of substantial democratic expansion. Threat theory, a key explanation of repression, holds that states respond proportionally to the threats they face. Yet Gutiérrez Sanín argues that in Colombia the state responded in a more muted manner than is often thought. Violence in Colombia has undoubtedly been widespread, and often intensely brutal. But as Gutiérrez Sanín shows, the state's formal institutional response to kidnapping was weak. Instead, the state responded through the informal and illegal mechanism of paramilitary violence. In this sense, by limiting the possibilities of a more intensive institutional response, democratic checks and balances contributed to the expansion of an illegal—and deadlier—form of repression. Gutiérrez Sanín traces the evolution of kidnapping alongside the development of democratic institutions in Colombia, and he documents the failed efforts by political elites to respond through democratic channels and the successful efforts by other elites to resort to illegal back channels instead.

In this sense, Gutiérrez Sanín's chapter accounts for an important element in the repertoire of violence by explaining the mechanisms that introduced it, shaped it, and helped it grow. Kidnapping in Colombia emerged from a complex and surprising interaction of structural and more contingent elements. Understanding these mechanisms, including the ways in which democratic institutions may have created unintended incentives that contributed to the expansion of violence, is a key step toward replacing the pessimism of necessity with the optimism of possibility. Gutiérrez Sanín focuses on the emergence of kidnapping in the decades before the recent peace process and subsequent accords. Since that time, rates of kidnapping in Colombia—along with other types of violence—have decreased.[31] While this is good news, Gutiérrez Sanín reminds us that if violence is not necessarily structural, neither is peace. Formal institutions and structures can have complex and surprising unintended consequences.

Finally, Jennifer Schirmer's chapter offers a firsthand account of a very concrete mechanism for the reduction of violence—directly engaging armed actors to persuade them to abandon violence for peace. Schirmer, a trained anthropologist, draws on her extensive experience and insight as a practitioner—indeed a participant—in peace dialogue efforts. A common view holds that "spoilers" cannot be changed, or at best can only be "bought off." The premise is that such actors are destined to remain intransigent, impeding progress toward peace and the consolidation of democratic institutions. Peacebuilding and democracy-promotion efforts often attempt to marginalize these actors by engaging and working with moderates to strengthen alternative networks and institutions. Schirmer challenges this view, suggesting that if peace processes marginalize armed actors, they may create a self-fulfilling prophecy that confirms armed actors' reasons for taking up arms in the first place.

Instead of ignoring or deliberately marginalizing armed actors, the *Conversatorios* (or dialogues) Schirmer describes directly engage them. Instead of assuming that structural forces doom some sectors of society to violence, *Conversatorios* are premised on the idea that actors can be understood and can change. The *Conversatorios* were a Norwegian government initiative in Colombia in which Schirmer herself participated. Her chapter provides an in-depth account based on her own experience in bringing together military officers, especially, with civilians and former guerrillas. Begun during the height of the armed conflict in the early 2000's and held off the record, the *Conversatorios* have engaged scores of officers in different dialogues. In this broad and peaceful exchange of views, actors come to understand and also challenge each other's views regarding violence. Schirmer shows that while the *Conversatorios* do not aim to produce a specific outcome, certain "ripple effects" led to more participants being willing to discuss increasingly difficult subjects with "those they originally believed to be fundamentally antagonistic to their own and their institution's interests." In this sense, even though not formally connected, the *Conversatorios* were direct precursors to the more formal peace negotiations between the Colombian government and the FARC, which culminated in the 2016 peace accord.

There are certainly limitations to the *Conversatorios*. If individual attitudes toward peace can change, they can also change back toward violence. And violence, moreover, is sometimes not simply the sum of individuals' preferences, but a more complex phenomenon that can occur in spite of what the sum of individuals in society might think. Yet the *Conversatorios* remind us that structural forces are not set in stone, and that in some cases individuals can bridge vast cognitive gaps to recognize and understand views radically opposed to their own. This kind of cognitive bridge-building is an example of agency at its deepest, reflecting individuals' capacity to transcend their frames of mind to reflect on their own experiences, values, and actions. We do not have to reject the importance of structural forces in general to recognize the significance of mechanisms like engagement and dialogue when it comes to breaking patterns of violence.

This book is not a handbook for how to reduce violence in Latin America, or anywhere else for that matter. Even if such a handbook were possible, it is beyond the scope of our task here. Instead, our aim is more modest: to question some of the structural assumptions embedded in a number of debates over the problem of violence in the region. Our perspective is less pessimistic than accounts that assume violence is structurally embedded in Latin American society. Violence is a complex and serious problem, but it is a contingent phenomenon, which depends on particular sets of mechanisms to emerge and develop. Latin America is not doomed. Our hope is that understanding these contingencies can be a first step toward changing the circumstances that created them.

NOTES

1   The Igarapé Institute notes that while Latin America has 8 percent of the world's population, it experiences 33 percent of the world's homicides, far more than any other region. See Robert Muggah and Katherine Aguirre Tobón, "Citizen Security in Latin America: Facts and Figures," *Igarapé Institute Strategic Paper 33* (April 2018), https://igarape.org.br/wp-content/uploads/2018/04/Citizen-Security-in-Latin-America-Facts-and-Figures.pdf; see also https://homicide.igarape.org.br/ (both accessed 15 November 2018).

2   E.g., Kees Koonings and Dirk Kruijt, *Societies of Fear: The Legacy of Civil War, Violence and Terror in Latin America* (London: Zed Books, 1999), and *Armed Actors: Organized Violence and State Failure in Latin America* (London: Zed Books, 2004); Juan Méndez, Guillermo O'Donnell, and Paulo Sergio Pinheiro, eds., *The (Un)Rule of Law and the Underprivileged in Latin America* (Notre Dame, IN: University of Notre Dame Press, 1999); Diane Davis and Anthony Pereira, *Irregular Armed Forces and their Role in Politics and State Formation* (New York: Cambridge University Press, 2003); Enrique Desmond Arias, *Drugs and Democracy in Rio de Janeiro: Trafficking, Social Networks, and Public Security* (Chapel Hill: University of North Carolina Press, 2006); Enrique Desmond Arias and Daniel Goldstein, *Violent Democracies in Latin America* (Durham, NC: Duke University Press, 2010); Lucia Dammert, *Fear and Crime in Latin America* (New York: Routledge, 2012); Graham Denyer Willis, *The Killing Consensus: Police, Organized Crime, and the Regulation of Life and Death in Urban Brazil* (Berkeley: University of California Press, 2014).

3   E.g., Guillermo O'Donnell and Philippe Schmitter, *Transitions from Authoritarian Rule: Tentative Conclusions about Uncertain Democracies* (Baltimore, MD: Johns Hopkins University Press, 1986).

4   E.g., Guillermo O'Donnell, "On the State, Democratization, and Some Conceptual Problems: A Latin American View with Some Glances at Postcommunist Countries,"

World Development 21, no. 8 (1993): 1355–69; Méndez, O'Donnell, and Pinheiro, *The (Un)Rule of Law.*

5   Anthony Giddens cited in Charles Tilly, *Explaining Social Processes* (Boulder, CO: Paradigm Publishers, 2008), 166.

6   Tilly, *Explaining*, 167.

7   Roberto Mangabeira Unger, *Social Theory: Its Situation and its Task* (New York: Cambridge University Press, 1987).

8   Eduardo Galeano, *Open Veins of Latin America: Five Centuries of the Pillage of a Continent* (New York: Monthly Review Press 1997).

9   Arias and Goldstein, *Violent Democracies.*

10 Mary Roldán, *Blood and Fire: La Violencia in Antioquia, Colombia, 1946–1953* (Durham, NC: Duke University Press, 2002).

11 Brian Loveman, *The Constitution of Tyranny: Regimes of Exception in Spanish America* (Pittsburgh: University of Pittsburgh Press, 1993); Brian Loveman and Thomas M. Davies, *The Politics of Antipolitics* (Wilmington, DE: Scholarly Resources, 1997).

12 Frank Safford and Marco Palacios, *Colombia: Fragmented Land, Divided Society* (New York: Oxford University Press, 2002)

13 Miguel Angel Centeno, *Blood and Debt: War and the Nation-State in Latin America* (University Park: Pennsylvania State University Press, 2002).

14 O'Donnell, "The State, Democratization, and Some Conceptual Problems"; Méndez, O'Donnell, and Pinheiro, *The (Un)Rule of Law.*

15 Arias and Goldstein, *Violent Democracies*, 5.

16 Daniel M. Goldstein, Gloria Achá, Eric Hinojosa, and Theo Roncken, "La Mano Dura and the Violence of Civil Society in Bolivia," in *Indigenous Peoples, Civil Society and the Neo-Liberal State in Latin America*, ed. Edward F. Fischer (New York: Berghahn Books, 2009), 49.

17 Arias, *Drugs and Democracy.*

18 E.g., Anthony Giddens, *Central Problems in Social Theory: Action, Structure and Contradiction in Social Analysis* (Berkeley: University of California Press, 1979), 59–65.

19 "How to stop the drug wars," *Economist*, 5 March 2009.

20 This distinction comes especially from Unger Mangabeira, *Social Theory.*

21 Bo Rothstein, *Social Traps and the Problem of Trust* (Cambridge: Cambridge University Press, 2005).

22 E.g., Michael J. Piore and Charles F. Sabel, *The Second Industrial Divide* (New York: Basic Books, 1984).

23 Maxwell A. Cameron, "Citizenship Deficits in Latin American Democracies," *Convergencia* 14, no. 45 (2007): 11–30.

24 Peter H. Smith, *Democracy in Latin America: Political Change in Comparative Perspective* (New York: Oxford University Press, 2005).

25 E.g., Yasha Mounk, *The People vs. Democracy: Why Our Freedom Is in Danger and How to Save It* (Cambridge, MA: Harvard University Press, 2018); Steven Levitsky and Daniel Ziblatt, *How Democracies Die* (New York: Penguin Random House, 2018).

26 Peter Hedström and Richard Swedberg, *Social Mechanisms: An Analytical Approach to Social Theory* (Cambridge: Cambridge University Press, 1998); Jon Elster, *Explaining Social Behavior: More Nuts and Bolts for the Social Sciences* (New York: Cambridge University Press, 2007).

27 Elster, *Explaining Social Behavior*.

28 Patrice McSherry, *Predatory States: Operation Condor and Covert War in Latin America* (Lanham, MD: Rowman and Littlefield, 2005).

29 Hedström and Swedberg, *Social Mechanisms*.

30 Catalina Smulovitz and Enrique Peruzzotti, "Societal Accountability in Latin America," *Journal of Democracy* 11, no. 4 (2000): 147–58; Catalina Smulovitz and Enrique Peruzzotti, *Enforcing the Rule of Law: Social Accountability in the New Latin American Democracies* (Pittsburgh: University of Pittsburgh Press, 2006).

31 Robert Muggah and Katherine Aguirre, "How Violence is Changing in Post-FARC Colombia," *Americas Quarterly*, 14 August 2017, https://www.americasquarterly.org/content/how-violence-changing-post-farc-colombia (accessed 15 November 2018).

PART I

Making Sense of Haiti's State Fragility and Violence: Combining Structure and Contingency?

Andreas E. Feldmann

On 12 January 2010 an earthquake measuring 7.0 on the Richter scale devastated Haiti, killing 158,000 people and displacing 1.3 million more.[1] The Haitian state was dealt a terrible blow as a significant number of state officers either died or were seriously injured; additionally, most of its infrastructural power (telecommunications, buildings, roads, bridges) was destroyed. The earthquake's devastating effects prompted fears, among Haitians and foreigners alike, that a massive wave of violence would descend over Haiti as criminals—urban gangs and escaped prisoners—took advantage of the anarchy. Yet the feared upsurge in violence did not materialize. Homicides, kidnappings, and crimes against property did not increase after the earthquake; only sexual violence saw a major rise, particularly in and around displaced persons camps.[2] In a rather perplexing development, the public's overall perception of security actually improved after the earthquake.[3]

As this phenomenon shows, the nature and characteristics of violence in Haiti remain puzzling. Despite rampant poverty, a history of acute political upheaval, ecological damage, and extensive organized crime activity, Haiti displays relatively moderate crime rates when compared to other Latin American and Caribbean countries.[4]

This chapter seeks to help decipher this puzzle by investigating the root causes of violence in Haiti, particularly since the end of the Cold War. In Haiti, different forms of violence coexist and reinforce each other. There is widespread state-orchestrated violence, notwithstanding the limited coercive capacity of the Haitian state.[5] Beyond that, a wide array of actors, including agents with loose ties to the state and various nonstate actors, also engage in acts of violence.[6] Homicides, gender violence, harsh prison conditions, and violent turf battles between criminal organizations are common.[7] In recent years, kidnapping has become a major problem.[8] Violence reigns unabated in Haiti because perpetrators enjoy virtually total impunity.[9]

Most of the studies in this volume lean toward arguing that the violence plaguing many Latin American states can be attributed to contingent rather than structural factors. The corollary to this proposition is that the region is not necessarily doomed—that violence can recede, be tamed, or even surmounted, and that there is, therefore, reasonable hope for the establishment of a socioeconomic and political context in Latin America that is hospitable to representative democracies with medium and high human development.[10]

Yet if there is one case that confirms the proposition that structural causes inform violence in Latin America, that case is Haiti. In other words, Haiti constitutes what Gerring calls a "crucial case"—that is, a case that confers validity on a given theory.[11] While acknowledging that structure plays a role in fueling violence in Haiti, this chapter argues that such a view is partial and incomplete. It posits, rather, that contemporary violence in Haiti results from a combination of structural and contingent factors. This argument is in line with authors who argue that unchangeable structures are very rare, and that the study of social phenomena—in this case violence—requires merging various interacting causal explanations that combine more rigid contextual conditions with contingent ones.[12]

Following Jack Levy, this chapter is presented as a hypothesis-generating case study.[13] Through a careful examination of the Haitian case, I seek to improve our understanding of the conditions informing violence in the region by questioning the proposition that violence in Latin America and the Caribbean obeys invariant structural conditions.[14] Drawing on Elster's seminal work,[15] the chapter seeks to disentangle the conditions informing violence by tracing how the combination of particular historical conditions—structural and contingent—have interacted through particular mechanisms (Elster's "causal chains") to create a distinct outcome: violence. More specifically, it is maintained that from within a historical interpretation, violence in Haiti follows what Elster conceptualizes as a "general causal pattern."[16]

In the Haitian case, this refers to the exclusion of the majority of the population by a small native elite that captured the state after the island gained its independence from France in 1804. Post-independence leaders could have transformed the violent, exclusive social order created by French colonialism; instead, they perpetuated many of the features of the old colonial system. From this perspective, the post-independence moment represents a "critical juncture"[17] in the country's history.[18] The new rulers engaged in predatory behavior, encouraging the creation of a parasitic state devised to serve their narrow political and economic interests rather than creating the basis for a modern state that would protect the wider population and address its urgent social and economic needs. Relying on a combination of coercion, co-optation, and clientelism, the rulers of independent Haiti inhibited the development of civil society, political parties, and, more broadly, opposing views of any kind. They thus deliberately curbed the development of formal institutions that could promote economic development and social well-being, regulate social relations, and arbitrate conflict through a fair, evenhanded process. Against this backdrop, structural conditions fostering violence flourished. These endogenous conditions, it is also maintained, were reinforced by the intervention of external powers that, in their keenness to retain influence in the country, collaborated with domestic ruling elites.

During the nineteenth and twentieth centuries, the principal agent of violence in Haiti was the state; with the demise of the Duvalier regime in the mid-1980s, patterns of violence became more complex and heterogeneous, much as the actors unleashing it. Structural conditions undoubtedly play a role in explaining changes in the patterns of violence, but the actual configuration derives from other, more contingent pressures associated with the process of globalization, including democratization and the development of a global organized crime industry.

In short, rather than an "either/or" explanation, it is argued that violence results from a combination of structural and contingent factors of an environmental, cognitive, and relational nature. Violence in Haiti can be explained against the backdrop of a state that has been ill-prepared to withstand the lethal combination of growing social pressure from a marginalized population and the weakening of state structures due to a complex pattern of globalization that propped up nonstate armed parties and led to the atomization and/or privatization of violence. The interplay between these conditions has set the stage for a qualitative change in the nature of violence, as witnessed in the mutation of traditional armed groups and the emergence of new, more lethal ones (paramilitaries, drug cartels, and transnational youth gangs) whose actions reinforce and recreate violence in ways not seen before in Haiti. A particularly salient factor is the emergence of powerful drug syndicates capable of openly challenging the state by combating and/or infiltrating its institutions (political parties, police, and judiciary) and fomenting a toxic culture of violence.

This chapter proceeds as follows. The first section briefly describes contemporary patterns of violence in Haiti. It then defines crucial terms before presenting evidence to support the proposition that structural and contingent factors have interacted through particular mechanisms to produce the patterns of violence that currently in Haiti. In the concluding section, the findings are discussed in the broader context of contemporary violence in Latin America and the Caribbean.

Patterns of Violence in Haiti

Haiti constitutes a fascinating case for the study of violence in Latin America, for several reasons. First, as indicated above, the nature, sources, and characteristics of violence are multidimensional, complex, and widespread.[19] Second, violence has been long lasting and relentless, haunting the country since its independence. Haiti has oscillated between periods of relative calm (1818-43, 1915-34) and acute violence, such as the long reign of the Duvaliers (1957-86), the regime of Generals Raoul Cedras and Michel François (1991-4), and part of Jean-Bertrand Aristide's second term (2003-4).[20] Third, levels of destitution, economic underdevelopment, and disenfranchisement make the country's sociopolitical situation desperate, something that has been exacerbated by severe ecological damage.[21] And fourth, the state's capture by unfit, venal rulers has crippled the development of formally institutionalized ways of dealing with social tensions and grievances.[22]

Data on violence in Haiti is sketchy.[23] In 2010, its homicide rate was 6.9 per 100,000 inhabitants, lower than that of other countries in the region, including Costa Rica (11.3), Ecuador (18), Brazil (22), Puerto Rico (26.2), and Trinidad and Tobago (35), and nowhere near Guatemala (42), Jamaica (52), El Salvador (66), or Honduras (82).[24] Data on kidnappings and sexual violence, though also not entirely reliable, shows a rather acute pattern.[25] While there are no statistics on mob violence, its brutal outcomes—at times orchestrated by political parties and strongpersons, at times spontaneous—is a common feature of the political landscape.[26] Violent riots are also common: in 2008, they paralyzed the country as people furiously protested soaring food and fuel prices in several cities. And yet it is very interesting to note that opinion polls show that the Haitian population's distrust of the state is very high, while the perception of insecurity is not.[27]

Organized entities that resort to violence to attain their objectives may be related to the state apparatus or linked to economic interests, organized crime, opposition groups, or to a combination thereof. Human rights organizations indicate that politically motivated killings, arbitrary arrests, extrajudicial executions, the murder of civilians, rape, beatings, threats, and extortion are regularly perpetrated by agents of the state and nonstate armed groups that operate with virtual impunity.[28] Journalists, human rights activists, aid workers, and even UN troops have been victims of the violence that reigns unabated in some pockets of the country. A substantive share of this violence stems from the unlawful actions of organized crime.[29] These syndicates target opposing groups and civilians who resist them. Civilians also often die in the crossfire as groups wage violent turf battles. Some of these groups have incorporated kidnapping into their repertoire of felonies.[30]

Since the end of the Cold War, Haiti has witnessed several major, and at times violent, political crises, and these have severely undermined security in the country. In 1990, the country elected Jean-Bertrand Aristide, a former Roman Catholic priest sympathetic to liberation theology. Aristide, who won with a wide margin of the vote (67 percent), became the first democratically elected president in the history of Haiti, and the only leader to rise to power without being a member of the country's economic and political elite. A few months after being sworn in to power, however, a military coup deposed him, pushing Haiti back into the dark days of military rule and prompting a major human rights crisis.[31] A puppet civilian regime controlled by a faction of the military led by General Raoul Cedras and supported by the neo-Duvaliérist militia (Le Front pour l' Avancement et le Progrès d'Haiti) took control of the country. To maintain its grip on power, it combined co-optation with the widespread use of terror. Cedras ruled for almost four years, reinstating kleptocratic practices, before being deposed by an international coalition led by the United States, which helped secure the return of President Aristide to finish his mandate.[32]

In 1995, Haitians overwhelmingly voted for René Préval (88 percent), Aristide's political protégé. During Préval's administration (1995–2000), Aristide broke ranks with his old party and created a new political movement, Fanmi Lavalas. In 2000 Aristide won the presidential elections again, although this time with a smaller margin. Now distanced from his foreign allies (France and the United States), and particularly from former local political allies, who accused him of irregularities, Aristide began his administration isolated and weak. Acrimony and mistrust prompted the beginning of a gradual but severe process of political polarization, which erupted violently in February 2004. That month, rebels from the Front Révolutionnaire pour l'Avancement et le Progrès Haïtien (FRAPH) initiated a military offensive from the northern city of Gonaïves that ended deposing the sitting government. As the FRAPH asserted control over the capital, Aristide was forced (again) to flee the country.[33]

The configuration of this short-lived internal armed conflict reflects the hybridity and complexity of violence in Haiti. Aristide's government confronted the FRAPH through the newly created Haitian National Police, which replaced the army Aristide disbanded during his first term.[34] On the government's side, other major players included pro-Aristide militias loosely associated with the former president through the Famni Lavalas, the *Chimères*. These parties were concentrated in areas where Aristide enjoyed wide popularity, such as Bel Air and Cité Soleil—two vast, marginal neighborhoods in Port-au-Prince. There is credible evidence that government forces and their allies committed serious crimes against the civilian population during the short-lived conflict.[35]

Opposition to Aristide's government, in turn, included a varied lot. Several paramilitary groups with ties to Haiti's economic elite and the dissolved army fought against Aristide. Several former members of the old security apparatus were also relevant players in the conflict. Groups of this nature included the Front de Reconstruction Nationale, which was controlled by the gangster Buteur Metayer and included former operatives of the infamous Cannibal Army; the Armée du Nord, led by Guy Phillippe; former paramilitary operatives under the control of Louis-Jodel Chamblain, the right hand of Phillippe's insurgent movement; paramilitary groups based in the country's Central Plateau and led by Remissanthe Ravix; the Front de Resistance du Sud; several armed organizations that operated in the countryside under the orders of former *chefs de section*, who ruled rural areas during the military regime; and, finally, multiple private militias organized under the order of powerful landowners who reclaimed by force land lost during the Aristide administration's land reform program. There is credible evidence that insurgent groups also perpetrated serious human rights violations, including summary executions and killings in pro-Aristide strongholds.[36]

In short, Haiti displays a level of violence that, while acute, is less than that of many other Latin American countries. Haiti, however, experienced a period of short-lived yet fierce internal armed conflict during which the country experienced an almost total breakdown of the state's monopoly on violence.[37] Fighting reached low urban warfare status as parties indiscriminately utilized assault rifles with massive firepower in densely populated civilian areas.[38] To address violence and a looming humanitarian calamity, in April 2004 the UN Security Council through resolution 1542 dispatched the United Nations Stabilization Mission in Haiti (MINUSTAH). MINUSTAH's mandate included assisting and protecting civilians; disarming armed parties; pacifying the country; helping the transitional government by strengthening and reforming institutions (e.g., the police, judiciary, and prison system) and buttressing the rule of law; endorsing the political process and organizing and monitoring free elections; and promoting human rights.[39] The presence of an internationally mandated peace enforcement mission such as MINUSTAH, along with several international humanitarian and development organizations working in situ, revealed the existence of a political and humanitarian crisis of vast proportions.[40]

MINUSTAH's presence helped to reduce levels of violence, though insecurity remains widespread across Haiti.[41] The country saw an important improvement in security conditions following the arrival of MINUSTAH in 2004 (the force stayed until 2017). The presence of UN peacekeepers helped to stabilize the country by deterring potential attacks by renegade armed parties, thus facilitating the transfer of power from the administration of President René Préval to that of Michele Martelly (2011-16).

Following the 2010 earthquake, the problem of how to avoid a major breakdown of law and order asserted itself with great force. Security in several of the displaced persons camps created multiple challenges, the most acute of all concerning gender violence: women and young girls were systematically beaten and raped by armed men, generally at night.[42] After the most acute phase of the humanitarian crisis faded, security returned to ex ante conditions characterized by state-orchestrated violence coupled with the activities of gangs and organized criminal groups and severe levels of nonlethal violence such as robberies, assaults, and riots.[43] General conditions of impunity continue to entrench societal violence, posing an enormous challenge to the new administration of President Jovenel Moïse (elected in 2017).[44]

The Root Sources of Violence in Haiti

As previously mentioned, in seeking to explain the sources of violence in Haiti this chapter asks two questions: 1) Are the root causes of violence structural, contingent, or a combination thereof? And 2) What accounts for the change in the configuration of violence from one prominently orchestrated by the state to one that is much more diffuse and complex? Mindful of the conceptual challenges posed by the investigation of violence,[45] I opt for a relatively broad definition that captures the particularities of this phenomenon in Haiti, a microcosm where multifarious expressions of violence arise simultaneously. In trying to strike a balance between excessively broad and too-narrow conceptualizations, for the purposes of this study, following Kalyvas, violence is restricted to its physical dimension. As such, it is defined as the premeditated victimization of people with the intent of killing or harming them for political or criminal motives.[46] But this definition differs from Kalyvas's in that it includes both situations of peace and internal armed conflict.[47] Nor do I distinguish rural from urban violence because, again, although they differ in their manifestations, they share most of the same roots. As far as the perpetrators are concerned, I include the state, actors with links to but not part of the state (i.e., death squads and paramilitaries), and nonstate armed actors.

I also purposefully include violence with political as well as criminal intent because the literature on violence and armed conflict has convincingly shown that drawing a clear line between these types of violence is very difficult.[48] Indeed, distinguishing between political violence and (nonpolitical) criminal behavior is particularly difficult in the Haitian case because heterogeneous forms of political violence (extrajudicial executions, targeted assassinations, torture, death threats, kidnappings, and forced disappearances) coexist with several manifestations of economically and sexually motivated crimes such as extortion, burglaries, robberies, theft, and rape, crimes that oftentimes display very high levels of violence.[49]

By focusing on the structural causes of violence, this chapter refers to long-lasting, consolidated social, historical, demographic, economic, and ecological conditions that shape the political landscape—including its institutions—and tend to endure over time. These include the state, whether strong or weak, the general distribution of wealth, access to public goods, and patterns of discrimination.[50] The conceptualization of contingency is intricate and its attributes often diffuse. It is not surprising, therefore, that there is little consensus on what the term really means beyond colloquial interpretations.[51] In discussing this matter, Schedler manifests that common interpretations of contingency view it as "accidental events that are under-determinate and unpredictable, even accidental events (causes) that have the potential of having big consequences."[52] In developing a more refined conceptualization of the meaning of contingency, Schedler posits that the concept stands on three abstract pillars: indeterminacy (i.e., it could be different), conditionality (it depends), and uncertainty (it is impossible to know).[53] Pettit, by contrast, argues that contingency is commonly understood as issues that are not strictly necessary for a given outcome; that is to say, they may happen in the actual world but do not figure in all conceivable worlds.[54]

This chapter also draws on Brown's useful typology regarding the sources of armed conflict. Brown distinguishes four clusters of factors (structural, economic, political, and cultural) that may prompt armed conflict, asserting that diverse permutations of all or some of them may prompt internal armed conflict. An important aspect of Brown's argument is that different permutations of these four clusters have to interact with some catalysts (i.e., leaders or opportunistic neighbors) to spark internal armed conflict.[55] This chapter complements Brown's categories with Tilly's work on the politics of collective violence, which discusses violence broadly by looking at the conditions informing it, not solely its most extreme manifestation as measured by the severity and intensity of armed conflict and genocide. Tilly develops several insightful categories of violence, including violent rituals, broken negotiations, coordinated destruction, scattered attacks, individual aggression, brawls, and opportunism.[56]

In sum, this chapter proposes to look at the root causes of violence following a broad conceptualization that includes both political violence and the more restricted category of internal armed conflict.

Structural Conditions

In examining the structural conditions informing violence in Haiti, this chapter looks at three main issues: the nature of the state, political conditions, and economic development. This approach follows Elster's advice to dig into a subject's history as if it were a black box.[57] A sound way to start examining the structural conditions informing violence in Haiti is by considering the development of its state. This provides information on the other key variables and mechanisms informing violence.

The Nature of the Haitian State

The literature on weak states posits that when (for a variety of reasons) states fail to fulfill their basic functions, conditions become ripe for social unrest, violence, and internal armed conflict.[58] The literature identifies two main functions states need to fulfill to curb violence. First, relying on

Weber's classical conception, it underlines that a state needs to rule over a specific territory and its people, effectively holding a monopoly on the means of coercion.[59] IR scholars also assert that states ought to be recognized by the members of the international society of states.[60] This classic conceptualization has been complemented with a more modern view that incorporates the notion that states ought to enable the conditions for the development of social life.[61] Rotberg claims that states ought to provide "political goods," including the development of the means to adjudicate disputes, basic infrastructure, and a functional economy that, regardless of its ideological stance, creates an environment that is conducive to the emergence of economic activity (banking system, currency, regulation). Following Weber, a modicum of legitimacy also represents an important element of state strength.[62]

According to this line of reasoning, states led by unprincipled rulers, characterized by rudimentary institutions, and unable to provide basic public goods foster the conditions for violence. The most critical factor explaining the emergence of violence is a state's inability to provide security and uphold the rule of law. This process may unleash a vicious cycle of insecurity by pushing communities to the brink, convincing them that the only option of guaranteeing their survival is the provision of their own security. This may generate what IR scholars characterize as "the security dilemma." This insight, originally used to depict an international order where no overarching authority exists among nations,[63] has also been used to describe domestic scenarios fraught with armed conflict in which the actions a community takes to increase its security (e.g., arming the population) are perceived as hostile by rival communities, thus sparking a chain reaction that ends up making everyone more insecure.[64] This line of argument has mostly been applied to explain the outbreak of ethnic conflict, but seems equally useful for explaining other cases of violence.[65]

Haiti clearly fits into this pattern. Its weak state is unable to control the multiple armed factions—political and criminal—that exercise influence and at times control sections of its territory. Widespread violence and criminality are compounded by an inefficient judicial system characterized by high levels of corruption, incompetence, and dehumanization.[66] According to Jean-Germain Gros, who has developed a very useful typology on state strength, Haiti represents a "counterinsurgency free anemic state."[67] Anemic states are able to partially fulfill their basic functions only in main urban areas. Anemic states result when dysfunctional development hamstrings the state's capacity to create adequate mechanisms and institutions to meet the challenges posed by modern societies.[68]

Why does Haiti have an anemic state? Most authors, both Haitian and foreign, point to the path taken by the country after the triumph of the 1791–1804 slave insurrection led by Toussaint L'Ouverture and his lieutenant, Jean-Jacques Dessalines. The defeat of Napoleonic France led to Haitian independence in 1804, making it the first postcolonial state in Latin America and the world's first modern independent black republic.[69]

The enormous expectations brought by independence were shattered as divisions in the victorious emancipation movement allowed a small elite to take power. In what became a common development among decolonization movements worldwide,[70] a native elite emerged from among those who had formerly occupied important positions during French rule. As large sugar estates collapsed as slaves refused to go back to their former masters, Haiti's new rulers had to develop a new mode of economic production. Unlike other countries in Latin America and the Caribbean, where oligarchy was associated with land tenure, in Haiti the elite engineered a rentier state based on an export-import-oriented economy. Most former slaves settled unclaimed land and/or areas abandoned by former landowners in the island's hinterland. There they created a collective system of production known as *corveé* and lived only at the subsistence level. A lack of organization and isolation kept liberated slaves disempowered. This, in turn, facilitated the new ruling elite's construction of mechanisms of economic control (in particular, a biased tax system) over the customhouses and urban markets where peasants had to sell their produce. This power was maintained and reinforced though force and intimidation.[71]

Soon after independence, the country's new rulers organized a national army and police force. It is no exaggeration to say that the national army became the most relevant institution in the country, operating as the highest arbiter of political controversy. Historically, the overwhelming majority of Haitian rulers have belonged to the ranks of the military. Yet the absence of any formal mechanisms for resolving disputes predisposed the country to continuous instability as factions within the elite jockeyed for political power by controlling the armed forces. Adams and Malone indicate that in its more than 200 years as an independent state, Haiti has had 22 constitutions and 42 heads of state, of which 29 were assassinated or overthrown, while 9 proclaimed themselves rulers for life.[72]

Nicholls explains that from independence until the 1915 US occupation, Haitian heads of state rose to power thanks to the power they garnered as military leaders. A few times, leaders were chosen as a compromise because no single military faction was able to impose its terms.[73] The story did not change after the United States withdrew from the island in 1934. On the contrary, the United States reinforced centralism and state-orchestrated violence. US troops and advisors collaborated in the creation of a new and more disciplined national army as well as rural police, the section chiefs (*chefs de section*), who became de facto rulers with virtually total autonomy from the central state. These section chiefs ruthlessly maintained order in the areas under their jurisdiction.[74]

Emancipation, it is argued, represents a critical juncture in Haiti's development, one that created the structural conditions, including the characteristics of the state and the political and socioeconomic system, that rendered the country prone to violence. This manifested itself in the creation of an illiberal political system with marked authoritarian tendencies and prone to resort to violence in order to resolve political disputes. Critical junctures are times of pivotal transformations derived from major crises or cleavages that arise from preexisting conditions and which create distinct outcomes or important legacies. It is relevant to underscore that this concept is not conceived as a particularistic historical episode, but rather as an event with cross-case significance. According to this line of reasoning, emancipation from colonial rule in Latin America (and elsewhere) opened the way for huge transformations of the political, social, and economic systems of the newborn countries.[75]

In Haiti, rather than correcting the injustices and biases of colonial rule, the state's capture by a greedy elite created the conditions for the development of an anemic state. Most slaves who had won their right to live as equal members of a social community were brought back to the *ex-ante* status characterized by submission to a small urban minority. The entire nation thus became hostage to the will of a capricious sector associated with economic power holders that had created institutions to perpetuate their grip on power and accrue the wealth and privileges associated with it.[76] To follow Tilly's approach, the mechanism informing violence in Haiti is relational because marginalization shaped connections among social units.[77] That is to say, the policies implemented by native leaders conspired against the development of a fair, inclusive political system based on institutions designed for the common good to create a state vulnerable to capture by leaders engaging in predatory practices.[78] The almost complete lack of constraints—save for intra-elite fighting—that Haiti's political system imposed on its rulers permitted predatory governance,[79] the most serious form of which was rent-seeking. Some authors argue that it is no exaggeration to claim that the rural hinterland became a colony of urban elites.[80]

Political Conditions

Structural explanations of violence in Haiti ought to take political factors into account. The literature underscores the salience of discriminatory practices that become institutionalized through the political system. This discrimination, generally conceptualized and justified on ideological, ethnic, national, or religious grounds, materializes in restrictions on electoral participation and inadequate representation in crucial institutions of the state. When sectors of the population are purposefully and blatantly excluded, they may resort to violence to redress the situation and create a different social order. Classic studies addressing this issue include those by Huntington, who emphasizes the disconnection between societal conditions and institutions, and Gurr, who develops the theory of relative deprivation following a period of rising expectations.[81] Another group of studies trace the political sources of violence to the role of power and the nature of leadership, emphasizing the existence of ambitious, opportunistic leaders or groups who through exclusion and manipulation seize power and cling to it.[82] Similarly, some studies point to intergroup rivalries based on incompatible goals, recalcitrance, and the lack of an accommodative spirit as political sources informing armed conflict.[83]

Many of the political elements identified by the literature as potential causes of conflict and violence are present in Haiti. The country developed insidious forms of discrimination that were institutionalized through its political system. Discrimination was conceptualized and justified on racial and cultural grounds, curbing representation of the peasantry and pauperized urban sectors in crucial institutions of the state. Racial distinctions were used to marginalize the majority of the population and prevent upward mobility. Skin color has also been used as a subtle mechanism of discrimination, creating an ominous type of caste system. At the expense of the vast majority of the population, Mulattos, a small but economically powerful minority, managed to attain economic supremacy and to share political power with a small number of urban blacks. This small, emerging black middle class rose to places of privilege in the twentieth century through marriage and economic success. Institutions such as the national army recruited peasants but curbed their professional development by preventing their advance through the ranks based on class and origin. Religion, too, was used as a tool of discrimination. The small ruling elite professed Catholicism and displayed a contemptuous attitude against voodoo, an "eclectic blend of Dahomian religions and Catholicism" and the religion practiced by the majority of the population.[84] Discrimination was further exacerbated by the use of language. The Haitian state introduced French as the official language. French was used in courts, universities, the bureaucracy, and government. As a way to keep peasants disempowered, the state did not extend the teaching of this language to the rural areas. This totally marginalized the vast majority of the population. Jean-Bertrand Aristide became the first president who spoke Creole as his mother tongue. Clientelistic arrangements devised to control dissatisfaction among the population were also widely used as tools of political control.[85]

Economic Development

Economic explanations of violence also apply to the Haitian case. Studies linking violence to economic factors have underscored the destabilizing effects of uneven wealth distribution and poor economic performance (i.e., endemic unemployment, stagnation, and the erosion of people's purchasing power). This literature also underlines how discriminatory economic practices denying parts of the population access to crucial resources and services provided by the state may increase the likelihood of violence.[86] A related strand in the literature identifies environmental factors as possible sources of conflict. These authors argue that access to and capture of scarce resources such as land and water are potential sources of conflict.[87] Other studies have underscored the economic functions of violence—that is, the utility that parties gain from a lawless scenario, while not necessarily a root cause of violence, is nevertheless a factor that explains why violence persists over time.[88]

For most of Haiti's national history, the vast majority of the population has endured economic misery as a result of exclusion and marginalization. Most of the rural population has lived at a subsistence level, lacking access to indispensable social services while enduring the heavy taxation of their meager resources. Basic infrastructure, including roads, sewage systems, power sources, schooling, health care, postal services, and transportation, among many others, were not provided, and this has seriously curbed the ability of the population to live a dignified existence. The rentier state economy offered very limited formal work opportunities for most of the population.[89]

The problems described above have created a dire situation in Haiti. Today, the majority of Haitians struggle to get by, deprived as they are of work and access to basic social services such as housing, health, education, drinking water, and public transportation.[90] If these conditions were not enough, natural disasters with devastating consequences, such as hurricanes, floods, and droughts, strike the country on a regular basis, further deepening the predicament of its population.[91]

Economic and diplomatic isolation caused by foreign powers, in particular France and the United States, reinforced Haiti's skewed, problematic socioeconomic development.[92] Aggravated by the loss of its colony, France demanded considerable economic compensation. Meanwhile, fearful of the Haitian precedent, the powerful pre–Civil War pro-slavery caucus successfully pressured the US government to diplomatically and economically isolate the embryonic state. These actions represented a heavy burden for Haiti, accentuating a perception of encirclement and further constraining its political options. Foreign pressure reinforced a perverse cycle whereby the elite felt isolated and attacked and thus resorted to every imaginable policy to secure its survival, even if that meant scarifying the rural population.[93]

The result of this combination of bad governance, economic mismanagement, elite abuse, and external pressures is breathtaking. Haiti registers the lowest human development in the Western Hemisphere. The country ranks 158 out of 187 countries per the Human Development Index, with indices such as life expectancy (61.2 years) and per capita income (US$ 1,102) among the lowest in the world.[94] The formal economy remains marginal and most of the population works in the informal sector. Incapable of collecting taxes, the state is unable to extend the most basic rights to the population. The country also suffers from severe ecological damage as a consequence of environmental degradation and resource shortages associated with population growth and unsustainable consumption patterns.[95]

Not surprisingly, emigration has become a major feature of Haiti's modern history. Up to a million Haitians live in the Dominican Republic, and there are sizable communities of Haitians in French Canada (Quebec), the United States (mostly in Florida), France, and other nations in Latin America. While most are considered economic migrants, repression and human rights abuses have created important flows of forced migrants.[96]

The New Shape of Violence in Haiti: Globalization and Contingency

The historical conditions informing violence in Haiti can be traced to several structural factors identified in the literature. The current patterns of violence in Haiti, however, are characterized by a different, much more complex configuration. Violence in Haiti has evolved in the context of a weak state, with limited legitimacy, incapable of satisfactorily fulfilling basic functions.[97] As in other Latin American states, a wide variety of violent actors have emerged in Haiti.[98] These include the military, the intelligence services, the police, agents that rely on "extralegal violence" to buttress the political status quo such as paramilitary forces or militias, guerrilla groups, and other anti-systemic forces, uncivil radicalized movements, and an archipelago of criminal organizations.[99]

As indicated above, during the nineteenth and most of the twentieth century, barring sporadic rebellions, mob violence, and factional fighting among the armed forces, the principal agent of violence in Haiti was the state. A lack of institutions to constrain the behavior of leaders who rose to power and used it to remain there played a pivotal role in the origin and nature of violence. Terror under Duvalier was only the most extreme manifestation of an enduring tale of violence discharged by the state against a disenfranchised, disempowered population.[100] Since the late 1980s, however, a steady, if gradual, proliferation of newer violent actors has changed the configuration of violence in the country.

This chapter posits that current patterns of violence arise from a combination of structural conditions discussed earlier with some more contingent elements that have acted as catalysts or mechanisms for generating violence. Structural conditions do not in and of themselves seem able to provide a full, convincing account for the changes in the nature of violence experienced in Haiti over the last two decades. The explanation, therefore, needs to be sharpened by looking into other contingent factors that act as intervening mechanisms to account for the transformation of violence. These contingent elements, it is claimed, derive from or are associated with the process of globalization.[101] They include 1) the transition to democratic processes and 2) the flourishing of global illegal industries helping to propagate organized crime.

The contingent factors just described are inextricably connected to the process of globalization. Globalization has had a big impact in the spread of liberal representative democracy as a political regime type.[102] Concerning the relation between violence and transitions to democracy, the literature approaches the matter from the viewpoint of democracies emerging from situations of armed conflict. These authors argue that states undergoing a process of democratization following an internal armed conflict (e.g., Sierra Leone, El Salvador, Afghanistan) normally endure difficult, destabilizing conditions that make them prone to violence.[103]

Many factors explain this development. First, weakened institutions such as the police and the judiciary may face growing difficulties enforcing the rule of law in a new democratic setting. Second, if what prompted the conflict in the first place was not resolved at the outcome of the conflict, and *ex-ante* conditions persist, aggravated parties may reengage in violence. Third, peaceful ways to resolve disputes and grievances, and the development of the capacity to undertake lawful economic activities, take time to become socialized. Therefore, unless conditions on the ground change dramatically, groups that participated in armed conflict oftentimes relapse into violence because they have a hard time adjusting to new conditions. Fourth, incentives to engage in illicit activities for economic gain persist in a situation of weak institutionalization, such as those that characterize postconflict transitions.[104] Lastly, studies find that previous patterns of armed conflict and violence normally foment violent practices that may lead to a relapse into war.[105]

Globalization has undoubtedly revolutionized many other aspects of life, and it should therefore come as no surprise that it has influenced patterns of violence and armed conflict around the world.[106] However, the complex relationship between globalization, violence, and armed conflict is not a straightforward one. Within the scholarly literature addressing this matter there is wide disagreement. On the one hand, neoliberals claim that the economic interdependence brought about by globalization favors prosperity and democracy—and therefore peaceful conditions—both in the domestic and global realms. They make this argument by using the analogy of liberal interpretations about international peace.[107] Marxists, structuralists, and dependency theorists, on the other hand, argue that open economies tend to increase the likelihood of conflict by exacerbating economic inequality, poverty, and injustice.[108] For them, the economic changes brought about by globalization have expanded social marginalization and alienated large swathes of society. The paradox is that although these sectors are passed over by the economic miracles of globalization, they remain largely exposed to them through mass media. Hegre, Gissinger, and Gleditsch review the merits of these positions, observing more empirical evidence supporting the liberal position, although they recognize that their findings are not conclusive.[109]

Although it is certainly beyond the scope of this chapter to settle the dispute between those who see globalization as a driver of violence and those rejecting this proposition, it is at least possible to list some influencing factors that seem clearly present in the Haitian case. First, changes in manufacturing, communication, and transportation derived from technological advances have led to new modes of economic interaction characterized by flexibility, outsourcing, and "just in time" production. This has prompted a major revolution in several key industries, including the arms industry. Held and McGrew argue that globalization has indeed brought about the transformation of warfare as "globalization, commercialization and criminalization" converged.[110] One aspect of this transformation concerns the privatization of the agents of violence, including mercenaries, pirates, and private security companies. Keohane refers to these actors as agents of informal organized violence.[111] The emergence of organized crime syndicates with transnational operations is particularly relevant. These groups are defined as organizations that engage in illegal activities for economic profit within more than two countries simultaneously.[112] Organized crime can be distinguished from other, more informal criminal organizations by the continuity, specialization, and sophistication of its activities, as well as by its corrupting power and capability to inflict violence. According to Lee, organized crime is an archipelago composed of organizations with different hierarchical and decentralized forms engaging in illegal activities, including prostitution, extortion, money laundering, kidnapping, slavery, piracy, and drug, arms, organ, and human trafficking. The emergence of these types of organizations constitutes a worldwide trend. By exploiting the voids left by weak states, these actors' lucrative activities normally worsen and prolong violence and armed conflict.[113]

Further, deregulation derived from a globalized economy has meant the near loss of control over the production and commercialization of arms, over which the state used to maintain a monopoly. This has permitted private agents to acquire an important share of the industry. The result has been a qualitative change in the arms industry, particularly a colossal growth in the commercialization of small arms.[114] The literature has examined the link between this development and patterns of armed conflict, establishing how the diffusion of technologically sophisticated small weaponry with enormous fire power (for example, rocket-propelled grenades and various models of assault rifle) has fed conflicts around the world, with particularly deleterious impacts of the well-being of civilians.[115]

With regards to the relationship between the aforementioned aspects of globalization and violence in Haiti, the links seem clear. Democratization in Haiti, while certainly welcomed, has spawned a number of problems, some of which are related to violence. The downfall of the Duvalier regime led to an anarchic era (there were five governments in four years until the election of Aristide in 1990) characterized by a resurgent army attempting to reassert its power. This period coincided with the end of the Cold War, something that decreased Haiti's strategic value, prompting a concomitant decline of US interest in the country. This would later change, however, as the chaos following the ousting of Aristide prompted a massive wave of Haitian asylum seekers to arrive on the shores of Florida.[116]

After Aristide assumed power, his government clashed violently with the old power holders supported by the Haitian army, which was intent on flexing its muscles. Most authors point out that the ambitious reformist agenda pushed by Aristide was perceived as a threat to the traditional economic and political elite. Cedras's violent coup was masterminded to derail the newly elected leader's political project without foreseeing that Aristide's many supporters were committed to violently resisting the coup. This resistance came about within the context of a debilitated state that, since Duvalier's departure in 1986, had lost its ability to monopolize (at least partially) the means of coercion. This created a window of opportunity for diverse forces to strengthen their ability to resist, both politically and militarily. At the same time, purged members of the former security apparatus were either recruited by Aristide, provincial *caudillos*, or simply turned to crime in order to make ends meet. Given their training, many soon mutated into structured armed militias that engaged in illegal enterprises. Corruption among the security forces and the disbanding of paramilitary forces that formerly supported the Duvalier regime prompted the dissemination of weapons through an incipient black market. In short, democratization in a highly deinstitutionalized context created political frictions that favored violence.[117]

This dynamic coincided with a fortuitous and quite unexpected development that played a significant role in shaping the contours of violence in Haiti: the advent of Colombian drug cartels during the early 1990s. As American authorities successfully shut down the smuggling of cocaine via Florida, the highly adaptable Colombian cartels moved to the Caribbean for the transshipment of drugs. Haiti—a transitional weak state characterized by endemic corruption and home to scores of unemployed men with military training—became an ideal hub.[118] In 2007, an estimated 10 percent of all cocaine destined for the United States passed through Haiti.[119]

The impact of this highly contingent event has been crucial for the development and configuration of violence in the country. The Haitian market has become awash with drug money. This money exacerbated corruption by financing payments to bureaucrats, judges, the police, and politicians. Haiti has the highest level of perceived corruption in the

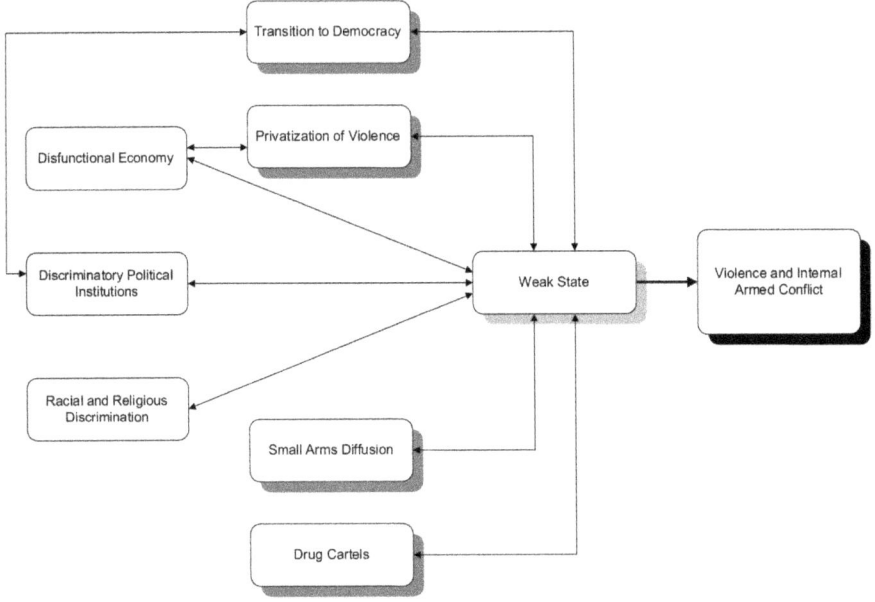

Figure 1.1
The Interplay Between Structural and Contingent Factors in Haiti.

Americas,[120] and among the highest in the world, according to Transparency International, a global corruption watchdog.[121] Drug money has also flooded the market with small arms. According to a credible estimate, there were around 190,000 small arms circulating among Haitian civilians in 2007.[122] While the ratio of arms ownership to population is comparatively low, the number of such weapons represents a major security threat in the context of a weak state. Violence tends to be concentrated in areas where there is large presence of organized crime. Daudelin refers to such places as "dysfunctional drug frontiers."[123] They have also helped create the conditions for the escalation of kidnappings.[124]

High rates of unemployment among a pauperized population, and the repeated disbandment of security forces following external international interventions in 1994 and 2004, has created an endless supply of people willing to fill the ranks of criminal organizations. Similarly, as part of a long Haitian tradition, influential political leaders continue to organize armed wings (uncivil movements) to assert their power and influence. The creation by former president Aristide of the *Chimères* is just one of the most recent examples of this trend. From the security standpoint, the consequences of these developments have been very negative. The multiplication of violent groups pursuing diverse interests has negatively impacted security in Haiti.[125]

Figure 1.1 presents a summary of the main argument. Structural conditions derived from a particular historical trajectory prompted by environmental, cognitive, and contextual factors, combined with harmful leadership, have fostered the development of an anemic state characterized by its inability to fulfill basic functions. Contingent variables associated with the process of globalization, the transition to democracy, the penetration of foreign organized crime, and the dissemination of small arms have further weakened the state, thereby making recent violence in Haiti much more complex, fluid, and intractable.

Conclusion

This chapter has assessed the conditions informing the most recent waves of violence in a seemingly ceaseless pattern played out across Haitian history. The main question addressed was whether the root conditions informing violence and armed conflict in Haiti obey structural or contingent conditions. Instead of answering in an either/or form, my analysis and the evidence presented here shows that violence in Haiti stems from a combination of both types of factors interacting through particular mechanisms. Following the seminal work by Elster, I show how the combination of particular historical conditions, both structural and contingent, interacted through particular "causal chains" to create a distinctly violent outcome.

In Haiti, a complex historical process derived from incompetent and selfish leadership, external pressure, and patterns of discrimination created a deeply flawed, parasitic state unfit to regulate social relations. Coercion, co-optation, clientelism, and violence became so widespread that they amounted to the normal state of affairs. All the while, the majority of the population was condemned to a life of destitution. The long rule of the Duvalier family epitomized this state of affairs. Francois and Jean-Claude Duvalier were only the most grotesque manifestation of a long tale of despotic, wicked rulers who brutally repressed opposition, undermined the creation of institutions, and lavishly wasted meager state resources while the general population lived in abject destitution.

Haiti's dysfunctional state and crippled economy are ill-prepared to withstand the forces associated with the process of globalization. New phenomena, including the diffusion of democracy, the penetration of foreign organized crime, and the dissemination of small arms, have created daunting challenges for Haiti. Whereas for most of its history, the principal agent of violence was the state, there has been a gradual though steady proliferation of other violent actors since the late 1980s. These include paramilitary organizations, organized criminal networks, and armed gangs related to diverse interests. Violence therefore has turned much more complex, fluid, and intractable.

Particular historical and cultural differences notwithstanding, the Haitian case illustrates the changing nature of violence in much of Latin America.[126] Reflecting the trials and tribulations of modern life, violence in Latin America has undergone a profound transformation in the last two decades. Before the latest wave of democratization in the 1980s, sociopolitical violence in Latin America was the result of confrontations between repressive and unresponsive elitist states and ideologically inspired armed and unarmed groups that opposed them.[127] Nowadays, Latin America experiences what Pinheiro terms "lawlessness"[128]—that is, a situation in which the most vulnerable groups of society, in particular destitute and marginalized children and women, bear the brunt of brutality and victimization at the hands of various armed groups. Kruijt and Koonings posit that this violence is not really a holdover of uneven systems that fostered cycles of insurrection and repression between the 1950s and 1980s.[129] According to them, there were certainly instances in that period where the border between politically motivated organized violence and criminal activity was hard to discern because they interacted and mutually reinforced themselves. Nonetheless, for the most part, it was possible to draw distinctions between them. Today, distinctions of this sort seem much more difficult to discern, as are the effective palliatives to this problem.[130]

This chapter has been presented as a hypothesis-generating case study. This careful examination of the Haitian case is meant to improve our understanding of the conditions informing violence. More generally, my aim is to use the Haitian case to contribute to the reflection on and discussion of the conditions prompting violence in Latin America. In combination with the other case studies contained in this volume, this material could be later tested through other methods to buttress and refine the proposition that violence in the Latin America context can be traced to a combination of structural and contingent factors that operate through specific mechanisms. This is meant to oppose the more negative and deterministic argument that violence in the region obeys invariable structural conditions, condemning Latin Americans to live indefinitely with this heavy burden.

Notes

This article is based on fieldwork conducted in 2013. A preliminary version was presented at Arms, Violence and Politics in Latin America: Past, Present, and Future, a conference held at the University of Calgary's Latin American Research Centre in May 2009. I acknowledge support from FONDECYT (project 1110565), Millennium Nucleus for the Study of Stateness and Democracy in Latin America (project NS 100014), and the International Development Research Centre (IDRC). I am grateful to Pablo Policzer, Rodrigo Mardones, Stephen Baranyi, Carlos Guevara-Mann, and Rudy Reserve for suggestions and comments on previous drafts. I acknowledge research assistance from Alex Micic, Dania Straughan, and Sebastián Briones, and editing assistance from Nikolai Stieglitz.

1   A. Kolbe, R. A. Hutson, H. Shannon, E. Trzcinski, B. Miles, N. Levitz, M. Puccio, L. James, J. R. Noel, and R. Muggah, "Mortality, Crime and Access to Basic Needs Before and After the Haiti Earthquake: A Random Survey of Port-au-Prince Households," *Medicine Conflict and Survival* 26, no. 4 (2010): 281–97. Government figures put the death toll at 222,000.

2   See *Small Arms Survey 2011: States of Security* (Cambridge: Cambridge University Press, 2011), 229–33. A partial exception was *Cité Soleil*, a suburb of the capital Port-au-Prince, where violence increased in the aftermath of the earthquake. See Luis Herns Marceline, "Cooperation, Peace and Reconstruction? A Tale from the Shanties," *Journal of Peacebuilding and Development* 6, no. 3 (2011): 17–31.

3   *Small Arms Survey 2011*, 229.

4   UN Office on Drugs and Crime, *2011 Global Study on Homicide: Trends, Contexts, Data*, https://www.unodc.org/documents/data-and-analysis/statistics/Homicide/Globa_study_on_homicide_2011_web.pdf.

5   Robert Muggah, *Securing Haiti's Transition: Reviewing Human Insecurity and the Prospects of Disarmament, Demobilization and Reintegration* (Geneva: Small Arms Survey, 2005), http://www.smallarmssurvey.org/fileadmin/docs/B-Occasional-papers/SAS-OP14-Haiti-EN.pdf, 2–10.

6. United Nations High Commissioner for Human Rights, *Taking Justice Into One's Own Hands: Or the Reign of Impunity in Haiti*, January 2017, https://www.haitilibre.com/docs/170117_exec_summary_haiti_-_taking_justice_into_ones_own_hands_-_en.pdf.

7. Louis Herns Marcelin, *Haiti Laid Bare: Fragility, Sovereignty and Delusional Recovery* (unpublished manuscript, 2010), http://www.rebatism.org/DOCUMENTS/Fragility%20and%20sovereignty.pdf.

8. Robert Muggah, "The Political Economy of Statebuilding in Haiti: Informal Resistance to Security First Statebuilding," in *Political Economy of Statebuilding, Power After Peace*, ed. Matts Berdal and Dominik Zaum (London: Routledge, 2013), 294.

9. See Human Rights Watch, "Haiti: Hundreds Killed Amid Rampant Impunity," 13 April 2005, http://www.hrw.org/en/news/2005/04/13/haiti-hundreds-killed-amid-rampant-impunity. See also Human Rights Watch, *World Report: Haiti*, 2008 http://www.hrw.org/en/node/79214.

10. For an interesting account of the relationship between democracy and violence in Latin America, see Enrique Desmond Arias and Daniel M. Goldstein, eds., *Violent Democracies in Latin America* (Durham, NC: Duke University Press, 2010); Gustavo Duncan, *Más Plata que Plomo: El Poder Político del Narcotráfico en Colombia y México* (Bogotá: Debate, 2015).

11. John Gerring, "Case Selection for Case Study Analysis: Qualitative and Quantitative Techniques," in *The Oxford Hand Book of Political Methodology*, ed. Janet M. Box-Steffensmeier, Henry E. Brady, and David Collier (Oxford: Oxford University Press, 2008), 645–84, and Harry Eckstein, "Case Studies and Theory in Political Science," in *Handbook of Political Science*, ed. Fred Greenstein and Nelson Polsby (Reading, MA: Addison-Wesley, 1975), 7: 79–138.

12. Charles Tilly, *The Politics of Collective Violence* (Cambridge: Cambridge University Press, 2003); Michael Brown, ed., *The International Dimensions of Internal Conflict* (Cambridge, MA: MIT Press, 1996).

13. Jack S. Levy, "Case Studies: Types, Designs, and Logic of Inference," *Conflict Management and Peace Science* 25, no. 1 (2008): 1–18.

14. For an interpretation of this type that uses cultural explanations, see Howard Wiarda, *The Soul of Latin America* (New Haven, CT: Yale University Press, 2001), and Howard Wiarda and Harvey Kline, *Latin American Politics and Development* (Boulder, CO: Westview Press, 1995).

15. John Elster, *Explaining Social Behavior: More Nuts and Bolts for the Social Science* (Cambridge: Cambridge University Press, 2008).

16. Elster, *Explaining*, 37.

17. Collier and Collier define critical junctures as periods of significant changes that manifests themselves in distinct ways creating diverse outcomes. See Ruth Berins Collier and David Collier, *Shaping the Political Arena: Critical Junctures, the Labor Movement, and Regime Dynamics in Latin America* (Princeton, NJ: Princeton University Press, 1991), 290. Critical junctures are not conceived as particularistic historical events, but rather as events with cross-case significance.

18 A recent study presents an alternative account and argues that the *critical juncture* determining Haiti's backwardness occurred much later. See Victor Bulmer Thomas, *The Economic History of the Caribbean since Napoleonic Wars* (Cambridge: Cambridge University Press, 2012).

19 Andreas E. Feldmann and Juan Esteban Montes, "Tribulaciones de Un Estado Colapsado," *Revista de Ciencia Política* 28 no. 1 (2008): 245–64.

20 David Nicholls, "The Duvalier Regime in Haiti," in *Sultanistic Regimes*, ed. H. E. Chehabi and Juan J. Linz (Baltimore, MD: Johns Hopkins University Press, 1998), 153–81.

21 See Thomas Homer-Dixon, "Environmental Scarcities and Violent Conflict: Evidence from Cases," *International Security* 19, no. 1 (1994): 5–40.

22 Robert Fatton Jr., "Haiti and the Limits of Sovereignty: Trapped in the Outer Periphery," in *Who Owns Haiti? People, Power and Sovereignty*, ed. Robert Maguire and Scott Freeman (Gainessville: University Press of Florida, 2017), 29–50; Andreas E. Feldmann, "The Phantom State of Haiti," *Forced Migration Review* 43 (2013): 32–4.

23 As with many other developing countries, the Haitian state lacks the capacity to consistently record data on violence and crime. Existing numbers clearly represent only a small subset of the violence afflicting the country. See *Small Arms Survey 2011*, 240–9.

24 United Nations Office of Drugs and Crime, *Annual Report: Homicide Statistics 2013*, http://www.unodc.org/unodc/en/data-and-analysis/homicide.html.

25 International Crisis Group, *Reforming Haiti's Security Sector: Rescuing the New Constitution and Democratic Stability*, Latin American Briefing no. 18 (2008), http://www.crisisgroup.org/~/media/Files/latinamerica/haiti/28_reforming_haiti_s_security_sector.pdf.

26 Crime is predominantly property related and perpetrated by gangs. The US Department of State reports that in 2017 there were 890 homicides, 79 percent in Port-au-Prince. See US State Department, *Haiti 2017 Crime and Safety Report*, 2018, https://www.osac.gov/Pages/ContentReportDetails.aspx?cid=23773.

27 See also Jean-Germain Gros, "Haiti's Flagging Transition," *Journal of Democracy* 8, no. 4, (1997): 99. Latin American Public Opinion Project, *Desafíos para la Democracia en Latino América y el Caribe: Evidencia Desde el Barómetro de las Américas 2006-7* (Nashville, TN: Vanderbilt University Press, 2006), 265–73; Latin American Public Opinion Project, "Haiti Questionnaire" (Nashville, TN: Vanderbilt University Press, 2006), http://sitemason.vanderbilt.edu/lapop/HAITIBACK; Dominique Pierre Martin Zéphyr, Yves-François Pierre, Abby Córdova Guillén, and Mitchell A. Seligson, *Culture Politique de la Démocratie en Haiti* (Nashville, TN: Vanderbuilt University Press, 2006), 70–95.

28 International Crisis Group, *Spoiling Security in Haiti* (Latin America/Caribbean Report no. 13), 31 May 2005, http://www.crisisgroup.org/~/media/Files/latin-america/haiti/13_spoiling_security_in_haiti.pdf.

29 Human Rights Watch, "Haiti: Hundreds Killed"; Inter-American Commission on Human Rights, *Haiti: Failed Justice or the Rule of Law? Challenges Ahead for Haiti and*

30 *the International Community*, 2005, http://www.cidh.oas.org/countryrep/HAITI%20 ENGLISH7X10%20FINAL.pdf; International Crisis Group, *Spoiling Security in Haiti*.

30 International Crisis Group, *Haiti: Saving the Environment, Preventing Instability and Conflict*, 2008, http://www.crisisgroup.org/library/documents/latin_america/aiti___saving_the_environment__preventing_instability_and_conflict.pdf. <<This link is broken, Please confirm url and provide access date.>>

31 International Crisis Group, *Haiti 2009: Stability at Risk*, Latin America and Caribbean Briefing No. 19, 31 March 2009, http://www.crisisgroup.org/library/documents/latin_america/b19_haiti_2009___stability_at_risk.pdf.

32 Jorge Hein and Andrew Thompson, "Introduction," in *Fixing Haiti: MINUSTAH and Beyond,* ed. Jorge Heine and Andrew Thompson (New York: United Nations University Press, 2011), 1–23.

33 Aristide, who sought asylum in South Africa, accused foreign powers—in particular the United States and France—of orchestrating the rebellion that ousted him. See Robert Fatton, Jr., "The Fall of Aristide and Haiti's Current Predicament," in *Haiti: Hope for a Fragile State*, ed. Yasmine Shamsie and Andrew Thompson (Waterloo, ON: Wilfrid Laurier University Press, 2006), 19–23.

34 Fatton, *The Fall of Aristide*, 21; Lotta Harbom and Peter Wallensteen, "Armed Conflict and its International Dimensions 1946–2004," *Journal of Peace Research* 42, no. 5 (2005): 625.

35 International Crisis Group, *Spoiling Security in Haiti*.

36 Human Rights Watch, "Haiti: Hundreds Killed"; Inter-American Commission on Human Rights, *Haiti: Failed Justice*.

37 Médecins *Sans Frontières, Haiti: Assisting Victims of Violence and Flooding*, 2004, http://www.msf.org/msfinternational/invoke.cfm?objectid=B8EDB9FA-EF79-467C-.

38 *Small Arms Survey 2007: Guns and the City* (Cambridge: Cambridge University Press, 2007); Inter-American Commission on Human Rights, *Haiti: Failed Justice*.

39 United Nations, "MINUSTAH Facts and Figures," 2011, www.un.org/en/peacekeeping/missions/minustah/.

40 Patricia Ezquenazi, "A Day of Dawning Peace in Haiti," *Americas* 58, no. 3 (2006): 8–11; Andreas E. Feldmann, Miguel Lengyel, Bernabé Malacalza, and Antonio Ramalho, "Lost in Translation: ABC Cooperation and Reconstruction in Haiti," *Journal of Peacebuilding and Development* 6, no. 3 (2011): 45–60; Stephen Baranyi, "Introduction: Peacebuilding and Reconstruction in Haiti," *Journal of Peacebuilding and Development* 6, no. 3 (2011): 3–16.

41 Kristian Hoelscher and Per M. Norheim-Martinsen, "Urban Violence and the Militarisation of Security: Brazilian 'Peacekeeping' in Rio de Janeiro and Port-au-Prince," *Small Wars and Insurgencies* 25, no. 5–6 (2014): 957–75.

42 Inter-American Commission on Human Rights, "IACHR Expresses Concern Over the Situation in Camps for IDPS in Haiti," Press Release No. 114/10 (2010); Feldmann, *The Failed State of Haiti*.

43 International Crisis Group, "Towards a Post-MINUSTAH Haiti: Making an Effective Transition," *Latin America/Caribbean Report N°44*, 2 August 2012, https://d2071andvip0wj.cloudfront.net/044-towards-a-post-minustah-haiti-making-an-effective-transition.pdf.

44 Human Rights Watch, *World Report 2018: Haiti*, 2017, https://www.hrw.org/world-report/2018/country-chapters/haiti.

45 Tilly underscores the difficulties of producing a complete characterization of collective violence by noting that it "resembles weather: complicated, changing, and unpredictable in some regards, yet resulting from similar causes variously combined in different times and places." Tilly, *The Politics of Collective Violence*, 4.

46 Stathis Kalyvas, "The Ontology of Political Violence: Action and Identity in Civil War," *Perspectives on Politics* 1, no. 3 (2003): 475–94.

47 Eriksson, Wallensteen, and Sollenberg define it as "contested incompatibility that concerns government or territory or both when the use of armed force between two parties results in at least 25 battle-related deaths/casualties. Of these two parties, at least one is the government of a state." See Mikael Erikssson, Peter Wallensteen, and Margareta Sollenberg, "Armed Conflict, 1989–2002," *Journal of Peace Research* 40, no. 5 (2003): 597.

48 See David Keen, *The Economic Functions of Violence in Civil Wars* (Adelphi Paper Series, Oxford University Press for the International Institute for Strategic Studies, 1998); Mary Kaldor, *New and Old Wars* (Stanford, CA: Stanford University Press, 2001); Harfried Münkler, "The Wars of the 21st Century," *International Review of the Red Cross* 85 (March 2003): 7–21; Andreas Feldmann and Victor Hinojosa, "Terrorism in Colombia: The Logic and Sources of a Multidimensional and Ubiquitous Phenomenon," *Terrorism and Political Violence* 21 (2009): 42–61; Hew Strachan and Sibylle Scheipers, eds., *The Changing Character of War* (Oxford: Oxford University Press, 2011), 1–24; Benjamin Lessing, *Making Peace in Drug Wars: Crackdowns and Cartels in Latin America* (Cambridge: Cambridge University Press, 2017); Angélica Durán-Martínez, *The Politics of Drug Violence: Criminals, Cops and Politicians Colombia and Mexico* (Oxford: Oxford University Press, 2018); Stathis Kalyvas, "How Civil Wars Help Explain Organized Crime—and How They Do Not," *Journal of Conflict Resolution* 59 no. 8 (2015): 1517–40.

49 Erica Caple James, *Democratic Insecurities: Violence, Trauma and Insecurity in Haiti* (Berkeley: University of California Press, 2010).

50 See Brown, *The International Dimensions of Internal Conflict*, 13–15.

51 Andreas Schedler, "Mapping Contingency," in *Political Contingency: Studying the Unexpected, the Accidental and the Unforeseen*, ed. Ian Shapiro and Sonu Bedy (New York: New York University Press, 2007), 57.

52 Schedler, "Mapping Contingency," 55.

53 Schedler, "Mapping Contingency," 70–3.

54 Philip Pettit, "Resilience and the Explanation of Social Theory," in *Political Contingency: Studying the Unexpected, the Accidental and the Unforeseen*, ed. Ian Shapiro and Sonu Bedy (New York: New York University Press, 2007), 79–98.

55 Brown, *The International Dimensions of Internal Conflict*, 1–15.

56 While most of these categories are self-explanatory, two merit clarification. "Opportunism" refers to the lifting of repressive means or surveillance that open up space for violence. Among its manifestations, Tilly includes looting, revenge killings, military pillage, and piracy. "Broken negotiations" concern violent events that generate retaliatory actions by one or several counterparts that harm people or damage infrastructure. Examples include protection rackets, military coups, demonstrations, and governmental repression. See Tilly, *The Politics of Collective Violence*, 15–16, 25–6. For another typology of violence, see Johan Galtung, *Transarmament and the Cold War: Essays in Peace Research*, vol 4. (Copenhagen: Christian Eljers, 1988).

57 Elster, *Explaining Social Behavior*.

58 Robert Rotberg, "The Challenge of Weak, Failing and Collapsed States," in *Leashing the Dogs of War: Conflict Management in a Divided World*, ed. Chester A. Crocker, Fen Osler Hampson, and Pamela Aall (Washington, DC: US Institute for Peace, 2007), 53–66; Jean-Germain Gros, "Towards a Taxonomy of Failed States in the New World Order: Decaying Somalia, Liberia, Rwanda and Haiti," *Third World Quarterly* 17, no 3 (1996): 455–71; William Zartman, *Collapsed States: The Disintegration and Restoration of Legitimate Authority* (Boulder, CO: Lynee Rienner, 1995); Robin M. Williams, Jr., *The Wars Within: Peoples and States in Conflict* (Ithaca, NY: Cornell University Press, 2003); Jeffrey Herbst, "Responding to State Failure in Africa," *International Security* 21, no. 3 (1996): 120–44. On the construction of states in Latin America, see Hillel Soifer, *State Building in Latin America* (Cambridge: Cambridge University Press, 2015).

59 Michael Mann, *The Sources of Social Power: A History of Power from the Beginning to AD 1760* (Cambridge: Cambridge University Press); Charles Call, "Beyond Failed State: Toward Conceptual Alternatives," *European Journal of International Relations* 17, no. 1 (2011): 303–26.

60 Hedley Bull, *The Anarchical Society* (New York: University of Columbia Press, 1977); Stephen Krasner, *Sovereignty: Organized Hypocrisy* (Princeton, NJ: Princeton University Press, 1999).

61 Gros, *Towards a Taxonomy of Failed States*, 456.

62 Rotberg, *The Challenge of Weak, Failing and Collapsed States*; Zartman, *Collapsed States*; Williams, *The Wars Within*.

63 John Herz, "Idealist Internationalism and the Security Dilemma," *World Politics* 2, no. 2 (1950): 157–80.

64 Barry Posen, "The Security Dilemma and Ethnic Conflict," *Survival* 35, no. 1 (1993): 27–47.

65 Brian Job, ed., *The Insecurity Dilemma: National Security of Third World States* (Boulder, CO: Lynne Rienner, 1992).

66 Haitian jails are a case in point. They distinguish themselves by their inhumane conditions, with most inmates being locked up without having been prosecuted, thereby violating a cardinal rule of due process. See Yasmine Shamsie and Andrew Thompson, "Introduction," in *Haiti: Hope for a Fragile State*, ed. Yasmine Shamsie and

Andrew Thompson (Waterloo, ON: Wilfred Laurier University Press, 2006), 2–4; see also Inter-American Commission on Human Rights, *Haiti: Failed Justice.*

67   The author distinguishes weak states along a continuum depending on their infrastructural capacities; see Gros, *Haiti's Flagging Transition,* 458–9. See also Kalevi Holsti, *Taming the Sovereigns: Institutional Chaos in International Politics* (Cambridge: Cambridge University Press, 2004).

68   Gros, *Haiti's Flagging Transition,* 459.

69   Malick W. Gachem, *The Old Regime and the Haitian Revolution* (Cambridge: Cambridge Press, 2012).

70   Herbst, *Responding to State Failure in Africa.*

71   See Thomas Skidmore and Peter Smith, *Modern Latin America*, 5th ed. (Oxford: Oxford University Press, 2001).

72   Marlye Gélin-Adams and David M. Malone, "Haiti: A Case of Endemic Weakness," in *State Failure and State Weakness in a Time of Terror*, ed. Robert Rotberg (Washington, DC: Brookings Institution Press, 2003) 287–304

73   Nicholls, *The Duvalier Regime in Haiti,* 155.

74   Nicholls, The Duvalier Regime in Haiti, 155.

75   Collier and Collier, *Shaping the Political Arena.*

76   Irwin Stotzky, *Silencing the Guns in Haiti: The Promise of Deliberative Democracy* (Chicago: University of Chicago Press, 1998).

77   Tilly, *The Politics of Collective Violence*, 20–1.

78   Michel-Rolph Trouillot, "État e Duvaliérisme," in *La République Haitienne: État des lieux et Perspectives,"* ed. Gérard Barthélemy and Christian Girault (Paris: Kartala, 1993).

79   Raimo Väyrynen defines predatory practices as "a strong form of political despotism and economic exploitation which pays little attention to the common good and neglects even its own reproduction." See Väyrynen, "Weak States and Humanitarian Emergencies: Failure, Predation and Rent Seeking," in W*ar, Hunger and Displacement: The Origins of Humanitarian Emergencies*, eds. Wayne Nafziger, Frances Stewart, and Raymo Väyrynen (Oxford: Oxford University Press, 2000), 2: 440.

80   Stotzky, *Silencing the Guns*, 60.

81   Samuel Huntington, *Political Order in Changing Societies* (New Haven, CT: Yale University Press, 1968); Ted Robert Gurr, *Why Men Rebel* (Princeton, NJ: Princeton University Press, 1970).

82   Charles King, "Power, Social Violence and Civil War," in *Leashing the Dogs of War: Conflict Management in a Divided World,* ed. Chester A. Crocker, Fen Osler Hampson, and Pamela Aall (Washington, DC: US Institute for Peace, 2007), 115–30.

83   Stephen Van Evera, "Hypothesis on Nationalism and War," *International Security* 18, no. 4 (1994): 5–39; Charles Tilly, "Does Modernization Breed Revolution?" *Comparative Politics* 5, no. 3 (1973): 425–47.

84 Skidmore and Smith, *Modern Latin America*, 296.

85 Nicholls, *The Duvalier Regime in Haiti*; Gros, *Haiti's Flagging Transition*.

86 See King, *Power, Social Violence and Civil War*.

87 See Mats Lundhal, "Haiti: Towards the Abyss? Dependence and Resource Depletion," in *War, Hunger and Displacement: The Origins of Humanitarian Emergencies*, ed. Wayne Nafziger, Frances Stewart, and Raymo Väyrynen (Oxford: Oxford University Press, 2000), 2: 10–19; Homer-Dixon, *Environmental Scarcities and Violent Conflict*.

88 David Keen, *Complex Emergencies* (Cambridge, UK: Polity, 2008).

89 Lundhal, *Haiti: Towards the Abyss?*; Yasmine Shamsie, "The Economic Dimension of Peace Building in Haiti: Drawing on the Past to Reflect on the Present," in *Haiti, Hope for a Fragile State*, ed. Yasmine Shamsie and Andrew Thompson (Waterloo, ON: Wilfrid Laurier University Press, 2006), 37–50; Stotzky *Silencing the Guns*.

90 United Nations Development Programme, "Haiti: Human Development Indicators," 2017, http://hdr.undp.org/en/countries/profiles/HTI.

91 Human Rights Watch, "Haiti: Hundreds Killed"; Inter-American Commission on Human Rights, *Haiti: Failed Justice*.

92 Fatton, *Haiti and the Limits of Sovereignty*.

93 Michel-Rolph Trouillot, "Haiti's Nightmare and the Lessons of History," *NACLA Report on the Americas* 27 (January/February 1994): 46–53; Malick W. Gachem, *The Old Regime and the Haitian Revolution* (Cambridge: Cambridge Press, 2012).

94 United Nations Development Programme, "Haiti: Human Development Indicators."

95 United Nations Development Programme, "Haiti: Human Development Indicators."

96 Arthur Helton, *The Price of Indifference* (Oxford: Oxford University Press, 2003), 86–102; Inter-American Commission on Human Rights, *Special Rapporteurship on Migrants and Their Families. Thematic Reports: Migration and Human Rights*, 2000, http://www.cidh.oas.org/Migrantes/chap.6.2000aeng.htm#IV.%20%20%20%20%20 MIGRATION%20AND%20HUMAN%20RIGHTS.

97 Louis Herns Marcelin, *Haiti Laid Bare*.

98 Kees Koonings and Dirk Kruijt, *Armed Actors: Organised Violence and State Failure in Latin America* (London: Zed Books, 2004), 9–11; Kees Koonings, "Armed Actors, Violence, and Democracy in Latin America in the 1990s: Introductory Notes," *Bulletin of Latin American Research* 20, no. 4 (2001): 401–8.

99 Koonings, "Armed Actors," 2001.

100 Nichols, *The Duvalier Regime in Haiti*.

101 David Held and Anthony McGrew, *Globalization and Anti-Globalization* (Cambridge, UK: Polity Press, 2007).

102 Samuel Huntington, *The Third Wave: Democratization in the Late Twentieth Century* (Norman: University of Oklahoma Press, 1991); Adam Przeworsky, Michael E. Alvarez, José Antonio Cheibub, and Fernando Limongi, *Democracy and Development: Political*

Institutions and Well-Being in the World, 1950–1980 (Cambridge: Cambridge University Press, 2000), 36–51.

103 Edward Mansfield and Jack Snyder, "Democratic Transitions and War: From Napoleon to Millennium's End," in *Turbulent Peace: The Challenges of Managing International Conflict* ed. Chester A Crocker, Fen Olser Hampson, and Pamela Aall (Washington, DC: United States Institute of Peace Press), 113–26.

104 Eriksson, Wallensteen, and Sollenberg, *Armed Conflict, 1989–2002*.

105 J. Michael Queen, David Mason, and Mehmet Gurses, "Sustaining the Peace: Determinants of Civil War Recurrence," *International Interactions* 33 no. 2 (2007): 167–93.

106 Held and McGrew, *Globalization and Anti-Globalization*; Kaldor, *New and Old Wars*; Mark Duffield, *Global Governance and the New Wars: The Merger of Development and Security* (London: Zed Books, 2001).

107 Daniel Deudney and John Ikenberry, "The Nature and Sources of Liberal International Order," *Review of International Studies* 25, no. 2 (1999): 179–96.

108 Duffield, *Global Governance*.

109 Havard Hegre, Reinveig Gissinger, and Nils Petter Gleditsch, "Globalization and Internal Conflict," in *Globalization and Armed Conflict*, ed. Gerald Schneider, Katherine Barbieri, and Nils Petter Gleditsch (London: Routledge, 2003), 251–76.

110 Held and McGrew, *Globalization and Anti-Globalization*, 56.

111 Robert Keohane, "The Globalization of Informal Violence, Theories of World Politics and the liberalism of Fear," in *Power and Governance in a Partially Globalized World*, ed. Robert Keohane (London: Routledge, 2002), 273–83.

112 Renaseer Lee III, "Transnational Organized Crime: An Overview," in *Transnational Crime in the America*s, ed. Tom Farer (New York: Routledge, 1999), 1–2.

113 Lee, "Transnational Organized Crime"; see also Duffield, *Global Governance*, and Kaldor, *New and Old Wars*.

114 *Small Arms Survey 2015: Weapons and the World*, http://www.smallarmssurvey.org/publications/by-type/yearbook/small-arms-survey-2015.html (accessed 12 March 2019).

115 Gargi Bhattcharyay, *The Illicit Movement of People* (London: Pluto Press, 2005).

116 Helton, *The Price of Indifference*; Gros, *Haiti's Flagging Transition*.

117 Juan Gabriel Valdés, Former UN secretary general special representative and head of MINUSTAH, interview by author, 8 July 2008 (Tape recording, Fundación Imagen País, Santiago, Chile); James Cockayne, "Winning Haiti's Protection Competition: Organized Crimes and Peace Operations, Past, Present and Future," *International Peacekeeping* 17, no. 1 (2009): 78–9.

118 Peter Smith, "Semi-organized Crime: Drug Trafficking in Mexico," in *Transnational Crime in the Americas*, ed. Tom Farer (London: Routledge, 1999), 193–216; Jorge Rodriguez-Beruff and Gerardo Cordero, "El Caribe: 'Tercera Frontera' y la Guerra

Contra las Drogas," in *Drogas y Democracia en América Latina: El Impacto de las Políticas de Estados Unidos*, ed. Coletta A. Youngers and Eileen Rosin (Buenos Aires: Editorial Biblios, 2005), 378; James Cockayne, *Winning Haiti's Protection*, 78–9.

119 Daniel Pou, *Armas Pequeñas y Livianas. Informe Sub-Regional Caribe* (Santo Domingo, DO: FLACSO República Dominicana, 2007).

120 Latin American Public Opinion Project, *Desafíos para la Democracia en Latino América y el Caribe: Evidencia Desde el Barómetro de las Américas 2006–7* (Nashville, TN: Vanderbilt University Press, 2006), 265–73; Latin American Public Opinion Project, "Haiti Questionnaire," 2006, http://sitemason.vanderbilt.edu/lapop/HAITIBACK; Zéphyr et al., *Culture Politique*, 70–95.

121 Haiti was listed 168 out of the 180 countries reviewed by Transparency International in 2017. See Transparency International, "Corruption Perception Index 2017," https://www.transparency.org/news/feature/corruption_perceptions_index_2017.

122 *Small Arms Survey 2007*, 174; Muggah, *Securing Haiti's Transition*. Other sources indicate that the number is higher. See Carlos Davia, Kathryn Travers, and Taina Christiansen, *Haiti's Predicament: Small Arms, Light Weapons and Urban Violence: Weapons of Mass Destruction and Small Arms. Disarmament, Non-proliferation, and Arms Control: Part I* (International Peace Studies, University for Peace, 2007).

123 Jean Daudelin, "Moving Frontiers: Patterns of Drug Violence in the Americas through a Property Rights Lens" (paper presented at Arms, Violence and Politics in Latin America: Past, Present, and Future, at the Latin American Research Centre, University of Calgary, May 2009).

124 International Crisis Group, *Reforming Haiti's Security Sector, Rescuing the New Constitution and Democratic Stability*, Latin American Briefing 18, 2008, http://www.crisisgroup.org/home/index.cfm?id=5499&l=4.

125 International Crisis Group, *Reforming Haiti's Security Sector*; Eduardo Aldunate, "My Experience as MINUSTAH Vice-Commander in Chief" (paper presented at Chile's Presence in Haiti: Exploring New Ways, at the Catholic University of Chile, December 2008); Zéphyr et al., *Culture Politique*, 96–127.

126 Koonings and Kruijt, *Armed Actors*, 9–11; Kees Koonings, "Armed Actors, Violence and Democracy," 403–5.

127 Koonings and Kruijt, *Armed Actors*.

128 Paulo Sergio Pinheiro, "Introduction," in *The (Un) Rule of Law and the Underprivileged in Latin America*, ed. Juan E. Méndez, Guillermo O'Donnell, and Paulo Sergio Pinheiro (Notre Dame, IN: Notre Dame University Press, 1996), 1–18.

129 Kooning and Kruijt, *Armed Actors*.

130 Diane Davis, "The Routinization of Violence in Latin America: Ethnographic Revelations," *Latin American Research Review* 53 no. 1 (2018): 211–16.

Operation Condor as an International System of State Violence and Terror: A Historical-Structural Analysis

J. Patrice McSherry

In the 1970s, Operation Condor—a covert, multinational "black operations" program organized by six Latin American states and secretly assisted by the US government—produced new patterns of politicized violence in the hemisphere. Condor operatives carried out the covert, cross-border abduction-disappearance of exiled dissidents, "rendition" to other countries, torture, and extrajudicial execution. Condor squads also assassinated, or attempted to assassinate, key political opposition leaders exiled in Latin America, Europe, and the United States. This chapter assesses the origins of Condor collaboration and methods of state terror in the context of a system of hegemony shaped by Washington in the post–Second World War era. Theoretically, the chapter explores the interaction of structural factors and human agency in the formation, functioning, and final waning of the repressive system known as Operation Condor, adapting concepts from Robert Cox and from Cardoso and Faletto as a framework.

After the Second World War, and especially after the 1959 Cuban Revolution, new progressive and nationalist movements in Latin America issued passionate calls for social justice, control of national resources, nationalization of foreign-owned businesses, greater political participation, land reform, an end to repression, free education, and equality for the oppressed. The 1960s in particular was a tumultuous time in which popular movements demanded new rights and a restructuring of political and economic power. Many workers, peasants, clergy, students, and teachers joined organizations demanding social change. Several guerrilla movements also emerged. As leftist and nationalist leaders won elections throughout Latin America in the 1960s and early 1970s, and new revolutionary and progressive movements gained strength, US security strategists feared a communist-inspired threat to US economic and political interests in the hemisphere. Local elites similarly feared that their traditional political dominance and wealth were at risk.

US officials reorganized the inter-American security system to combat the forces of revolution and social change, expanding the US military presence in the region, incorporating Latin American partners within a dense matrix of hemispheric security institutions, and launching counterinsurgency efforts. The Cold War counterinsurgency regime unified the continent's military, police, and intelligence forces under US leadership in a mission of "internal defense and development"[1] undergirded by fierce anticommunism. While a number of Latin American militaries had previously been political actors, going so far as to take power and preside over military regimes, the new continental security system modernized military capabilities and legitimized a central political role for the armed forces—and justified the harsh repression and the use of extralegal methods against so-called internal enemies. US policymakers often prized their foreign counterparts more for their commitment to anticommunism than to human rights or democratic principles. While some military sectors resisted US influence, over time armed institutions throughout the region adopted the counterinsurgency mission. In the 1960s, '70s, and early '80s US-backed armed forces carried out coups throughout Latin America, moving to obliterate leftist forces and extirpate their ideas. While the forms of repression used in each country differed, the counterinsurgents shared key goals: namely, to eliminate actual and potential "internal enemies," and to reorganize their states and societies to consolidate military power.

The Condor prototype was formed within the inter-American system by early 1974, coalescing after the Uruguayan coup (June 1973) and the Chilean coup (September 1973). Tens of thousands of people from these countries and others fled to Argentina—the last outpost of democracy (under Juan Perón)—to escape severe repression. The military governments in Chile, Bolivia, Uruguay, Brazil, and Paraguay, as well as the CIA, were acutely concerned about these exiles, fearing their activities against these regimes and the probability of international sympathy for pro-democracy movements. Condor was their weapon against them. One former CIA officer, Philip Agee, noted that in the 1960s the CIA had routinely spied on refugees and exiles from the Southern Cone countries and gave lists of suspects to the security forces to round up. "We had many Paraguayans under surveillance in Montevideo," he said. "Montevideo was the place for Brazilians, Argentines, and Paraguayans in the 60s and we had them all under surveillance."[2] Such spying was later subsumed under Operation Condor. Agee said he was sure that the CIA acted within Condor.

Condor, "officially" institutionalized in November 1975, filled a crucial function in the inter-American counterinsurgency regime. While the militaries carried out massive repression within their own countries, the transnational Condor system silenced individuals and groups that had escaped these dictatorships to prevent them from organizing politically or influencing public opinion. The anticommunist mission of which Condor was a part ultimately crushed democratic as well as radical movements and individuals. Latin American elites and military commanders, for the most part, enthusiastically adopted the internal security doctrines, countersubversive mission, and unconventional warfare methods promoted by the United States.[3] Thus, to understand the counterinsurgency regime, as well as the violence and terror sown by Condor in this era, both system- and state-level analysis must be considered. Condor was not solely a Latin American (or Chilean) initiative; nor was it simply an instrument of Washington.

I posit that four key factors led to a continent-wide wave of state terror during the Cold War, including Operation Condor. First, a shared Cold War ideological framework and counterinsurgency orientation, energetically fostered in inter-American facilities and by US Mobile Training Teams. Second, an acceptance of harsh, illegal methods as a legitimate part of an all-out struggle to eliminate perceived existential enemies. Third, the willingness among Condor commanders across the region to allow foreign military and intelligence operations on their soil in the pursuit of enemies across borders, even if suspending sovereignty rights (and violating asylum and human rights norms). Finally, the impetus and resources from a powerful state to train, assist, finance, and arm security institutions and facilitate the development of a covert transnational organization. This analysis suggests that Condor was a product of a contingent set of factors—although it was created largely to preserve the existing structures of wealth and power in the region.

This chapter argues that structural and contingent factors should not be considered an either-or question. Long-term structures form the context and the parameters within which human agency operates. Structural conditions influence, constrain, and shape, but do not determine, decisions made by states and individuals. Decision-makers are presented with both opportunities and limits posed by structural conditions, but their decisions are not preordained. Historical developments are the product of the complex, reciprocal interaction between structures—long-term power relations in political, military, and economic spheres—and contingent choices, which can also shape structures. Structures are not permanent; they can shift, especially during wars or economic crises, or when a critical mass of political opposition generates significant challenges to the existing system of power relations, creating what Robert Cox calls "counterhegemony."

Theoretical Context: Structure and Agency

I define structural conditions as long-term economic, military, and political systems of power relations and dominant ideologies, including long-standing socioeconomic conditions such as poverty, inequality, and exploitation. My analysis draws from Cox[4] as well as Cardoso and Faletto.[5] Cox's model, which builds on Gramsci, illuminates the ways in which power, ideology, and economic (production) relations combine to produce world-historical structures or blocs. By highlighting the interaction between global and state-level factors, Cox bridges the span between comparative and international politics. Cardoso and Faletto also offer a nondeterminist, nuanced analytical framework through which to understand power relations and the dynamics of structure and agency. They argue that "although enduring, social structures can be, and in fact are, continuously transformed by social movements," and assert that their historical-structural approach "emphasizes not just the structural conditioning of social life, but also the historical transformation of structures by conflict, social movements, and class struggles."[6] They add:

> The emphasis on the structural aspect can convey the impression that situations of dependency are stable and permanent.... Our approach should bring to the forefront both aspects of social structures: the mechanisms of self-perpetuation and the possibilities for change. Social structures impose limits on social processes and reiterate established forms of behavior. However, they also generate contradictions and social tensions, opening the possibilities for social movements and ideologies of change.... Subordinated social groups and classes, as well as dominated countries, try to counterattack dominant interests that sustain structures of domination.[7]

Cardoso and Faletto recognize that structures are not permanent or inevitable, but are shaped and reshaped through a process of social change and struggle by social and political actors moving to assert their interests and escape domination and dependency.

Cox's complex model also avoids the pitfalls of determinism that plague some structural theories, such as Kenneth Waltz's neorealism.[8] Waltz argues that the distribution of capabilities in a system essentially determines state behavior; international structures compel states to act in predictable ways no matter which individuals or parties are in power. In contrast, Cox stresses the potential of social forces to influence and transform structural constraints and historic blocs. Structures condition; they affect calculations of interest by elites and non-elites; they can be changed through human agency. Cox defines a "counterhegemonic force" as the combination of an "increase in material resources available to subordinate groups and a coherent and persistent articulation of the subordinate group's demands that challenges the legitimacy of the prevailing consensus."[9]

Cox emphasizes the institutions of power that enforce and advance economic models, positing linkages among ideas and ideology, material capabilities (power), and institutions on a world scale, which may result in either hegemonic or coercive regimes. During the Cold War US interests and actions powerfully shaped international and hemispheric structures. Washington's strategy combined both hegemonic and coercive elements. In Latin America and elsewhere, Washington's foreign policy promoted US-style market capitalism, adherence to the political orientation of the United States, and adoption of an anticommunist security doctrine that particularly targeted "the enemy within." Those political, military, and economic agendas became an integral part of hemispheric relations and national politics and economics in Latin America. While some Latin American governments diverged from Washington in important interest areas, such as economic policy, US leaders had substantial success in their efforts to integrate the region's military and security forces into a more cohesive whole within the counterinsurgency regime. That development was unusual in historical terms. Given the asymmetrical power resources that characterized hemispheric relations, Washington was often able to shape outcomes in ways beneficial to US interests. Moreover, many Latin American elites shared Washington's anticommunism and its fear of social mobilization, especially after the Cuban Revolution. Such leaders were often more responsive to Washington than to their own citizens. When reformist or radical challenges to the dominant order arose, Washington and its Latin American allies often employed coercion—legal and extralegal—to quell them.

Thus, in Latin America during the Cold War a historical structure, in Cox's terms, emerged, dominated by anticommunist ideological concepts and a set of continental institutions backed by US power capabilities. Those structural conditions help to explain why the Condor states, some of which had formerly been adversaries, united for the first time to jointly pursue "subversives" outside the rule of law and beyond their own borders. Previously these militaries had jealously guarded their sovereignty and harbored suspicions of their neighbors. But during the Cold War, military commanders came to share an overarching security doctrine that stressed "ideological frontiers" rather than national borders. They agreed to meld together secret intelligence and "hunter-killer" units to operate in one another's territories, an unprecedented development. Condor was also unprecedented because it wholly left aside any pretense of lawful methods and instead used terror to intimidate and eliminate perceived enemies extraterritorially.

In short, Condor was organized as a covert counterterror apparatus at a particular historical moment, when there was a broad convergence of interests between Washington and the right-wing military regimes of South America and a readiness to combat so-called subversion by whatever means necessary. Since the 1950s Washington had moved to foster and support such like-minded regimes, and weaken or oust leftist or progressive leaders, using its enormous resources in pursuit of a foreign policy designed to shore up US hegemony in the hemisphere in the context of the Cold War. Latin American elites pursued their own perceived interests but were also forcefully and incessantly pressured by Washington. Domestic social conflicts were transformed into continental security crises under the Cold War hegemonic framework.

Given these structural conditions, shaped by US power through both incentives and threats, many of the Latin American political leaders had a fairly narrow range of choices. Many were happy to take advantage of opportunities presented by Washington's agenda to seize more power, secure their economic positions, and consolidate their grip on society. Others who were less accommodating faced threats of termination of economic or military aid, blocking of credits through the IMF or World Bank, covert sabotage, or even overthrow. A number of Latin American leaders who defied or differed from the US agenda were subject to covert action to undermine and/or oust them (Árbenz in Guatemala, Goulart in Brazil, Allende in Chile, the Frente Amplio in Uruguay, and so on). US forces also worked to enhance the influence of those hardline military officers aligned with US goals, to promote the counterinsurgency sector of the region's armed forces over more constitutionalist sectors.

Yet Condor as an active hunter-killer organization declined and disappeared in the early 1980s in South America (although key Condor officers relocated to Central America, where they set up a Condor-like system as revolutionary movements gained strength there in the '80s[10]). The parastatal structures and forces that had played a powerful role for some eight or nine years faded from view. Several explanations can be proposed.

First, Washington's alliance with Britain (rather than Argentina) during the 1982 Falklands (or Malvinas) War angered many Latin American militaries. Second, mass social and political opposition movements in South America had been largely extinguished (although important new human rights organizations were emerging)—that is, Condor's objectives had been largely fulfilled. Third, outside forces such as the United Nations and international human rights organizations, as well as officials in the Carter administration, were aware of Condor and were beginning to investigate and push back.

The Condor case indicates that structures that are powerful at their peak can change, weaken, and finally pass into history. The repression itself engendered new forms of opposition. These observations support the proposition that Condor was a result of a contingent set of factors within the broader structural framework of the Cold War. The combination of a fierce and ruthless internal security doctrine with the capabilities provided by hemispheric military-security institutions and the US government conditioned the choices made by governments in the region in ways that suited both US and Latin American elite interests in preserving existing political and economic hierarchies.

After the end of the Cold War these structural conditions shifted again, opening possibilities for new forms of agency in Latin America. Latin Americans were able to seize new opportunities in part due to the failures of the US-promoted model. New norms and counterhegemonic movements arose based on the popular rejection of key components of the US-sponsored global order and the historical memory of the dirty wars. In the twenty-first century, Latin American states have taken increasingly independent positions. Given the new configuration of social forces and political actors in the region, it seems unlikely at the time of this writing that Condor could be reconstituted there in the foreseeable future. I return to this discussion presently.

The United States in the Cold War Inter-American Security System

As in Europe and Asia, Washington promoted a regional security strategy in the Western Hemisphere. Document NSC-141 (1952) outlined US policy for the Americas as follows:

> We seek first and foremost an orderly political and economic development which will make the Latin-American nations resistant to the internal growth of communism and to Soviet political warfare.... Secondly, we seek hemisphere solidarity in support of our world policy and the cooperation of the Latin-American nations in safeguarding the hemisphere through individual and collective defense measures against external aggression and internal subversion.[11]

Washington had begun urging military collaboration in the hemisphere after the Second World War through organizations such as the US Army Caribbean School—created in 1946 and later renamed the School of the Americas (SOA)—and agreements such as the Rio Pact of 1947, which proclaimed the concept of hemispheric defense. Other institutions that integrated the continent's armies included the Inter-American Defense Board and the Conferences of American Armies. The Conferences were initiated by US commanders in 1960 to fuse together the region's militaries against subversion and revolution during the Cold War. The 1959 Cuban Revolution had spurred an enhanced sense of threat among conservative sectors throughout the region, leading to deeper coordination and the noteworthy redefinition of the primary mission of the Latin American armed forces from *national defense* to *internal security*. Indeed, the curriculum of the SOA was completely transformed in 1961 to emphasize the threat posed by "internal enemies." US and French personnel reorganized and trained the Latin American militaries to undertake aggressive counterinsurgency operations within their own societies. The US security establishment dramatically reoriented, reshaped, expanded, and mobilized the existing hemispheric system to turn these national militaries inward.

The United States had previously carried out covert paramilitary operations and regime changes in the region, such as the subversion and overthrow of Jacobo Árbenz in Guatemala in 1954, via proxy forces, while the French had begun teaching counterinsurgency doctrine in Argentina and Brazil in the 1950s. The CIA had been developing new methods of "psychological torture" since 1950 and refining tactics of unconventional warfare initiated in the Second World War.[12] US counterinsurgency training and doctrine incorporated these methods and fostered the use of terrorism, sabotage, and subversion as tools of paramilitary warfare,[13] tactics that were enthusiastically adopted by many Latin American security forces. The 1960s saw the rapid development and implementation of a counterinsurgency paradigm in the region under both French and US influences. The CIA and the Special Forces became the key advocates, trainers, and advisers of unconventional warfare in Latin America. Much documentation exists on the instrumental role of US advisors in assisting Latin American militaries to create centralized intelligence and operations units, hunter-killer teams, and other secret forces to fight "subversives" during the Cold War.

Colombia provides an early case study. A US military advisory team visited in 1959 to provide advice on constructing a new internal security capability, developing "counter-guerrilla training, civil action programmes, intelligence structures, and communications networks," and aiding the Colombians "to undertake offensive counter-insurgency and psychological warfare operations."[14] US advisors led the reorientation of the Colombian army from conventional to unconventional warfare and the reorganization of its forces to focus on internal security. They also helped to create and organize elite Ranger commandos based on the Special Forces model, a new national intelligence structure, and new PSYWAR and civil action units. US Mobile Training Teams, composed of Special Operations Forces and intelligence advisors, assisted in the creation of "Intelligence/Hunter-Killer teams," which included both military and civilian operatives, to pursue so-called subversives. The US team also recommended "paramilitary, sabotage, and/or terrorist activities against known communist proponents."[15]

A similar US mission was undertaken in Bolivia in 1962. The US government signed an agreement with Bolivia "to make available to the

Government of Bolivia defense articles and defense services for internal security,"[16] and a US Army Military Group was dispatched to create and train a new unit. "Special action" training—or covert unconventional warfare and counterterror training, specifically to pursue and eliminate Che Guevara—was to be provided by the 8th Special Forces Group of Green Berets, as outlined in point 2 of the accord:

> Recognizing a request from the Armed Forces of Bolivia for special training assistance during the initial organization and training phase of this unit, there will be provided a training team of U.S. Specialists from the 8th Special Forces, U.S. Army Forces, Panama, Canal Zone. . . . The mission of this team shall be to provide a rapid reaction force capable of counterinsurgency operations.[17]

The 8th Special Forces Group, based at Fort Gulick, Panama Canal Zone, was the US army's only Special Action Force (specializing in counterinsurgency and counterterror operations, subversion and sabotage, unconventional warfare, and psychological warfare), and it was tasked with providing training to Latin American militaries.[18] The Bolivian Ranger commando unit that captured and executed Che Guevara was set up and trained by the Mobile Training Team from the 8th Group. A CIA paramilitary officer, Cuban exile Félix Rodríguez, was also with the Bolivian unit at the time of Che's capture and killing. Significantly, advisor Walt Rostow noted in a memo to President Johnson that Che's killing "shows the soundness of our 'preventive medicine' assistance to countries facing incipient insurgency—it was the Bolivian 2nd Ranger Battalion, trained by our Green Berets from June-September of this year, that cornered him and got him."[19] Such elite, covert commando organizations—some of which essentially became death squads—dramatically reshaped the state and its relation to society in Latin America and severely impacted human rights.

US military and CIA officers played crucial roles in creating other intelligence and operations organizations in the region, including the Serviço Nacional de Informações in Brazil, the Dirección de Inteligencia Nacional in Chile, la Técnica in Paraguay, and the Dirección Nacional de Información e Inteligencia in Uruguay, among others. These intelligence organizations became key proponents of human rights violations and terror in their countries, and they later formed the nucleus of Operation Condor.

US personnel, notably CIA officers, also played a key role in linking these units together. As one representative State Department policy document advised in 1971,

> Public Safety and military assistance programs providing funds for the training of Uruguayan personnel in the U.S. and Panama... and the maintenance of in-country advisors will continue to provide the bulk of U.S. assistance.... It is especially desirable that such neighboring countries as Argentina and Brazil collaborate effectively with the Uruguayan security forces and where possible we should encourage such cooperation.... To improve the capability of services to successfully detain, interrogate and imprison suspected terrorists, we should consider advisability of providing expert advice, preferably through TDY [temporary duty, possibly contracted] personnel and utilizing third country specialists.... To improve the intelligence capacity of the DNII [the Uruguayan Dirección Nacional de Información e Inteligencia], U.S., or, if possible, third country agencies should provide training.[20]

Latin American Actors in the Inter-American System

Anticommunist actors in the region were quite willing to accept US largesse to fortify their rule (or oust progressive leaders) and quell the rising tide of demands from newly politicized social sectors. The "internal enemies" doctrine targeted legal social movements, leftist political parties, elected leaders, activists, and dissidents, as well as insurgents, all of which were perceived to threaten existing configurations of political and economic power. It is important to see that the right-wing reaction, including Condor, was not solely a response to guerrilla movements. The record shows that the counterinsurgents greatly feared the possibility of *elected* leaders who would pursue a nationalist or leftist agenda through constitutional channels.

That fear of elected leaders is well illustrated by declassified documents detailing discussions between Richard Nixon and Brazilian military dictator Emílio Garrastazu Médici in December 1971.[21] The two like-minded leaders plotted to undermine or overthrow leftist and progressive leaders throughout the hemisphere via covert operations that would hide the hand of the United States. Nixon told Médici that "there were many things that Brazil as a South American country could do that the U.S. could not"—implying that Brazil could act on behalf of Washington—to undermine leftist leaders in Chile, Bolivia, Uruguay, Cuba, and Peru, all of which they discussed. Médici proposed that Brazil and the United States collaborate to stop the "trend of Marxist and leftist expansion," and Nixon pledged to "assist Brazil when and wherever possible," specifically with funds and resources to undermine the leftist government of Salvador Allende in Chile. Médici told Nixon that Brazil was working with Chilean officers to overthrow Allende (this was two years before the 1973 coup), and Nixon responded that it was "very important that Brazil and the United States work closely in this field" so that they could "prevent new Allendes and Castros and try where possible to reverse these trends."[22] The two agreed to set up a secret back channel for communications (to prevent unauthorized persons from reading explosive top-secret exchanges and avoid a paper trail), and Nixon said that he would appoint Henry Kissinger as his liaison.

These documents, released in August 2009, provide new evidence of the ways in which powerful anticommunist leaders conspired to sabotage elected progressive governments promoting social change in the region. Brazil was clearly willing to use "the threat of intervention or tools of diplomacy and covert action to oppose leftist regimes, to keep friendly governments in office, or to help place them there in countries such as Bolivia and Uruguay," as a secret 1972 CIA National Intelligence Estimate put it.[23] Significantly, one concerned Brazilian general told a CIA contact that he thought "the United States obviously wants Brazil to 'do the dirty work,' "[24] thereby expressing internal qualms about Brazil's expanding role as Washington's surrogate in subverting Latin American governments. Despite such occasional reservations, however, the Brazilian military played a major role as a counterrevolutionary actor in the region. Such forms of cooperation laid the groundwork for Operation Condor.

In 1973 or early 1974, before the apparatus acquired its code name and formal structure, the counterinsurgents created the prototype of Operation Condor, a coordinated system for disappearing, torturing, and illegally transferring exiles across borders.[25] Between 1973 and 1975, cross-border disappearances and forcible, extralegal transfers of exiles ("renditions") by multinational squadrons commenced under an unwritten agreement enabling the associated militaries to pursue individuals who had fled to neighboring countries. This was the essence of Condor, as yet unnamed. Chilean colonel Manuel Contreras, head of Chile's Dirección de Inteligencia Nacional (DINA), was a key Condor organizer. He called for a founding meeting to institutionalize the Condor prototype in 1975. In 2000 the CIA acknowledged that Contreras had been a paid CIA agent between 1974 and 1977, a period when the Condor network was planning and carrying out assassinations in Europe, Latin America, and the United States.

In Argentina, Perón himself apparently mandated Argentine participation in the Condor prototype. Evidence suggests that he authorized joint cross-border operations before his death in July 1974. A declassified US document noted that

> Perón authorized the Argentine Federal Police and the Argentine intelligence to cooperate with Chilean intelligence in apprehending Chilean left-wing extremists in exile in Argentina. Similar arrangements had also been made with the security services of Bolivia, Uruguay, and Brazil. This cooperation among security forces apparently includes permission for foreign officials to operate within Argentina, against their exiled nationals. . . . This authority allegedly includes arrest of such exiles and transfer to the home country without recourse to legal procedures . . . [and includes] the formation of paramilitary groups to act extralegally against the terrorists, including the utilization of abduction, interrogation, and execution.[26]

In 1974 a Uruguayan abduction-disappearance squadron took up residence in Buenos Aires, where it worked with its Argentine and Chilean counterparts to seize, torture, interrogate, and illegally transfer exiles (many of whom had protected status with the United Nations) to their home countries. Selected Uruguayan navy units began to coordinate secret repressive actions with personnel from the notorious Argentine Navy Mechanics School (ESMA) in 1974, and an ESMA delegation traveled to Uruguay that year to train officers in torture techniques in counterinsurgency courses.[27] Later, Condor officers in Argentina used an abandoned auto repair shop, Orletti Motors—code-named OT [Operaciones Tácticas] 18—as a secret torture and detention center for foreign detainees. Survivors reported seeing Bolivians, Chileans, Uruguayans, as well as two Cuban diplomats, imprisoned and tortured there. Orletti was under the operational control of the Argentine intelligence organization Secretaría de Inteligencia del Estado (SIDE), which reported to the top commanders of the Argentine dictatorship.

In August 1975, organizers of the eleventh Conference of American Armies held a preliminary planning meeting in Montevideo, and in October the inter-American military summit took place in that city. These secret conferences were a major venue for secret planning among the army delegates, including Condor operations. Conferences had "mandatory themes" including "The Establishment of a Communications Net to Transmit and Exchange Information on Subversive Movements" (1963); "Administration of Training and Intensifying Preparations of Armies in Revolutionary Wars" (1964); "Communist Subversion in the Americas/Democratic Education and Instruction on Fighting a Revolutionary Battle" (1969); "Strategies Against Subversion in the Americas for the Security of the Hemisphere" (1973); and "Psychological Warfare Guarantee from Member Armies Not To Permit Subversive Elements From Other Countries to Operate in Their Country" (1981).[28] The theme for the 1975 conference was "Rules of the CAA [Conference of American Armies] and Integral Education System in the Americas (To Contribute to the Eradication of Subversion)."

The commander of the Uruguayan Joint Chiefs, Luis Queirolo, saluted his "grand nucleus of friends and comrades in arms" at the preparatory conference and lauded the unified mission of the militaries, proclaiming that "the only thing separating us is our uniforms, for the men of the armies of America, I believe, have never before understood one another as we do at this moment. . . . There exists a coordination among the armies of the continent to combat and impede Marxist infiltration or whatever other form of subversion."[29] General Julio Vadora—Uruguayan army chief, president of the 1975 conference, and a Condor commander—gave a fiery speech at the October session and, significantly, endorsed "the regional integration" of the armed forces. He added, "Marxist theories have no place, with their class struggles, generational confrontations, conflicts between owners and workers, just as there is no place for violence, hate, lies, and corruption, breaches of authority, anarchy, illiteracy, misery or hunger. The armies are the instruments of national integration." A 6 November memo from the Uruguayan Embassy in Santiago about the army conference noted that the de facto civilian president of Uruguay, Juan María Bordaberry, had given a speech as well.[30] Bordaberry had dissolved Congress and cooperated with the military to close down Uruguay's democracy and institute a civil-military dictatorship in 1973.

Between 6 and 12 October, the Conference of Intelligence Commanders took place in Uruguay's Hotel Carrasco, and on 29 October the Conference of Commanders in Chief was held. Here Manuel Contreras of the Chilean DINA launched his proposal for institutionalizing the Condor prototype. He circulated an agenda, dated 29 October, and a recommended structure for the transnational repressive alliance and called for a formal founding meeting in Santiago in November. Contreras noted in his invitation that previous combined operations had taken place on the basis of "gentlemen's agreements" and that more permanent, sophisticated structures were needed. Contreras's proposal reflected the apocalyptic language of the national security doctrine:

> Subversion, for some years, has been present in our Continent, sheltered by politico-economic concepts that are fundamentally contrary to History, Philosophy, Religion, and the traditions of the countries of our Hemisphere. This described situation recognizes no Frontiers or Countries, and the infiltration penetrates all levels of National life. . . . It is to confront this Psycho-political War that we have deter-

mined that we must function in the international environment not with a command centralized in its internal functioning, but with an efficient Coordination that will permit an opportune interchange of intelligence and experience as well as a certain level of personal relations among the chiefs responsible for Security.[31]

At the Santiago meeting military delegations from Argentina, Bolivia, Chile, Paraguay, and Uruguay signed what was essentially the charter document of the Condor organization. (Brazil, with observer status, became a full member soon afterward.) The original proposals were adopted, a coordinating structure and encrypted communications system organized, and security procedures agreed upon. The participants pledged to initiate "rapid and immediate contact when an individual was expelled from a country or when a suspect traveled in order to alert the Intelligence Services" of the other Condor countries. Point 5G of the agreement recommended installing intelligence operatives in each country's embassies, where they would be fully accredited and, moreover, would be in a position to monitor and control Condor operations. Point 5L stated that the "present organism is denominated CONDOR, approved unanimously in conformity with the motion presented by the Uruguayan delegation in honor of the host country."[32]

In recent years much documentation has been discovered in the Paraguayan police's "archives of terror," in Uruguayan, Argentine, Chilean, and Brazilian archives, and in declassified US files on the growing collaboration among the militaries, their shared hatred of and alarm at the "subversive threat," and their regular intelligence meetings in the 1970s. The Paraguayan archives include lists of thousands of persons—including children—suspected to be subversives, and thousands of photos of "seditionists," many from neighboring countries. Lists of Chileans, Uruguayans, Brazilians, and Bolivians exiled in Misiones Province, Argentina, filled one police file. Some photos carried a red slash and the handwritten words "Muerto" or "Capturado."[33]

An August 1975 intelligence report discovered in Uruguay in 2006, written by notorious Uruguayan Condor operative Colonel José Gavazzo, further documented Condor operations. Gavazzo had always denied involvement in Condor despite being identified by numerous survivors of Orletti. The report confirmed his role as a key Condor commander as it discussed intelligence gathered on the activities of revolutionary groups, including the Junta Coordinadora Revolutionaria, and persons from Chile, Bolivia, Argentina, and Uruguay, and reported on the abductions of some of them in Argentina.[34] Gavazzo was also implicated in cables from 1976 released in Uruguay in 2009. The decoded cables between "Condor 1" (Argentina) and "Condor 5" (Uruguay), were marked "Secret-Very Urgent" and conveyed requests for intelligence about suspects. Gavazzo signed one cable as "Jefe de CONDOROP" (Chief of CONDOROP).[35] Journalist Roger Rodríguez noted that the acronym was in English (CONDOROP) rather than Spanish (OPCONDOR) and wondered whether it reflected the covert US role in Condor.[36] These cables were turned over to the Uruguayan courts in 2009.

Another series of intelligence reports, written by Condor officer Enrique Arancibia Clavel—Chilean DINA agent and torturer stationed in Argentina during the 1970s—showed the massive toll of military extermination efforts. He reported:

> Attached is a list of all the deaths during the year 1975. The list is classified by month. It includes the "official" deaths as well as the "unofficial." This work was done by Battalion 601 of Army Intelligence located at Callao and Viamonte, which depends on *Jefatura II de Inteligencia* of the General Command of the Army. The lists correspond to annex 74888.75/A1.EA. and annex 74889.75/id. Those that appear NN are those whose bodies were impossible to identify, almost 100% of which correspond to extremist elements eliminated by the security forces extralegally. There are computed 22,000 between dead and disappeared from 1975 to the present.[37]

Thousands of exiles from many countries were under threat in each of the Condor countries and beyond. In August 1977, for example, the UN Human Rights Commission representative said she had placed under UN protection some fifty refugees in Rio de Janeiro, most of them Argentine, and sent them to third countries.[38] In another case, an Argentine living in Rio reported to the UNHCR that he had been kidnapped by a group of Brazilians and Argentines and tortured with electric shocks in an unknown location before being released.[39] In 1979 Bolivian human rights leaders said there were hundreds of Bolivians missing as a result of "repressive coordination" among the South American dictatorships, and they specifically cited Operation Condor.[40] The Condor regime was lethally effective—due, in no small measure, to covert US assistance.

US Involvement in Condor

Washington acted as a secret partner and sponsor of Condor, particularly during the Nixon and Ford administrations. A number of declassified documents show that top US leaders and national security officials considered the Condor system an effective and valuable weapon in the hemispheric anticommunist crusade. The strategic concept of Condor as a covert special operations force fit neatly within US unconventional warfare doctrine. One military analyst defines special operations as "unorthodox coups ... unexpected strokes of violence, usually mounted and executed outside the military establishment of the day, which exercise a startling effect on the enemy: preferably at the highest level."[41] Such operations are conducted "outside the normal legal conventions governing war," as one analyst delicately put it.[42] Another defines a special operations force in terms of its "strategic utility" in providing "significant results with limited resources" and having a "disproportionate impact" as a force multiplier, thus "expanding the options of political and military leaders."[43] A fourth asserts that Special Operations Forces have large roles in three key missions: preemptive action, domestic counterterrorism, and unconventional warfare. Unconventional warfare includes "a broad spectrum of military and paramilitary operations ... conducted by, with, or through indigenous or surrogate forces who are organized, equipped, supported and directed by an external source."[44]

Many declassified US documents of the time referred to Condor in favorable language. One 1976 Defense Intelligence Agency (DIA) report noted that a Condor assassination unit was "structured much like a U.S. Special Forces Team," and matter-of-factly described Condor's "joint counterinsurgency operations" to "eliminate Marxist terrorist activities."[45] Military and CIA cables reported on secret Condor operations, including the forced disappearance of dozens of members of the Uruguayan Partido de la Victoria del Pueblo (PVP) in Buenos Aires in 1976, indicating close relations with key Condor hunter-killer units.[46] In this case, the Uruguayan army tried to camouflage the PVP disappearances with a psychological operations campaign, claiming that the exiles had returned to Uruguay clandestinely in a planned "invasion" of the country. Colonel Gavazzo and other Condor officers staged a spectacular fictitious capture of the disappeared and tortured activists, bringing them from secret detention centers in Uruguay to local hotels and then ostentatiously parading them before the press, with large numbers of weapons that they said belonged to the PVP members.[47]

The CIA provided telex machines and, later, state-of-the-art computers to the Condor system, coding and decoding devices, and other technology, while US security agencies provided intelligence cooperation, including lists of suspects. Declassified documents show that US personnel were directly involved in some Condor abduction-disappearances and "renditions." The Rettig Commission of Chile learned, for example, that the capture of Chilean militant Jorge Isaac Fuentes Alarcón in Paraguay was a cooperative effort by Argentine intelligence services, personnel of the US Embassy in Buenos Aires, and Paraguayan police.[48] In another case, Argentine Condor operative Leandro Sánchez Reisse, testifying before a congressional subcommittee in 1987, stated that there was a central inter-American intelligence body called the Intelligence Advisory Committee that included delegates from the Latin American intelligence services as well as the CIA and the DIA. This body apparently discussed individuals who were considered political enemies and threats in the region; some of them disappeared.

In recent years the attorneys of Condor operatives in both Chile and Argentina have argued before judges that the tactics of torture, abduction, terrorism, and sabotage used in the dirty wars were legitimate and lawful under the existing military governments and part of authorized military doctrine and training. The lawyer for Chilean Condor torturer Miguel Krassnoff asserted in 2004, for example, that "the State instructed" Chilean officers to use such methods and that therefore his client should not be held accountable. He went so far as to show military manuals to the court as evidence—and to argue that army doctrine at the time drew directly from counterinsurgency techniques elaborated in the United States and taught in the School of the Americas. In 2005 an Argentine lawyer made an identical argument before a court on behalf of his clients, thirty dirty war officers, including General Santiago Riveros (a Condor commander). He cited passages from an Argentine army manual on psychological warfare that referred to the use of torture, sabotage, threats, and kidnappings.[49] In 2009, when the manual in question was made public, retired Argentine colonel Horacio Ballester, president of the Center of Military Men for Democracy, said that it seemed to be a direct translation of a US manual used in the School of the Americas during the Cold War.[50]

There was an even more stunning indication of covert US collaboration with the Condor apparatus: Condor units operated from the major US military base in the Panama Canal Zone. The base was the regional counterinsurgency center, often serving as a platform for US intervention in Latin American countries. The site hosted some fourteen US military installations at the time, including the School of the Americas, the headquarters of the Southern Command, bases for the four armed services, and a large CIA station. Moreover, Condor officers were granted authorized access to the US continental communications system housed at the base.

A Paraguayan general told Ambassador Robert White in 1978 that Condor agents used "an encrypted system within the U.S. telecommunications net[work]" on the base, which covered all of Latin America, to "coordinate intelligence information."[51] White immediately linked the operation to Condor. The base's powerful communications capability gave Condor agents the ability to monitor, track, and seize individuals across a vast geographical area—and demonstrated deep US engagement and involvement with the Condor system. The provision of a top-secret, encrypted, dedicated channel for communications on an important US base indicates that the Condor network was considered a high-risk, highly classified black operation that served the interests of Washington. As I have argued previously, this degree of US involvement is one of several crucial pieces of evidence that Condor was a top-secret component of the continental counterinsurgency regime, sponsored and led by Washington.

As the US government, the regional hegemon, facilitated the militarization of Latin America, it also supplied crucial sustenance to the Condor organization that functioned covertly within the inter-American system.

Analyzing Contingent and Structural Factors

Washington perceived a threat to its hegemony in Latin America, and its anticommunist partners in the region also feared popular protest and movements demanding structural change. The developing world was viewed as the key battleground in the East-West conflict, and the US government interpreted any challenge to US orientations and its preferred form of market capitalism to be subversive, whether nationalist, social democratic, or even neutralist. At the same time, traditional elites and conservative military officers in Latin America were alarmed by the rise of social mobilization within their countries.

During this era Latin American and US military and political elites made calculated decisions to bypass legal methods in order to demobilize societies and eliminate potential, or actual, power contenders. Brutal methods were considered legitimate, even noble, in a zero-sum struggle with "subversion." As Brian Loveman points out, in some countries secret police had resorted to practices like torture in earlier eras. But during the counterinsurgency period torture, disappearance, extrajudicial execution, and assassination became institutionalized, and human rights crimes became widespread. The creation and use of parastatal forces and structures instilled dread and fear within broad populations, disorienting and disarticulating them. The systematic use of death squads and mass "disappearances" appeared first in Guatemala in the 1960s, part of a counterinsurgency strategy encouraged by US advisors. Indeed, death squads appeared in several countries where US police training programs were largest in the 1960s and '70s: in Guatemala, Brazil, Uruguay, and the Dominican Republic.[52] These squads were parallel forces created and used by states as counterinsurgency tools. As local elites sought to preserve or increase their wealth and power they often chose alignment with Washington as their best option, at times even opportunistically inflating the threat of "communism" to win US backing.

There was a convergence of interests in preempting radical or even social democratic alternatives to the prevailing politico-economic systems. The Condor system was perceived to have "strategic utility" and to be cost effective. Washington had helped to create the environment for unconventional warfare and covertly facilitated Condor's formation and its subsequent operations. It is unlikely that the Latin American military states themselves could have constructed, or perpetuated, such a sophisticated continental hunter-killer program as Condor without Washington's political, technological, and intelligence resources. US sponsorship served as a link among the Latin American countries, and Washington was a key proponent and enabler of anticommunist repressive operations across the region. Conversely, US opposition to such hemispheric death squad operations could have greatly weakened or stopped them, given the substantial support and sustenance (e.g., the Panama communications network) that Washington was providing. This observation is important because it locates Condor within the system of hegemonic power relations at the time, and it highlights the key role that Washington played in the production and perpetuation of particular patterns of political violence.

The continent's militaries were united in a "holy war" against subversion during the Cold War. US forces worked to deepen this unity of interests and ideology within the inter-American security institutions and through the strategic use of enormous resources to provide incentives and threats. Many of the militaries embraced the messianic role and new national powers provided by the counterinsurgency regime. Challenges to elite rule would be met lethally, lawlessly, and brutally, outside of previously recognized limits. Condor was a black operation within the counterinsurgency effort, and it had a powerful supporter.

Longitudinal Comparisons: Changing Historic Blocs and Structures

In the early twenty-first century, however, survivors of the dirty wars had ascended to the presidencies of Argentina, Brazil, Chile, and Uruguay, and leftists also governed in Bolivia, Ecuador, Venezuela, Paraguay, El Salvador, and Nicaragua. Preventing this scenario had been a crucial goal of Washington's hemispheric policy during the Cold War. How can this change be explained? True, most of these new leaders deliberately cultivated a moderate stance and avoided the more radical policies embraced by Hugo Chávez of Venezuela and a few others. It was also true that US policy and military resources were focused on wars in the Middle East. But it seemed clear that Washington's previous hegemonic influence and its model of world order had weakened in Latin America. Moreover, Condor had a beginning and an end. Why? It is not enough to observe that Latin Americans were now exercising agency in new ways and choosing leaders, and new paths, that diverged from Washington's preferences. To understand *how* and *why* this situation came about we must also look to changing structural factors and the rise of counterhegemony in the region.

First, much information had emerged documenting Washington's links to military coups and dictatorships during the Cold War. Such information tarnished the reputation of the United States in the eyes of many Latin Americans, as did the US obsession with drug trafficking and other security-oriented agendas after the end of the Cold War. Second, the US-sponsored economic model of free-market neoliberalism had been challenged in Latin America, in a gradually cumulative process, since the 1980s. During the 1980s and '90s the linkage of discredited military regimes with neoliberal economic policies; the debt crisis; the policies of structural adjustment; the overbearing role of the IMF and World Bank; the increasing poverty and inequality in Latin America; the collapse of social welfare programs and public institutions such as schools and hospitals; the financial meltdowns in several key countries: all of these developments led to widespread rejection of "the Washington consensus" in the region. Masses of people, sectors of the media, political organizations, and other social forces pushed back against the existing model of power relations, which was impoverishing large majorities, and over time succeeded in challenging it. Leaders who had aligned themselves with that consensus were defeated (or ousted through "people power," as in Ecuador and Argentina). New leaders were elected who rejected the neoliberal model and acted to redirect state resources domestically, to a greater or lesser extent. In short, the Cold War model of repressive military rule coupled with internationally linked free markets entered into crisis in the 1980s and '90s in the region and gradually became delegitimized. While poverty and inequality, and new forms of violence, persisted, Latin America provides an example of the power of popular movements' ability to not only confront structural systems of power, but also to alter them over time. As the structural conditions shaped by US hegemony in the hemisphere entered a state of flux, new opportunities arose for Latin Americans to choose alternative paths, which had been closed to them earlier. Counterhegemonic movements were further strengthened by significant public rejection of the George W. Bush administration's "War on Terror," its doctrine of preemption, its invasion of Iraq, and its lawless methods, which many of the world's people condemned.

Global structures were changing as well. With the "unipolar moment" that began with the collapse of the USSR, an ascendant force in US politics—the neoconservatives—had urged that the country move to assume world dominance and prevent the rise of any other power.[53] They also pushed relentlessly for an invasion of Iraq and the establishment of US hegemony in the Middle East. But this hegemonic project created new countermovements. Much of the world rejected the preemptive incursion into Iraq and condemned the methods used in the so-called War on Terror. The United States entered a crisis of legitimacy under the Bush administration and became increasingly isolated politically. The severe financial crisis and recession that began in 2007 cost Washington and its dominant model of structuring global economic relations even more credibility. These developments signified a gradual shift in global power structures that was still unfolding as this chapter was being written. As the US politico-economic model entered into crisis, new opportunities opened for less powerful states to stake independent positions and pursue independent policies. The "unipolar moment" seemed to be ending as new power centers emerged in the world in opposition to US policies.[54]

Moreover, human rights norms and institutions had grown stronger internationally since the end of the Cold War. The 1990s saw many advances in the global human rights regime, including the arrest of General Pinochet under the principle of universal jurisdiction, and the creation of the International Criminal Court (ICC). After the terrible toll of the dirty wars, important sectors of the Latin American public were pro-democracy and very much aware of human rights issues. Many Latin American states, in an impressive show of defiance toward the Bush administration, refused to sign bilateral agreements exempting US personnel from the

ICC's jurisdiction, even when Washington threatened to cut off military aid (and did). Argentina, Venezuela, Bolivia, and Uruguay withdrew their officers from SOA training programs. Ecuador closed the US military base at Manta. When Colombia entered Ecuador in 2008 in a preemptive strike against Colombian guerrillas, its action was roundly condemned by Latin American leaders and the OAS—despite support for Colombia from the United States. In August 2009, all the Latin American presidents strongly opposed a US-Colombia plan allowing US military forces access to seven military bases for operations in that country and for continental counter-drug operations that used to be based in Manta. In short, Latin American leaders were challenging US policies and defining their own agendas in new ways. Opposition had assumed a critical mass, leading to new configurations of power or, in Cox's terms, a counterhegemony. Such expressions of independence—even when risking US threats and penalties—signaled important changes in overarching structures and power relations as well as new forms of agency.

Latin America thus reflects the dynamic interaction between structural and contingent factors. Rising challenges to central pillars of existing power relations led to the emergence of a new configuration of power in the hemisphere. Washington became relatively weaker and unable to impose its preferred model in the region. As the US-dominated political-economic global order (or historic bloc, in Cox's terms) entered a crisis of legitimacy, new possibilities for Latin American agency emerged, and Latin Americans seized them to pursue their own interests, even if defying Washington's preferences.

Even the security forces of the region changed to some extent. There were still intransigent elements within the region's military, police, and intelligence institutions (as well as within US forces). The mystique of elite units operating outside the law continued to appeal to some military sectors. But the militaries were wary of the Bush administration's attempts to promote the War on Terror as an all-encompassing continental mission and paradigm, similar to Cold War national security doctrine, and essentially they refused to accept US pressure to adopt it.

In short, power relations between the United States and Latin America were less asymmetrical than before, due to the changed configuration of social forces, institutions, ideologies, economic relations, and norms.

Key actors were choosing *not* to align with US interests and agendas as changing structural conditions opened new opportunities to pursue national interests. All these developments suggested that any sort of reconstitution of a Condor organization in Latin America was unlikely in the contemporary historical moment. Latin Americans were very aware of the horrors of the past, and they wanted to lead the way in the struggle for truth and justice so as to prevent future dirty wars and future Condors. The rejection of Washington's security paradigm in the region had real consequences. Large movements of people had effects in terms of shaping new structures and making alternative choices. Latin America well illustrates the insight that not only do structures affect the decisions of actors, but actors can change structures, or create new ones.

Conclusion

The question of structural and contingent factors is a complex one. During the Cold War era the latitude for contingent choices available to Latin American leaders and movements within the prevailing structures was quite restricted. US policymakers made deliberate decisions to back leaders in Latin America whose main assets were anticommunism and a pro-US orientation, and to oust leaders who challenged US policy preferences. Hemispheric structures drew the armed and intelligence forces together in an anticommunist mission with extensive repercussions in the region. Military and civil-military governments of the era employed vicious repression and worsened social stratification and inequality. Condor was formed within this convergence of Cold War interests, ideas, and institutions. Elites made strategic choices, calculating—within the matrix of threats and incentives from Washington—that extralegal forms of violence were the most efficient way to preserve their power and crush opposition. Condor was judged to have "strategic utility"—that is, its benefits outweighed its costs. While such elite decisions were not inevitable, there were powerful forces at work that shaped the options available to Latin American leaders in military and security matters.

This line of reasoning suggests that the specific type of organized violence represented by Condor was a contingent phenomenon having much to do with structural conditions, including US objectives and methods in the region, the hemispheric counterinsurgency regime, and the correlation of forces at the time. A Cold War historic bloc existed, to use Cox's terms. The Cold War hegemonic structure was a prism through which most elites interpreted events. Labor strikes, peasant protests, and student demonstrations were all considered signs of communist subversion, even though many of the militant movements targeted by repressive governments were demanding more democracy, more inclusion, and more social equality. These were legitimate demands that governments could have accommodated. The problem was the overarching military-political structure and its accompanying ideological assumptions, which "internationalized" what were actually domestic conflicts. That historic bloc has undergone transformation since the 1980s.

Understanding the specific forms of state-sponsored violence represented by Operation Condor thus requires a perspective blending system and state levels and a dynamic understanding of the reciprocal interaction between structures and contingent choices. As Cardoso and Faletto argue, this sort of analysis avoids "the two fallacies frequently found in similar interpretations: a belief that the internal or national socio-political situation is mechanically conditioned by external dominance; and the opposite idea that all is due to historical contingency."[55]

During the Cold War the United States, as the hemispheric hegemon, was able to shape a historic bloc and strongly influence the economic, political, and military directions of Latin American countries, in many cases inducing them to accept US preferences. In Cardoso and Faletto's terms, Washington, aided by its Latin American allies, employed specific mechanisms and processes of domination to maintain existing structures of wealth and power in the hemisphere.[56] Condor represented a powerful new structure that generated new patterns of violence and had a far-reaching impact upon thousands of people. Yet Condor came to an end when new divisions appeared between Washington and Latin American governments and when new international institutions and social forces (both local and international) began to publicly denounce and act against the repression. The actors involved in the Condor system eventually opted to disengage. Clearly, the operation's costs had reached the point of overshadowing its benefits. Condor effectively became dormant in the early 1980s in South America—although the Condor model was transplanted to Central America by Condor officers, where it functioned throughout the 1980s.

New Condor-like systems of illicit violence could possibly be resurrected, although the prospects seem slim at this historical moment in Latin America. The counterweight to such a development is rooted in human agency: aware and active people and organizations, informed by historical memory, that oppose parastatal forces and extremist security doctrines and act to forestall them through law, through education, through organized action, and through strengthening the powers of democratic domestic and international institutions.

Notes

The author is grateful to the director of the Armed Groups Project, Pablo Policzer; to all the members of the group, especially Raúl Molina Mejía and Susan Franceschet; and to her colleague Rose Muzio, for their valuable comments on this chapter.

1   See, for example, John Child, *Unequal Alliance: The Inter-American Military System, 1938–1978* (Boulder, CO: Westview Press, 1980).

2   Stella Calloni, "La CIA actuó en la Operación Cóndor contra las izquierdistas de América Latina: ex agente," *La Jornada* (Mexico), 9 May 2006.

3   For a nuanced perspective, see the introduction to *When States Kill: Latin America, the U.S., and Technologies of Terror*, ed. Cecilia Menjívar and Néstor Rodríguez (Austin: University of Texas Press, 2005).

4   It should be noted that Cox and Cardoso and Faletto place large emphases on production relations and economic development, respectively, while my analysis here adapts their concepts to analyze primarily political-military developments. This chapter draws on a 1998 paper of mine, which also used Cox's framework. See McSherry, "The Argentine Military-Security Forces in the Era of Globalization: Changes and Continuities," International Congress, Canadian Association for Latin American and Caribbean Studies/Canadian Association for Mexican Studies, Vancouver; Robert W. Cox, "Social Forces, States, and World Orders: Beyond International Relations Theory," *Millennium: Journal of International Studies* 10, no. 2 (1981): 126–55; republished with a postscript in Robert O. Keohane, ed., *Neorealism and Its Critics* (New York: Columbia University Press, 1986); see also Cox, *Production, Power, and World Order: Social Forces in the Making of History* (New York: Columbia University Press, 1987).

5   Fernando H. Cardoso and Enzo Faletto, *Dependency and Development in Latin America*, expanded and amended ed. (Berkeley: University of California Press, 1979).

6   Cardoso and Faletto, *Dependency and Development*, x.

7   Cardoso and Faletto, *Dependency and Development*, x–xi.

8   Kenneth Waltz, *Theory of International Politics* (Reading: Addison-Wesley, 1979).

9   Robert W. Cox and Timothy J. Sinclair, *Approaches to World Order* (Cambridge: Cambridge University Press, 1996), 364.

10 See McSherry, *Predatory States: Operation Condor and Covert War in Latin America* (Lanham, MD: Rowman and Littlefield, 2005), Chapter 7.

11 Cited in Brian Loveman, *For La Patria: Politics and the Armed Forces in Latin America* (Wilmington, DE: Scholarly Resources, 1999), 151.

12 See, for example, Alfred McCoy, *A Question of Torture: CIA Interrogation, from the Cold War to the War on Terror* (New York: Metropolitan Books/Henry Holt, 2006); Christopher Simpson, *The Science of Coercion: Communication Research and Psychological Warfare, 1945-1960* (Berkeley, CA: Oxford University Press, 1996).

13 See Michael McClintock, "American Doctrine and Counterinsurgent State Terror," in *Western State Terrorism*, ed. Alexander George (New York: Routledge, 1991): 121-54; Michael McClintock, *Instruments of Statecraft: U.S. Guerrilla Warfare, Counterinsurgency, Counterterrorism, 1940-1990* (New York: Pantheon Books, 1992), especially chapter 2.

14 Dennis M. Rempe, "Guerrillas, Bandits, and Independent Republics: US Counter-insurgency Efforts in Colombia 1959-1965," *Small Wars and Insurgencies* 6, no. 3 (Winter 1995): 304-27.

15 Rempe, "Guerrillas, Bandits, and Independent Republics," 308.

16 "Memorandum of Understanding Concerning the Activation, Organization and Training of the 2nd Ranger Battalion – Bolivian Army," 28 April 1967, www.gwu.edu/~nsarchiv/NSAEBB/NSAEBB5/che14_1.htm (accessed 23 November 2007).

17 "Memorandum of Understanding Concerning the Activation, Organization and Training of the 2nd Ranger Battalion – Bolivian Army."

18 Fred J. Pushies, Terry Griswold, D. M. Giangreco, and S. F. Tomajczyk, *U. S. Counter-Terrorist Forces* (Minneapolis, MN: Crestline Imprints, 2002).

19 Walt Rostow memorandum for the President, "Death of 'Che' Guevara," 17 October 1967, from National Archives and Records Administration (NARA) files.

20 epartment of State, Secret Airgram, To State Department, From U.S. Embassy, Montevideo, "Transmission of a Preliminary Analysis and Strategy Paper – Uruguay," 25 August 1971, p. 17.

21 See National Security Archive, "Brazil Conspired with U.S. to Overthrow Allende," *National Security Archive Electronic Briefing Book No. 282*, 16 August 2009, http://www2.gwu.edu/~nsarchiv/NSAEBB/NSAEBB282/index.htm (accessed 17 August 2009).

22 "Memorandum for the President's File," from Henry Kissinger, 9 December 1971, p. 5. See also McSherry, *Predatory States*, 53-8.

23 CIA, National Intelligence Estimate 93-72, Secret, "The New Course in Brazil," 13 January 1972.

24 Secret CIA Memorandum, "Alleged Commitments Made by President Richard M. Nixon to Brazilian President Emilio Garrastazu Médici," n.d.

25 See McSherry, *Predatory States*, for evidence of this conclusion, including discussion of a secret February 1974 meeting of Condor representatives in Buenos Aires.

26 C. M. Cerna, "Summary of Argentine Law and Practice on Terrorism," US State Department, March 1976, cited in Martin Edwin Andersen, ed., *Dossier Secreto: Argentina's Desaparecidos and the Myth of the "Dirty War"* (Boulder, CO: Westview, 1993), 108. See also Horacio Verbitsky, "El Vuelo del Cóndor," *Página/12*, 28 January 1996; and Miguel Bonasso, *El presidente que no fue: Los archivos ocultos del peronismo*, 2nd ed. (Buenos Aires: Planeta, 2002), 819.

27 A former navy officer testified about this covert relationship in a 2008 trial in Uruguay. See "La Armada ya coordinaba con la ESMA," *La República* (Montevideo), 19 August 2008.

28 The 1981 theme is interesting, since it was a major Condor function. See Spanish website for the Conferences of American Armies, http://www.redcea.org\CycleInformation.aspx?Language=1&Cycle=11&Type=Mandatory (accessed 15 June 2006).

29 *Círculo Militar* (Montevideo), *El Soldado* (September 1975): 13, reviewed by author in Montevideo, August 2005.

30 Documents discovered by scholar Fernando López in Uruguayan Foreign Ministry files in August 2009, which he generously shared with the author. Caja 33, Embajada Uruguaya en Chile, Carpeta 6 "Conferencia de Ejercitos Americanos," November 1975.

31 "Primera Reunión de Trabajo de Inteligencia Nacional: Indice," document no. 00022F 0156, 29 October 1975, obtained by author in Paraguayan police archives in 1996.

32 This document was discovered in the Ministry of Foreign Relations in Chile in 1999 and published in the daily *La Nación* (Santiago), 16 June 1999.

33 Author's notes from 1996 examination of Book 007, D1, in Paraguayan archives.

34 Copy of the report in author's possession. See Walter Pernas, "La autoincriminación de José Gavazzo en la Operación Cóndor," *Brecha* (Montevideo), 30 June 2006; Stella Calloni, "Gavazzo fue figura clave en la Operación Cóndor en Argentina," *La Jornada* (Mexico), 25 June 2006.

35 Róger Rodríguez, "Uruguay era el 'Cóndor 5' y Gavazzo figura como 'el jefe' de 'CONDOROP,' " *La República* (Montevideo), 5 January 2009.

36 Personal correspondence with author, 6 January 2009.

37 Arancibia Clavel files, document in author's possession. See also National Security Archive, http://www.gwu.edu/~nsarchiv/NSAEBB/NSAEBB185/full%20%5BReport%20on%20Argentina%20disappeared%5D.pdf (accessed 22 January 2008).

38 US Consulate to Secretary of State, "Argentine Refugees in Brazil," 25 August 1977.

39 US Consulate, Rio, to Secretary of State, "Argentine Refugees in Brazil," 30 August 1977.

40 US Embassy in La Paz, to Secretary of State, "Concern over Bolivian 'disappeared' in Argentina and Chile," 18 October 1979.

41 M. R. D. Foot, "Special Operations, 1" in *The Fourth Dimension Resistance*, ed. E. Elliott-Bateman (Manchester: Manchester University Press, 1970), 19, cited in Captain Malcolm Brailey, "The Transformation of Special Operations Forces in Contemporary Conflict: Strategy, Missions, Organisation and Tactics," *Land Warfare Studies Centre Working Paper No. 127*, November 2005.

42 Brailey, "Transformation," 20. This author is an advocate of Special Forces operations. He cites, for instance, the role of Special Forces Mobile Training Teams in El Salvador in the 1980s as an example of great success.

43 C. Gray, "Handfuls of Heroes on Desperate Ventures: When Do Special Operations Succeed?" *Parameters* no. 2 (Spring 1999), cited in Brailey. "Transformation."

44 US Department of Defense Joint Publication 1-02, cited in K. D. Dickson, "The New Asymmetry: Unconventional Warfare and Army Special Forces," *Special Warfare* (Fall 2001): 16–17.

45 Defense Intelligence Agency, "Special Operations Forces," US Army, Defense Intelligence Agency (Washington, DC), 1 October 1976.

46 Defense Intelligence Agency, "Special Operations Forces."

47 A defector from the Uruguayan Servicio de Información de Defensa (Defense Intelligence Service) testified to this black operation. See "Declaraciones de Julio Cesar Barbosa Pla: Ex Integrante del SID," nd (1977?). Obtained by author in Buenos Aires from Argentine Commission on Historical Memory, 2005. See also McSherry, *Predatory States*, 122–25.

48 Fuentes Alarcón was seized by Paraguayan police as he crossed the border from Argentina to Paraguay in May 1975. Fuentes, a sociologist and a leader of the Chilean revolutionary group Movimiento de Izquierda Revolucionaria, was traveling with Amílcar Santucho, a brother of the leader of the Ejército Revolucionario del Pueblo of Argentina. Fuentes was transferred to Chilean police, who brought him to Villa Grimaldi, a notorious DINA detention center in Santiago. He was last seen there, savagely tortured. A declassified letter from the US Embassy in Buenos Aires (written by Robert Scherrer) informed the Chilean military of Fuentes's capture and provided the names and addresses of three individuals residing in the United States whom Fuentes had named during his interrogation. The letter stated that the FBI was conducting investigations of the three. This letter, among others, confirms that US officials and agencies were cooperating with the military dictatorships and acting as a link in the Condor chain.

49 Jorge Escalante, "Defensa de Krassnoff dice que el Ejército le enseñó a torturar," *La Nación* (Santiago), 15 September 2004; Marcos Taire, "El Ejército fue instruido para el secuestro, el terrorismo, la tortura y el asesinato," *ARGENPRESS*, 11 March 2005.

50 Adriana Meyer, "Un manual para represores," *Página/12*, 26 July 2009. Riveros was convicted in August 2009.

51   See secret "Roger Channel" cable from Ambassador Robert White to Secretary of State, "Second Meeting with Chief of Staff in Letelier Case," 13 October 1978, http://foia.state.gov/documents/StateChile3/000058FD.pdf (accessed 7 February 2001); see also Diana Jean Schemo, "New Files Tie U.S. to Deaths of Latin Leftists in 1970s," *New York Times*, 6 March 2001.

52   Michael Klare and Nancy Stein, "Police Terrorism in Latin America: Secret U.S. Bomb School Exposed," *NACLA Latin America and Empire Report* 8, no. 1 (January 1974): 21.

53   See, for example, the 1992 Defense Planning Guidance of the first Bush administration, prepared by neoconservatives in Secretary of Defense Cheney's office, which was leaked to the media. Many of the neocons assumed strategic positions in the Bush II administration and fiercely advocated the invasion of Iraq.

54   For more analysis of these events, see John Ehrenberg, J. Patrice McSherry, José R. Sánchez, and Caroleen Marji Sayej, *The Iraq Papers* (Berkeley, CA: Oxford University Press, 2009).

55   Cardoso and Faletto, *Dependency and Development*, 173.

56   Cardoso and Faletto, *Dependency and Development*, x.

PART II

3

Written in Black and Red: Murder as a Communicative Act in Mexico

Pablo Piccato

In the fourth part of his novel *2666*, Roberto Bolaño writes about the remains of women found dead in a northern border city. Page after page, he describes clothes, details from the place of discovery, bones. There is little else: only traces of victims' identities, no unfolding resolution of a mystery, no detective able to find the murderer. The problem with murder, Bolaño suggests, is not discovering the truth behind it, but understanding its meaning, as if killing was a public statement by an unknown speaker we must nevertheless acknowledge. The mystery is less who did it (impossible to know, most likely) as what they meant by it. Unlike other predatory crimes, homicide excludes the victim from any subsequent exchange about its consequences, whether that involves punishment or forgiveness. The living are left to deal with it.[1]

I will argue in this chapter that the living give meanings to criminal violence by talking about murder, and that this operation informs the uses of that violence: murder is committed not only as an instrument to obtain advantages in politics or drug trafficking, but also as a way to convey specific messages. This means considering murder not only as a public-health or criminal-justice problem but also as a communicative act intended to be received and decoded by an audience. Homicide is the center of a field of public discourse that, out of a strong sense of moral condemnation of the crime, makes explicit the ineptitude of the police and judicial system, and is therefore critical of the government in ways in which other, more strictly "political" areas of debate, are not.

A similar approach was proposed by Thomas de Quincey in the fictional lectures of the Society of Connoisseurs in Murder. De Quincey provoked readers by assessing the aesthetic values of blood and crime scenes. What do killers intend to say? How should their act be interpreted? The answers to these questions in contemporary Mexico, I believe, are central to understanding the relationship between civil society and the state. We should remember that, already by De Quincey's time, aesthetic judgment was essential to the development of a modern public sphere as a space of critical debate. By proposing an amoral perspective on crime he stressed the artificiality of dividing debates about art from those about other matters of public interest. Contemporary scholars have explored the value of criminal acts and languages as communication across media and social groups.[2] A similar effect can be found in homicide in twentieth-century Mexico to the extent that it creates a field of public discussion, engaging audiences and transforming the rules for their critical exchanges with the state. Yet this story is not only about modernization. In the case of Mexico, the public use of homicide has contributed to an unprecedented increase of violence in recent years. Thus, in order to understand the changing rules of that public discussion and the weight of the past on contemporary circumstances, it is necessary to look at the meanings of murder in a historical framework.

It might seem redundant to defend the value of a historical perspective on crime, but in the case of present-day Mexico it is necessary. The rise in crime since the 1990s and the subsequent moral panic has generated a cottage industry of consultants, think tanks, research projects. It offers "consumable" advice to federal and local governments, which in turn pay for most of the research.[3] The result is the predominance of policy-oriented perspectives that seldom look at evidence older than the ten or so years available in surveys or statistical databases, some of them of dubious quality but strong public impact.[4] The problem is compounded by the fact that criminology in Mexico has not established itself as an academic discipline with its own standards and institutional support.[5] Paradoxically, the subject of "perceptions" of crime is increasingly important in the field of *seguridad pública* studies. Polls gather information about the public's views on the problem of insecurity without serious questioning of the categories used, and yet it is assumed that their results should have policy implications because they faithfully reflect actual variations in criminal practices. Polls and independent studies are necessary, it is argued, because official statistics are not reliable.[6]

The questions raised by contemporary levels of violence seem so urgent that audiences have no reason to consider the relevance of the past: it has never been so bad, we hear; memory provides only a golden age to contrast against the present. I will argue, instead, that a historical approach shows that homicide in twentieth-century Mexico has been a key theme in the relationship between civil society and the state and in public discussions about justice and transgression.[7] Looking at changes in the meanings of murder during the twentieth century, I will suggest that the new modalities of violence, insofar as they respond to codes of meaning that are themselves the product of the historical evolution of murder as a communicative act, are in fact not so new.

This chapter will first examine that evolution in broad strokes: an overview of the trends in murder rates across the country will be contrasted with public views of increasing danger throughout the century. This will lead to an examination of the rules and media of public discourse defined around crime. The third section will suggest an explanation and a way to look at contemporary violence linked to drug trafficking. I will conclude by returning to the interpretations of murder in literary fiction and suggest ways in which they can be useful to understand the present.

Perceptions, Trends, and Practices

Murder has been too frequent in Mexico, but not to the extent that many people think. That is suggested by published judicial statistics since the late nineteenth century—the best long-term indicator, although by no means a complete accounting. Qualitative evidence indicates that murder was a concern during the nineteenth century, although not the national obsession it would become by the late twentieth. The paradox is that, even though the worry about murder has probably become more acute in the last hundred years, the statistical evidence shows that its frequency has been steadily declining. It is not clear yet how that long-term decline has

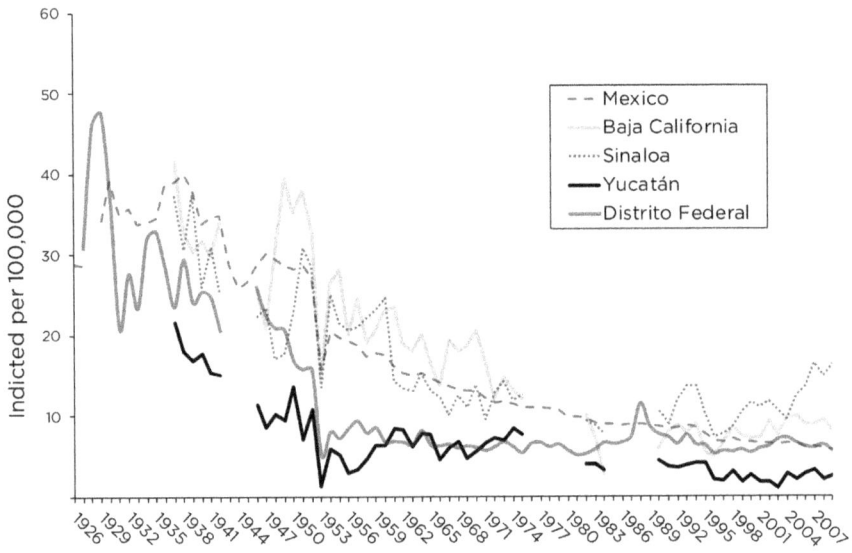

Figure 3.1
Homicide Indicted, Rates per 100,000 Population. Mexico, 1926–2009.
Source: Pablo Piccato, Sara Hidalgo, and Andrés Lajous, "Estadísticas del crimen en México: Series Históricas 1926–2008," https://ppiccato.shinyapps.io/judiciales/.

been affected by the recent spate of drug-related violence. Secretario de Seguridad Pública Genaro García Luna recognized the dissonance between decreasing rates of murder and increasing concerns about it, explaining it as a consequence of organized crime's goal of spreading fear and demonstrating its power.[8]

The difference between perception and actual trends is not new. Figure 3.1 shows national rates of persons indicted for homicide per total population, indicating a decline in homicide during most of the twentieth century.[9] Although rates are high today, they seem to be much smaller than in the years before and immediately after the 1910 revolution. In the Ciudad de México, where that information is available for persons sentenced, the rate of homicide per 100,000 inhabitants was 46, on average, between 1885 and 1871, 31 in 1909, and climbed to 37 in 1930, decreasing thereafter.[10] The decline corresponds with that of criminality in general in the country, as witnessed by the trends of other crimes.[11] Homicide seems to have continued a steady decline until the present. The number of homicides known to authorities (always larger than the number of people indicted, as many cases do not lead to arrests) has decreased in recent years, from a national rate of 37 per 100,000 inhabitants in 1997 to 33 in 2011.[12] Figure 3.1 also suggests that, even if homicide has been a stable problem throughout the twentieth century, it has changed its places and trends in recent years. The Ciudad de México now has rates higher than the national rate, as do states like Sinaloa and Baja California—both clearly impacted by the expansion of the drug business and correlated violence—all of them contrasting with the historically low levels of Yucatán. The problem is serious but not as bad as in other places: a recent UN comparison gives 18 homicides per 100,000 inhabitants in Mexico, against 33 in Colombia, 66 in El Salvador, and 5 in the United States.[13]

Decreasing and relatively low rates of homicide in Mexico are counterintuitive. Although homicide is commonly held to be a crime that is easy to count, while other crimes like theft and rape can easily escape the attention of institutions, in the case of Mexico we have to take this certainty with a grain of salt. Today, undercounting of homicides is widespread, and is linked to broader institutional problems. The frequency of disappearances has increased significantly, according to anecdotal evidence but no formal count. If we compare the number of homicides identified as the cause of death by health authorities with the number of people indicted for homicide, the latter is consistently and amply higher. The difference—an average of 65 percent more for the country between 1926 and 2005, and 91 percent more for the Ciudad de México—suggests that justice only reaches a limited number of cases. According to the Instituto Ciudadano de Estudios Sobre la Seguridad, between 1997 and 2003 the number of persons sentenced for homicide was on average 20 percent of the number of investigations opened for the crime.[14] This is a greater problem in certain regions, such as the northern border in recent years. The work of other scholars suggests that the number of crimes never reported and prosecuted is very high, although it is not clear whether this situation has worsened in recent years due to the lack of long-term victimization surveys.[15] There is no conclusive evidence, however, that the limited number of prosecutions for murder could explain the declining rates: most likely, if we consider the qualitative evidence described below, the problem of impunity has been constant throughout the century.

Public concern about murder has never diminished during the century. On the contrary, it grew as evidence of the corruption and ineptitude of the police and the judiciary was publicized and became a political issue. Famous cases of unsolved homicides and the evidence of impunity seem to have had more impact than any statistical analysis in creating concern among the general public. Another reason for this paradoxical difference between trends and fears are the patterns by which murder was committed and the ways in which civil society responded to it.

Civil society plays a central role in the prevention of crime and the resolution of the conflicts generated by it. My own work on Mexico City and that of other scholars shows that communities that often lack the institutional support of a reliable police or justice system have found ways to deal with transgression, sometimes through the use of collective violence, sometimes by ignoring domestic abuse, but more often through shaming and different modes of informal reintegrative justice that try to restore a sense of safety to victims. These mechanisms, invisible to official statistics and victimization surveys, are less effective when dealing with murder, particularly if violence includes powerful weapons or a weak state response. The increasing use of guns and the highly organized behavior of killers might explain part of the difference between trends and perceptions.[16]

The practices of murder in Mexico have changed during the century, with the increasing use of firearms over knives and blunt objects. Street-corner brawls were the most visible form of homicidal violence early in the twentieth century. A knife fight between two men, provided that certain basic rules were followed, expressed the courage of both rivals, independently of the outcome. Although the vocabulary was different, the rules of honor were the same as in elite duels. Guns modified these rules, as they made it harder to express equality or even deliberate coordination between fighters: fewer people owned a gun—which could kill from a distance without exposing the body of the shooter.[17] Guns, however, did not make homicidal violence random or arbitrary. After the revolution, when many former revolutionaries came to respectable official positions, the image of the *pistolero* was associated with murder and impunity: he was the bodyguard and enforcer for politicians or criminals, close to if not a member of the police, an expert in violence always beyond the reach of justice. The use of *pistoleros* against political opposition, union leaders, or students constituted a kind of artisanal deployment of violence, yet a highly visible one, and thus symbolic of the informal monopoly on violence exercised by the Mexican state and the local ruling *camarillas*. The dapper *pistolero* used his gun to demonstrate his political clout, without any pretense of fair play but without shying away from his reputation. The gun in the waist was part of his outfit, a symbol of power similar to his badge.[18]

In recent years, less individualistic and more efficient *sicarios*, usually working for organized crime, have come to represent the evolution and privatization of the *pistolero*. The gang known as Los Zetas is the best example: its founders came from an elite Mexican army unit trained in the United States. They still recruit new members from the armed forces, sometimes advertising with banners on city streets. They kill with overwhelming use of force and little concern about police obstruction. Drug lords are making increasing use of this new brand of professionals of violence. From the beginnings of their large-scale transnational business in the first half of the twentieth century, drug traffickers tried to isolate their commercial operations from bloodshed, which they saw as a cost that should be kept at a minimum; bribes were always preferred to outright violence. Some groups, like the Arellano Félix clan in Tijuana, began to use careless violence in minor transactions in the 1980s. This lack of discipline, and the more aggressive yet still disoriented enforcement by the state in the last decade, has given the experts in violence a power of their own: the Zetas started selling their services to the Gulf Cartel, in Tamaulipas, but now engage in other activities such as kidnapping, robbery, commissioned killings, and human trafficking. It was, in the words of one journalist, as if the organization of Don Corleone had been put in the hands of Luca Brasi.[19]

Murder and Publicity

This new brand of violent criminals can be defined not only by their use of powerful weapons, abundant funds, and a complex, military-like organization, but also by their deliberate use of the media to further their goals. Regardless of the number of crimes they commit, their impact on public debates about crime is very high.[20] This is possible because, as practices and practitioners of criminal violence evolved during the twentieth century, changing public interpretations of murder became the center of a distinct field of public discourse that found in the *nota roja* its best medium, first in the police section of newspapers, then through illustrated magazines and, in more recent years, on television. The genre got its name when an editor in Guadalajara had a hand smeared with red ink printed on the cover of his newspaper in the 1880s. Scholars and art critics have explained the great commercial success of police news in Mexico by the attraction of gore and sex, the modernization of traditional narrative forms, and its ability to popularize criminological knowledge. This analysis has stressed the visual elements of its language: lurid crime scenes satisfied readers' anxieties and other shameful pornographic needs and provided cues for direct, visceral responses to crime.[21]

Homicide was the center of the *nota roja* because its consequences could be depicted visually in a way impossible to emulate in other crimes. The twentieth century in Mexico, as in other places, saw the development of a graphic language that filled newspaper pages with naked or decomposed cadavers, suspects' mug shots, and the objects and traces of death. Illustrations echoed the stark contrasts and frontal framing of forensic shots, but added a sense of drama by their association with written narratives. Victims, even the ones who were alive, could not escape the public display of the humiliation to which they had been subjected.[22] In recent years the graphic imagery of death and murder has become an object of aesthetic and even commercial value, particularly through the work of photojournalists like Enrique Metinides and performance artists like SEMEFO and Teresa Margolles.[23]

Without disputing the attraction of images, I would argue that, during the middle decades of the twentieth century, the *nota roja* was meant to be read, not just looked at, and that reading it involved a critical consideration

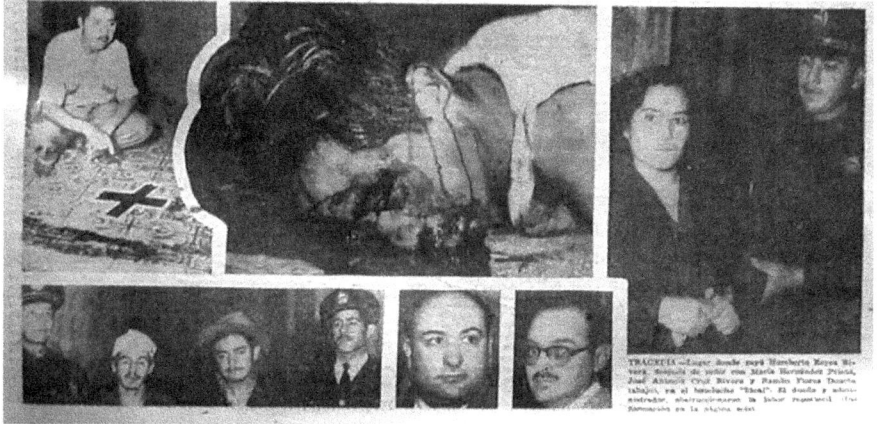

FIGURE 3.2
Crime Scene Images. *La Prensa*, 8 January 1953. Courtesy of *La Prensa*, Fototeca, Hemeroteca y Biblioteca Mario Vásquez Raña, Organización Editorial Mexicana.

of the political impact of murder. Around or below the image, the headlines contain a pun, convey moral outrage, or synthesize the crime in the most direct words. They characterize victims or criminals in memorable ways: "The plumber who killed a cobbler in an absurd fight"; "He wanted to have fun and they destroyed his face with bottles"; or the famous "Violóla, matóla, enterróla" (He raped her, he killed her, he buried her).[24] The text of the article usually contains a wealth of detail that might contradict the moralizing bent of the photographs, captions, and headlines. When readers bought *Alarma!*, the most popular magazine in the country since the 1960s, we can assume that they planned to take some time to go through the abundant copy, coming to associate one shocking image with one complex story. Figure 3.2 exemplifies the combination of narrative and images in the *nota roja*. Closely cropped we see, clockwise from right, the female suspect, held by a police officer; the administrator and owner of the hotel where the events took place; the two other suspects, also surrounded by police agents; the exact place where the victim fell; and the body of the victim. The ensemble combines gore, the objectivity of crime scene investigation, and the shaming of mug shots. Events, consequences,

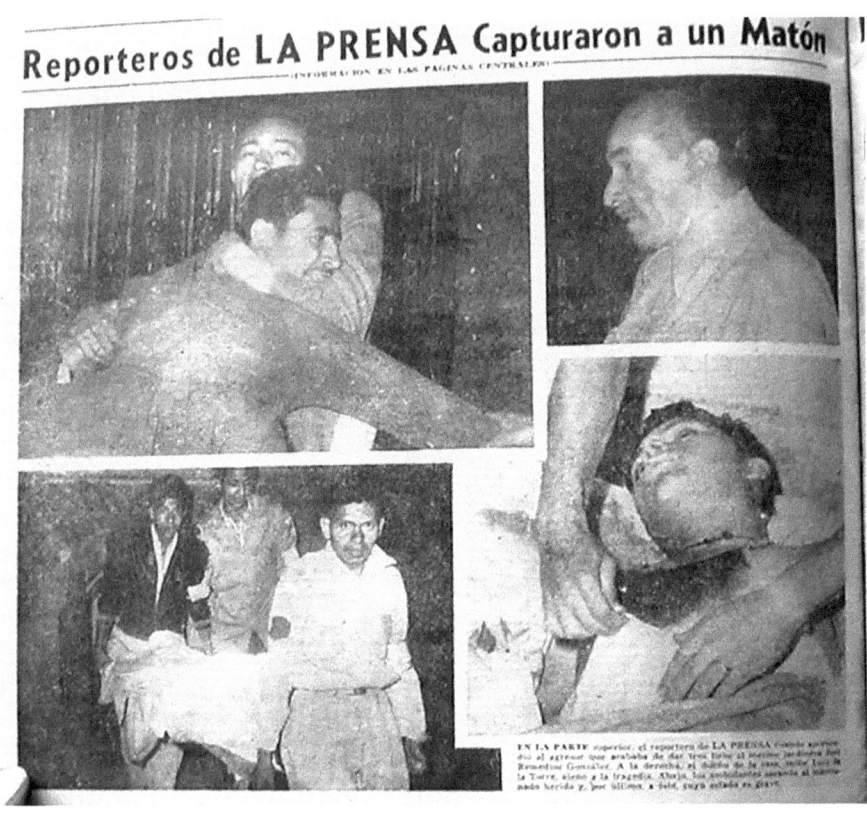

FIGURE 3.3
Reporter Captures Suspect. *La Prensa*, 17 March 1959. Courtesy of *La Prensa*, Fototeca, Hemeroteca y Biblioteca Mario Vásquez Raña, Organización Editorial Mexicana.

and responsibility could not be depicted in a more economical way. The story explained the circumstances of the crime in considerable detail.[25]

A careful reading was in order because press accounts were the basic public testimony of crime. They tended to adopt the perspective of the police, which provided much circumstantial detail. Stories were tightly organized around shocking events and disturbing personalities; victims were defined in a few strokes, as were other less prominent witnesses or suspects. Detectives, prosecutors, and judges were praised or criticized. Police news highlighted the role of the reporter. The hotel staff in figure 3.2

were portrayed in such an unflattering way because they "obstructed the job of reporters." Although government agencies, sports, or social news were more desirable assignments for journalists, police reporters had a unique proximity to the story and some of them achieved some fame thanks to the sensational cases they covered. Reporters came to expect judges to give them unfettered access to suspects (which they could interview and photograph at will, often on the presumption of their guilt) and to the records and evidence of trials. *Nota roja* reporters were so closely identified with the police and suspects that sometimes people mistook them for detectives surveying the crime scene and interviewing witnesses.[26] In one case, documented in Figure 3.3, a reporter from *La Prensa* was portrayed subduing a suspect.

Reporters were important because they expressed readers' right to have an informed opinion about a case, just like detectives or judges did. Reports included meaningful data that invited readers to produce hypotheses different from those put forth by the authorities. It is commonly argued that the *nota roja* is a genre in which moralistic opinion and morbid images hide the full political and social implications of crime, or where irrationality prevails. If we look at the coverage of some homicides during the golden years of the genre, however, we find detailed narratives that faithfully convey a diversity of voices and opinions. Police sections assumed, and required, a high level of engagement from readers. Small features in their pages revealed myriad interactions between readers and editors: letters denouncing daily problems of life in the city and trying to elicit official action; photographs of suspects or lost children, asking those who knew anything to call a telephone number. Press reports documented each crime, regardless of the official response to it. When relatives of victims wrote to presidents asking that murders be investigated, they added press clippings to prove that the case was real. Police news, in sum, conveyed a strong sense of urgency. It dealt with issues that, although not involving sovereignty or the overall political system, reflected directly on the issues of everyday life, such as security, urban services, and domestic relations.[27]

We should keep in mind that the regime that dominated Mexico between 1929 and the last decades of the century controlled political news in newspapers with little need for direct censorship, relying instead on advertising, loans to companies or editors, and envelopes thick with cash distributed to reporters. As a result, the political sections of newspapers barely covered social movements like the railroad workers' strikes of the 1950s, or the student movements of the 1960s, and all but ignored the fierce repression these actions met. The *nota roja* could report on the crimes committed by powerful politicians or their relatives, and expand on the private vices that would turn them into victims. Police news was popular because it had pragmatic, engaged readers. It was a guide to the dangers of everyday life, from domestic violence to street delinquency, from brutal policemen to corrupt judges.[28] People dealt with government representatives through the roles of victims or suspects. In Mexico, this constant game (who got caught and who did not, who became a helpless victim and who avoided the danger) frames the reading of police news and the exercise of citizenship. The importance of the media in the context of contemporary violence is a consequence of the development of the *nota roja* as a prime scenario for political debate in twentieth-century Mexico.

The political meaning of murder is fully spelled out in presidential archives. A homicide's dramatic consequences and the fact that the perpetrator often enjoyed impunity prompted citizens to demand justice from authorities, and gave victims' relatives a political agency seldom associated with the victims of other crimes. Regardless of their social background, these indirect victims were not afraid to name corrupt or complicit officials and to argue that impunity meant loss of legitimacy for the government. Citizens' petitions to the president in relation to a homicide came from individuals and organizations such as unions or neighbors' associations. These petitions, part of a long tradition of public discourse in Mexico, asked for justice, and they seldom failed to refer to police news and to allude to the political implications of their demands. The archives of Mexican presidents, particularly from Lázaro Cárdenas (1934–40) to Adolfo López Mateos (1958–64), at the National Archives, hold many of these letters—an average of 1,189 files per six-year presidential period. Considering the numbers of indicted persons provided by judicial sources, at least 3 percent of all homicides in the country found their way to the president's desk. Presidents took an active role, forwarding letters to the attorney general, following up on certain cases, and even offering security to relatives of victims threatened by freed murderers.[29] Nobody saw this as a violation of due process. Sometimes it was necessary to take justice into one's own hands, or at least to give it a nudge.

These letters provide detailed narratives of the aftermath of a murder—in contrast with judicial records, which are only concerned with its causes, and with press reports, which seldom pay attention to the social cost of the crime. Petitioners tried to convey the impact of the crime on the lives of people beyond the courtroom and the crime scene. In doing so, they could not but express the uncomfortable fact that judicial authorities were helpless in front of the real power of *pistoleros*, *caciques*, or corrupt officials. Appealing to the president meant that lower authorities had caused "disappointments" to those who were seeking justice. Balentina Esquevel denounced the local bosses who killed her son and shot her in the leg yet escaped punishment because they offered "beer and a good lunch" to the prosecutor.[30] Murder gave some people enough courage to tell ugly realities to the president. In 1958, according to the relative of one of his victims, air force pilot Sergio García Núñez bragged that a judge was going to acquit him soon because the judge had received 50,000 pesos. Another suspect was paying 9,000 pesos a month to avoid indictment. All letters were more or less explicit about a basic political reasoning: eventually the legitimacy of the president himself depended on his handling of such cases. Or, in the words of one of these letter writers, "the people get tired, Mr. President, of so many García Nuñezes."[31]

Presidents were prompted to respond, we might speculate, by their sense of duty, but also by the fact that petitioners were not afraid to warn that their pursuit of justice would continue in front of the press. Such threats may sound strange given the extent of presidential power in Mexico during the twentieth century. But homicide opened up debates that were not easy to control. Murderers at large were a stain on the reputation of police and judges, all of them political appointees, and a symptom of authorities' limited power. Such revelations could have an impact on investigations: when a case of grievous impunity was mentioned in the pages of newspapers, the game shifted in favor of the complainants. Keeping homicides quiet was therefore useful for suspects. The above-mentioned García Núñez bragged that "by explicit orders of the Presidency newspapers remain silent about everything concerning his case."[32] He did not have an alibi, but he had political clout and a media strategy.

With the same basic language and themes, the field of public discourse centered on homicide continued to expand during the twentieth century. It has been the space, for example, of denunciations against human rights abuses by police agencies since the late 1970s; it has provided the context for perceptions of the weakening of the Partido Revolucionario Institucional (PRI) regime, particularly the unity of the *familia revolucionaria*, following a string of high-profile murders in 1993 and 1994. While the *nota roja* continued as a popular print genre, TV shows emulated the same graphic resources and critical bent of the press—at least to the extent possible in the duopolistic and loyally pro-government television industry. President Ernesto Zedillo, who reached office precisely because of one of those murders (that of PRI candidate Luis Donaldo Colosio), and who would preside over the transition to the first post-PRI president, pressured a TV network to cancel a tabloid show (*Duro y directo*) in 1999. Videos of homicides had been broadcast even before they became common on the Internet.[33] Recent years have seen the continuity of the communicative uses of homicide, although now in a context that intersects with the booming economy of drug trafficking and the diversification of electronic media used to convey explanations of murder. Thanks to wide access to Internet video, television is no longer the privileged source for gruesome images associated with crime in Mexico.

Continuities

Since the 1980s drug traffickers, with their abundant cash and help from US gun suppliers, have introduced many and more powerful weapons into the practice of homicide. Again, as with the widespread use of guns after the revolution, the new tools did not result in uncontrolled and meaningless violence. Murder became instead the expression of organization: anonymous, targeted, even if increasingly frequent. Professional killings have developed codes meant to be interpreted in specific ways: the message is now conveyed by the violence inflicted on bodies (mutilations, usually decapitation) or the method used to dispose of them (wrapped in blankets, inside a trunk or a barrel); such are the consequences of failing to pay debts or show respect to those who control a territory. In some cases the crime scene is assembled in such a way as to convey a message, usually a note on the body. According to *New York Times* correspondent Mark Lacey, "When Mexican homicide investigators pull up at the scene of the latest drug-related slaughter, they go through a mental checklist: How many corpses? What sort of wounds? And, finally, where is the note scrawled by the killers?"[34] In order to convey specific images, bodies are mutilated or disposed of in certain ways. The Zetas and other groups post banners to recruit soldiers, or to take or disclaim responsibility for specific attacks—the now famous *narcomantas*. Criminal organizations have even published ads in newspapers.[35]

The relationship between drug traffickers and journalists demonstrates the importance of these messages. Both money and threats are used to influence coverage and thus create the impression of control or, alternatively, of rivals' weakness. Murder is used against those who refuse to follow orders, and Mexico is today one of the most dangerous countries for journalists.[36] Drug traffickers might want journalists to cover a murder with ample visual resources, or not to cover it at all. In one case, a journalist was ordered by two rival gangs, under threat of death, to do both—to cover and ignore—the presence of a body dropped next to a highway. Criminal organizations might also use the press to put pressure on government officials.[37]

Impunity defines drug-related murder. A police officer in Culiacán, Sinaloa, told me in 2008 that as soon as detectives see any sign that a homicide is connected to drug trafficking they close the investigation. The novels of Elmer Mendoza, a writer from the same city, borrow this fact to give new intensity and verisimilitude to the murder genre. His detectives, in *Balas de plata* and other novels, are robbed of the very questions they are trying to answer by the more powerful narcotics agents or by the narcos themselves.[38] Public opinion sees policemen, prosecutors, and judges as corrupt—and evidence to the contrary is only anecdotal. A murdered cop is always thought to have been associated with criminals. There have been exposés of corruption in the press and dutiful reports of the purges and moralization campaigns within police institutions. Yet a large majority of self-reported victims of other crimes tell pollsters that they do not bother to present complaints or press charges. The women killed in Ciudad Juárez that inspired Bolaño only reinforce the skepticism. The growth of the drug business and its use of violence in recent years now pose nothing less than a challenge for the political system to recover its legitimacy.[39]

Contemporary violence must therefore be examined in the context of the transformation of the Mexican public sphere during the twentieth century. This thesis is not intended to undermine other approaches to the problem of violence that emphasize socioeconomic or institutional factors. As with other aspects of the study of crime and violence, a multidisciplinary perspective is not a choice but a necessity. Yet looking at homicide as a communicative act should introduce a caveat that we could formulate, in simple terms, as the criminal imbrication of practices and public discourse: all crimes have explanations, yet explanations shape crimes.

In twentieth-century Mexico, murder created a field of public discourse, a space of debate that was open to diverse voices and not dominated by one particular authoritative perspective; it was inherently critical of state institutions and agents. Murder generated narratives full of stark characters and visually strong scenes. Through the press, literature, and radio, homicide attracted broad audiences and constituted them into vocal publics that addressed the media and political authorities.[40] Although the frequency of homicide decreased during the twentieth century, its visibility and impact on the public sphere only grew. This is the specific contribution of the approach presented here. Scholars have not been very good at reading the back sections of newspapers; looking for causes of crime, they have failed to explain consequences; their understanding of the *nota roja* has been biased by a view of crime reporters and readers as somewhat inferior intellectually. Criminals, however, have continued to produce narratives, using old and new media, and the public has kept on consuming them.

Recognizing the imbrication of discourses and practices of crime is a necessary operation in any comprehensive attempt to understand violence in Mexico today and in other contemporary societies where insecurity has become a central political theme. Placing crime in the public sphere means considering its dialogical aspects, the communicative effects of violence, and demands for justice. Clearly this implies a critique of models that see criminal violence merely as a social or psychological pathology, the effect of irrationality, or the object of policies intended to control its threat. A public-sphere approach requires an analysis that pays attention to the reciprocal interactions between multiple variables, some of them cultural, others socioeconomic. Located in the public sphere, crime and violence can be considered part of the interactions between civil society and the state that shape policies.

A specific area in which this interaction is taking shape pertains to the problem of truth and justice vis-à-vis the tens of thousands of homicides associated with drug violence over the past couple of decades. Diverse voices have acquired prominence through their demand that the lack of investigations and the impunity that characterizes the contemporary situation be redressed. The lack of information about most murders suggests a degree of participation on the part of the armed forces and paramilitary groups that is already framing an agenda of memory, accountability, and the right to truth that will likely continue into the presidency of Andrés Manuel López Obrador. The need for a truth commission has been mentioned by Olga Sánchez Cordero, López Obrador's choice for *secretaria de gobernación*.[41]

By the end of the fourth part of Bolaño's *2666*, a Mexican politician, frustrated by the lack of action on the murders of women, pleaded with journalist Sergio González Rodríguez to continue publishing about the murders. She sees no other option: she cannot give the information to US authorities because she is Mexican; and because the Mexican police will do nothing, she concludes that "I am left with the press." The journalist answers: "here nobody censors and nobody reads, but the press is a different thing. Newspapers are read, at least the headlines."[42] González Rodríguez was a real journalist who sent Bolaño, then writing in Spain, the information about the Ciudad Juárez killings he needed for his novel. González Rodríguez also wrote his own book about the case, *Huesos en el desierto*. It starts and ends with an old proverb that today we can read as a reflection on the meaning of murder for those who survive it: "Let others know what you remember; they will thus be able to read what is recorded in red ink in order to understand what is written in black."[43]

Notes

This paper was initially presented at Arms, Violence and Politics in Latin America: Past, Present, and Future, a conference held at the University of Calgary's Latin American Research Centre in May 2009. I thank all the participants for their comments, and in particular Pablo Policzer. I also thank Roberto Santamaría for his invaluable assistance in updating and improving the manuscript.

1. Roberto Bolaño, *2666* (Barcelona: Editorial Anagrama, 2004).

2. Thomas De Quincey, *On Murder* (New York: Oxford University Press, 2006). See Cuauhtémoc Medina, "Alarma!," *Poliester* (1993). Although the concept of the public sphere as formulated by Jürgen Habermas is central to my approach, there are several departures from his model. The most obvious is that, as I suggest, the rational exchanges that can take place in the public sphere do not exclude violence. See Jürgen Habermas, *The Theory of Communicative Action*, vol. 1, *Reason and the Rationalization of Society*, trans. Thomas McCarthy (Boston: Beacon Press, 1984); and Habermas, *The Structural Transformation of the Public Sphere: An Inquiry into a Category of Bourgeois Society* (Cambridge, MA: MIT Press, 1991). For an analysis of communicative acts among criminals that focuses on understanding communications among criminals rather than more publicly, see Diego Gambetta, *Codes of the Underworld: How Criminals Communicate* (Princeton, NJ: Princeton University Press, 2009).

3. See Arturo Alvarado, ed., *La reforma de la justicia en México* (Mexico City: El Colegio de Mexico, 2008); Wayne A. Cornelius and David A. Shirk, *Reforming the Administration of Justice in Mexico* (Notre Dame, IN: University of Notre Dame Press, 2007). Systematic attempts to compile and expand data to contribute to informed decisions have been made by the Instituto para la Seguridad y la Democracia, AC, and the Project on the Administration of Justice at the Transborder Institute.

4. One extreme example of this superficial assessment is the counting of the "executed" in the recent wave of drug-related violence. There is no clear criterion against which to measure how executions are distinguished from other crimes. The periods used are presidential terms, suggesting that the violence started because of political causes but without providing a comparison with earlier periods. For an example of the confusion between the number of *muertes violentas* counted by official sources, and the number of *ejecuciones* committed by rival drug cartels, see "Ejecuciones en México equivalen a un tercio de muertes en Irak desde 2003," *El Universal* (Mexico City), 5 June 2007. The Secretaría de Seguridad Pública defines and counts *ejecuciones* as those crimes committed by narcotraffickers, or, in its words, "homicidio doloso efectuado con un alto grado de violencia, vinculado a la delincuencia organizada." The definition, admits the SSP, has no legal basis. See Gustavo Castillo, "Se logró 'frenar y revertir' el número de *ejecuciones* en México durante 2007," *La Jornada* (Mexico City), 29 December 2007, http://www.jornada.unam.mx/2007/12/29/index.php?section=politica&article=014n1pol (accessed 27 October 2018). A criticism of the count can be found in Miguer Carbonell, "¿El gobierno es adivino?," *El Universal* (Mexico City), 24 January 2012. The government responded by suspending the official count. See David Luhnow, "Mexico Drug Violence Shows Decline," *Wall Street Journal* (New York), 13 June 2012, http://online.wsj.com/article/SB10001424052702303822206

4577464821699025772.html?KEYWORDS=DAVID+LUHNOW (accessed 27 October 2018).

5   For recent efforts to systematize and share information about security and justice, it is worth mentioning the Instituto Igarapé (https://igarape.org.br/en/about/about-igarape/); see also Justice in Mexico (https://justiceinmexico.org/).

6   In a survey commissioned by México Unido contra la Delincuencia, an organization focused on impacting state policies, interviewees are asked if they fear being victims of crime and about their trust in state institutions. See "Encuesta Mitofsky de Percepción Ciudadana sobre la Seguridad en México," http://www.mucd.org.mx/Encuesta-Mitofsky-de-Percepci%C3%B3n-Ciudadana-sobre-la-Seguridad-en-M%C3%A9xico-c67i0.html (accessed 17 July 2012). For victimization surveys as corrective of official statistics, see Instituto Ciudadano de Estudios sobre la Inseguridad (ICESI), AC, "Encuestas Nacionales sobre Inseguridad, "El costo de la inseguridad en México," Cuadernos de ICESI, https://www.wilsoncenter.org/sites/default/files/Cuadernos%20del%20ICESI.pdf (accessed 27 October 2018).

7   Historical studies include Elisa Speckman, *Crimen y Castigo: Legislación Penal, Interpretaciones de la Criminalidad y Administración de Justicia (Ciudad de México, 1872–1910)* (Mexico City: El Colegio de México, 2002); Pablo Piccato, *City of Suspects: Crime in Mexico City, 1900–1931* (Durham, NC: Duke University Press, 2001); Robert Buffington, "Forging the Fatherland: Criminality and Citizenship in Modern Mexico" (PhD diss., University of Arizona, 1994); Robert Buffington and Pablo Piccato, *True Stories of Crime in Modern Mexico* (Albuquerque: University of New Mexico Press, 2009). On civil society and crime, see Heather Strang and John Braithwaite, *Restorative Justice and Civil Society* (Cambridge: Cambridge University Press, 2001). This is a basic argument of Pablo Piccato, *A History of Infamy: Crime, Truth and Justice in Mexico* (Berkeley: University of California Press, 2017).

8   "Versión estenográfica de la participación del Secretario de Seguridad Pública, Ingeniero Genaro García Luna, durante la Novena Reunión Ordinaria de Trabajo de la Comisión de Seguridad Pública de la LX Legislatura de la Cámara de Diputados," 25 April 2007, http://www.pfp.gob.mx/portalWebApp/ShowBinary?nodeId=/BEA%20Repository/250008//archivo&pathImg=%2FBEA+Repository%2Fimport%2FSecretaria+de+Seguridad+Publica%2FDocumentos+de+Comparecencias (accessed 12 February 2009).

9   "Indicted," or *presunto*, means those suspects charged and imprisoned but not sentenced, and they represent the most reliable figures available to compile long-term series. Even though they may not represent the entire number of homicides, indicted suspects are more important in public perceptions of crime than those found guilty, and certainly more visible than those not arrested. Source: Pablo Piccato, Sara Hidalgo, and Andrés Lajous, "Estadísticas del crimen en México: Series históricas, 1901–2008," https://ppiccato.shinyapps.io/judiciales/.

10 Piccato, *City of Suspects*, ch. 4; Dirección General de Estadística, *Estadística del ramo criminal en la República Mexicana que comprende un periodo de quince años, de 1871 a 1885* (Mexico City: Secretaría de Fomento, 1890); *Anuario Estadístico de la República Mexicana 1895* (Mexico City: Secretaría de Fomento, 1896).

11 For basic information and other crimes, see database at http://www.sandiego.edu/peacestudies/tbi/resources/data_portal.php, and Piccato, "Estadísticas del crimen."

12 See Secretaría de Gobernación, "Incidencia Delictiva Nacional, Fuero Común," http://www.secretariadoejecutivosnsp.gob.mx/es/SecretariadoEjecutivo/Incidencia_Delictiva_Nacional_fuero_comun (accessed 17 July 2012); for 2011 population, INEGI, "Mexico en Cifras," http://www.inegi.org.mx/sistemas/mexicocifras/default.aspx (accessed 17 July 2012). According to United Nations Office of Drugs and Crime (UNODC) statistics, the homicide rate in Mexico has decreased to 16.35 in 2015 from a recent peak of 22.61 in 2011. UNODC statistics, https://data.unodc.org/#state:1 (accessed 6 July 2018). 2018, however, is on course to be the year with more homicides in Mexican history.

13 See "2011 Global Study on Homicide," UNODC, http://www.unodc.org/unodc/en/data-and-analysis/statistics/crime/global-study-on-homicide-2011.html (accessed 6 July 2018). Latin America has six countries among the ten countries with the highest levels of homicide in the world. National rates, however, hide important intranational variations. See also UNDOC, "Global Study on Homocide," 2013, https://www.unodc.org/documents/gsh/pdfs/2014_GLOBAL_HOMICIDE_BOOK_web.pdf (accessed 6 July 2018).

14 See ICESI, "Estadísticas ENSI," http://www.icesi.org.mx/documentos/estadisticas/estadisticasOfi/sentenciados_por_homicidios_1997_2003.pdf (accessed 17 July 2012). We develop some of these points in Andrés Lajous and Pablo Piccato, "Tendencias históricas del crimen en México," *Nexos*, 1 April 2018, https://www.nexos.com.mx/?p=36958.

15 Guillermo Zepeda Lecuona, *Crimen sin castigo: Procuración de justicia penal y ministerio público en México* (Mexico City: Fondo de Cultura Económica-Cidac, 2004).

16 Piccato, *City of Suspects*; Pablo Piccato, "Communities and Crime in Mexico City," *Delaware Review of Latin American Studies* 6, no. 1 (2005), http://www.udel.edu/LAS/Vol6-1Piccato.html, (accessed 28 October 2018); John Braithwaite, *Crime, Shame and Reintegration* (New York: Cambridge University Press, 1989); Alfonso Quiroz Cuarón, José Gómez Robleda, and Benjamín Argüelles, *Tendencia y ritmo de la criminalidad en México, D.F.* (Mexico City: Instituto de Investigaciones Estadísticas, 1939).

17 Piccato, *City of Suspects*, ch. 5. See for example *El Universal* (Mexico City), 1 October 1920, 6.

18 Benjamin T. Smith, *Pistoleros and Popular Movements: The Politics of State Formation in Postrevolutionary Oaxaca* (Lincoln: University of Nebraska Press, 2009); Alan Knight, "Habitus and Homicide: Political Culture in Revolutionary Mexico," in *Citizens of the Pyramid: Essays on Mexican Political Culture*, ed. Wil G. Pansters (Amsterdam: Thela Publishers, 1997); Piccato, *A History of Infamy*, ch. 5. According to a newspaper, the *pistolero* "Su función es la de asesinar y cuando su jefe les dice que eliminen a determinada persona, van y con toda tranquilidad lo hacen; y luego vuelven a repetir el crimen cuando se les ordena otra vez." See *Ultimas Noticias* (Mexico City), 22 September 1942, 1.

19 Jon Sistiaga, "Narcoméxico: Corrido para un degollado," (video, nCuatro, 2008). On the Arellano Félix family, see Jesús Blancornelas, *El cártel: Los Arellano Félix, la mafia más*

poderosa en la historia de América Latina (Mexico City: Debolsillo, 2004). On the Zetas' origins as US-trained special forces in the Mexican army co-opted by the Gulf Cartel, see "Reinica EU capacitación de soldados mexicanos," *Milenio* (Mexico City), 6 August 2009, http://impreso.milenio.com/node/8620045 (accessed 28 August 2018). Luca Brasi is the inarticulate but fearsome enforcer for Vito Corleone in Mario Puzo's novel and Francis Ford Coppola's movie *The Godfather*.

20 See for example a video distributed by an organization, and dutifully broadcast by national television station, in which a captured rival speaks about organization, business, murders, and the relations of his organization with journalists: "Matando Zetas," 29 March 20097 http://www.youtube.com/watch?v=GvF0zSSEXzk (accessed 5 September 2009). See also, "Gente Nueva ejecutaron a los dos ensabanados del Puerto de Veracruz," *Enlace Veracruz 212*, 29 March 2007, http://archivo.vazquezchagoya.com/?p=2202 (accessed 28 August 2018).

21 Francesc Barata and Marco Lara Klahr, *Nota(n) roja: La vibrante historia de un género y una nueva manera de informar* (Mexico City: Random House Mondadori, 2009), 32; Jesse Lerner, *The Shock of Modernity: Crime Photography in Mexico City* (Mexico City: Turner, 2007); Piccato, *A History of Infamy*, ch. 2.

22 For the most successful magazines since the 1930s, see Carlos Monsiváis, *Los mil y un velorios: Crónica de la nota roja* (Mexico City: Consejo Nacional para la Cultura y las Artes, 1994), 30–1. Another list, including detective fiction series, can be found in Ilan Stavans, *Antihéroes: México y su novela policial* (Mexico City: Joaquín Mortiz, 1993), 76–8. Eduardo Téllez Vargas and José Ramón Garmabella, ¡Reportero de policía!: El Güero Téllez (Mexico City: Ediciones Océano, 1982).

23 Enrique Metinides, Geoff Dyer, Néstor García Canclini, Gabriel Kuri, and Photographers' Gallery, *Enrique Metinides* (London: Ridinghouse, 2003).

24 *El universal gráfico*, January 1947, 5; *El Universal Gráfico*, January 1955, 5; Monsiváis, *Los mil y un velorios*, 31; Medina, "Alarma!"

25 The caption reads: "TRAGEDIA—Lugar donde cayó Humberto Reyes Rivera después de reñir con María Hernandez Prieto, José Antonio Cruz Rivera y Ramón Flores Duarte (abajo), en el hotelucho 'Ideal'. El dueño y administrador obstruccionaron la labor reporteril." See *La Prensa* (Mexico City), 8 January 1953, 1.

26 Téllez Vargas and Garmabella, ¡Reportero de policía!

27 *La Prensa* (Mexico City), 4 March 1959, 26. Archivo General de la Nación, Fondo Presidentes, Manuel Ávila Camacho (hereafter AGN, MAC), 13 January 1941, 541/57. This characterization runs counter much of the current literature about (or against) police news. For a view of *nota roja* as irrational and "que apela al subsonsciente colectivo," see Barata and Lara Klahr, *Nota(n) roja*, 58.

28 See, for example, the case of Ema Martínez, who killed Senator Rafael Altamirano and revealed some seedy practices among the federal bureaucracy: *La Prensa* (Mexico City), 7 March 1959, 2. On journalism and politics, see Julio Scherer García and Carlos Monsiváis, *Tiempo de saber: Prensa y poder en México* (Mexico City: Aguilar, 2003). Studies of crime and punishment in Mexico City and other modern Latin America societies show that the police and judiciary have long been the agents of the most

frequent and direct relationships between citizens and the state. See, for example, Osvaldo Barreneche, *Dentro de la ley, todo: La justicia criminal de Buenos Aires en la etapa formativa del sistema penal moderno de la Argentina* (La Plata, AR: Ediciones al Margen, 2001); Amy Chazkel, *Laws of Chance: Brazil's Clandestine Lottery and the Making of Urban Public Life* (Durham, NC: Duke University Press, 2011).

29 Manuel Ávila Camacho instructed the Mexico City chief of police to tell suspect Manuel Sáenz de Miera to stop bothering the mother of a homicide victim,12 January 1942, AGN, MAC, 541/430. A mother denouncing a police officer freed after killing her son in Macrina Estrada Aguirre a presidente Adolfo López Mateos, DF, 11 June 1959, Archivo General de la Nación, Fondo Presidentes, Adolfo López Mateos (hereafter AGN, ALM), 541/93. Taxi drivers in telegrama José González a presidente López Mateos, DF, 28 April 1959, AGN, ALM, 541/79. Chauffeurs in Francisco Macario Lucero, Confederación de Inquilinos y colonos de la República Mexicana a Presidente de la Rep. Mexico, 11 August 1955; Archivo General de la Nación, Fondo Presidentes, Adolfo Ruiz Cortines (hereafter AGN, ARC), 541/254. Trabajadores de Caminos to Cárdenas, 11 March 1936, Archivo General de la Nación, Fondo Presidentes, Lázaro Cárdenas (hereafter AGN LC), 444.92/42.

30 Balentina Esquivel al "Jefe de la Defensa Nacional" Agustin Castro, Mexico DF, 22 Sep. 1940, Archivo General de la Nación, Dirección General de Gobierno, 2/012.2 (29)/5, caja 78 exp. 6. For another mother demanding justice in the murder of her son by a policeman, see 24 Apr. 1945, AGN MAC, -549.44/149, 24.abr.45: aguilar rivera guadalupe. See also, for a son killed by the police, AGN, ALM, 541/93, Macrina Estrada Aguirre a presidente ADLM, DF, 11 Jun. 1959.

31 Lic. Javier Torres Pérez, Mexico DF, a presidente, 28 Ago. 1958, AGN, ARC, 541/1003; Jorge Vélez to president Alemán, Port Isabel, 26 Sep. 1948, Archivo General de la Nación, Fondo Presidentes, Miguel Ávila Camacho, 541/50.

32 Lic. Antonio Gómez Pérez to Lic. José Aguilar y Maya, DF, 7 Ago. 1958, AGN, ARC, 541/1003.

33 For assassinations, see the murder of Cardinal Juan Jesús Posadas Ocampo, in May 1993, of presidential candidate Luis Donaldo Colosio, in March 1994, and of PRI Secretary General José Francisco Ruiz Massieu in September of the same year. All of them were characterized by much debate about the true culprits. On the cancellation of the show, see Mary Beth Sheridan, "Mexico's Reality TV Presses Some Hot Buttons," *Los Angeles Times*, 10 July 1999, http://articles.latimes.com/1999/jul/10/news/mn-54663 (accessed 28 October 2018). On "muerte en directo," see Barata and Lara Klahr, *Nota(n) roja*, 42–3.

34 Marc Lacey, "Grenade Attack in Mexico Breaks From Deadly Script," *New York Times*, 24 September 2008, http://www.nytimes.com/2008/09/25/world/americas/25mexico.html?_r=1&scp=1&sq=crime%20mexico%20drugs&st=cse&oref=slogin (accessed 28 October 2018).

35 Alejandro Jiménez, "Estrategia de cárteles: difusión y propaganda: Mediante un empírico manejo de crisis, los narcotraficantes mexicanos ganaron los primeros espacios comunicativos," *El Universal* (Mexico City), 26 September 2008, http://www.

eluniversal.com.mx/nacion/162611.html (accessed 28 August 2009); see also Sistiaga, "Corrido para un degollado."

36 See *Attacks on the Press in 2008: A Worldwide Survey by the Committee to Protect Journalists* (New York: Committee To Protect Journalists, 2009). Again, the phenomenon is not entirely new. For one 1977 example, see Luis Alejandro Astorga Almanza, *El siglo de las drogas: el narcotráfico, del Porfiriato al nuevo milenio*, 1st ed. (Mexico City: Plaza y Janés, 2005), 116–17. An overview can be found in Pablo Piccato, " 'Ya Saben Quién': Journalism, Crime and Impunity in Mexico Today," in *Mexico's Struggle for Public Security: Organized Crime and State Responses*, edited by Susana Berruecos and George Philip (London: Palgrave Macmillan, 2012).

37 José Carreño Carlón, "El crimen, medios y motivos de Calderón," *El Universal* (Mexico City), 15 May 2008, http://www.eluniversal.com.mx/columnas/71411.html (accessed 28 August 2009); Alejandro Jiménez, "Estrategia de cárteles: difusión y propaganda," *El Universal* (Mexico City), 26 September 2008, http://www.eluniversal.com.mx/nacion/162611.html (accessed 30 September 2009).

38 Élmer Mendoza, *Balas de plata*, 1a. ed. (Barcelona: Tusquets Editores, 2008).

39 Zepeda Lecuona, *Crimen sin castigo.*, 9, 19, 45. Before being approved by the Senate as Federal Attorney General, Arturo Chávez was questioned by multiple organizations because of his lack of support for the resolution of the Juárez murders while Chihuahua state attorney. Andrea Becerril and Víctor Ballinas, "Hay clamor general de rechazo a la ratificación de Arturo Chávez," *La Jornada* (Mexico City), 24 September 2009, http://www.jornada.unam.mx/2009/09/24/index.php?section=politica&article=009n2pol (accessed 28 October 2018).

40 On the construction of publics, see Michael Warner, *Publics and Counterpublics* (New York: Zone Books, 2002).

41 "Comisiones de la verdad estarían constituidas por sociedad civil: Sánchez Cordero," *El Financiero* (Mexico City), 21 June 2018, http://www.elfinanciero.com.mx/elecciones-2018/comisiones-de-la-verdad-estarian-constituidas-por-sociedad-civil-y-expertos-sanchez-cordero (accessed 16 July 2018). See the movement lead by poet Javier Sicilia and the editorial effort of the website *Nuestra Aparente Rendición*, http://nuestraaparenterendicion.com/. On the right to truth, in the context of the transition out of authoritarian regimes, see Carlos Santiago Nino, *Radical Evil on Trial* (New Haven, CT: Yale University Press, 1996).

42 Bolaño, *2666*, 789.

43 Sergio González Rodríguez, *Huesos en el desierto* (Barcelona: Editorial Anagrama, 2002), 286.

Protest and Police "Excesses" in Chile: The Limits of Social Accountability[1]

Michelle D. Bonner

In 2006 Chilean high school students mobilized and called for changes to the educational system, including national standards for secondary education and the elimination of the fee required to take university entrance exams. Their tactics included cultural events, "days of reflection," school occupations, and street protests. One of their largest actions took place on 30 May. On that day, 739,000 students and their supporters across the country took to the streets. The Chilean national police, the Carabineros de Chile, were there to maintain order. To this end, the Carabineros used what was described by the media as "excessive violence," particularly against protesters in the center of Santiago.

The Carabineros used water cannons and tear gas against the protesters, they beat people as they were detaining them in police buses (almost seven hundred people were arrested), and they also beat bystanders and journalists covering the event.[2] While media reports were unclear about exactly how many people were beaten or how badly, a few examples of overzealous police action illustrate the seriousness of the tumult. Three journalists—Libio Saavedra, Marco Cabrera, and Fernando Cidler—were beaten and injured by Carabineros.[3] Further, an individual Carabinero was alleged to have forced three students (two aged seventeen and one sixteen-year-old) to undress before registering them in a humiliating manner.[4]

The Chilean media coverage of this event was significant. It was the first time in over forty years (since before the 1973 coup) that the national media were so widely critical of the police's management of protests. The coverage signaled to the police, political leaders, and the public that repressive protest policing might no longer be perceived as broadly acceptable, as it was in the past.

The right to social protest is a defining feature of democracy. Yet police use of violence against protesters is not limited to authoritarian regimes, and thus cannot be considered a structural problem limited to postauthoritarian Latin American countries. Even in established democracies protesters can be killed or injured by what I refer to in this chapter as police violence. A more common police approach in established democracies is the use of other tactics (violent or otherwise) to limit free speech, and in this chapter such methods are referred to as police repression. Police repression may include arbitrarily arresting large numbers of protesters without charges, moving the route of a protest by using barricades or other obstacles, using police sirens to drown out protest chants and singing, using a disproportionate number of police officers, or deploying nonlethal weapons, including tear gas. That said, the literature on established democracies has noted a significant decline over the last fifty years or so in the use of repressive tactics by police against social protest. The media are one of the key variables identified in the literature on protest policing in established democracies that explains the reduction in repression. That is, rather than being structurally determined, police repression of social protest is in part contingent upon the role played by the media.

The literature on protest policing in established democracies has found that the greater the number of journalists present and the greater the media coverage, the lower the level of police repression of social protests.[5] Media presence can have an immediate effect on police reactions to protest, and such accumulated police experience can lead to police using less repression when confronting future protests. In other words, the media act as a mechanism of accountability on protest policing. Enrique Peruzzotti and Catalina Smulovitz refer to this role of the media as social accountability.[6]

Drawing on the work of Peruzzotti and Smulovitz, as well as the literature on the media and protest policing, we can identify three principal ways the media keep police accountable. First, wrongdoers can be identified, shamed, and forced to account for their actions. This is what Andreas Schedler calls the "answerability" aspect of accountability.[7] Second, media coverage of police repression can lead to the activation of horizontal accountability. Horizontal accountability refers to state institutions holding wrongdoers accountable through such mechanisms as judicial trials, official inquiries, and forced resignations. This is what Schedler refers to as the "enforcement" aspect of accountability, whereby sanctions are imposed on wrongdoers.[8]

Third—and often overlooked in analyses of accountability, but addressed substantially in the literature on protest policing—the media play an important role in affecting public opinion. They do so by reframing police repression of social protest as wrongdoing. Public opinion matters when police rely on good relations with the public to do their job. It also matters to politicians who hope to be reelected; public opinion can influence politicians' choices regarding activating (or not) state mechanisms of accountability. In the literature on protest policing, public opinion is most often measured through the media.[9] Indeed, one author defines public opinion on protest policing as "repeated statements expressed in the public sphere."[10]

While the literature on protest policing recognizes the media's powerful role as a mechanism of accountability, it also recognizes that the media's influence does not necessarily favor reduced levels of police repression in all cases. The literature widely recognizes two competing frames used in the media to explain protest policing, which are often referred to as the "civil rights" versus the "law-and-order" frames. The civil rights frame emphasizes the right to protest, the need for police to refrain from violence and repression, and the need for police reform. The law-and-order frame tends to vilify protesters and support police using whatever levels of violence and repression they deem necessary to control protesters and restore law and order.

Research demonstrates that when the media champions the civil rights frame, police repression decreases.[11] The choice of the media to emphasize one frame over the other can be influenced by a number of factors, including bias against the group protesting, police stage-managing incidents to gain public sympathy, and the degree to which social movement groups gain (or fail to gain) access to the media.[12] Another major factor is the choices made by journalists regarding primary sources. The more journalists rely on the police and public officials for their primary source of information, or when journalists are confined to watching from behind police lines, the more likely the law-and-order frame will predominate.[13] Clearly there are limits to the media's ability to act as a mechanism of accountability on protest policing.

In new democracies, protest policing is also framed by the media in terms of "civil rights" or "law-and-order," but the choice of one frame over the other is influenced by additional factors. In particular, the police forces in new democracies such as Chile have very often undergone little reform, and many of the structures, personnel, laws, and practices from previous authoritarian regimes persist. Similarly, the media may also face important residual restrictions in their work. That is, there are structural factors that explain the persistence of high levels of police repression against social protest in postauthoritarian countries, and these structural factors can impede change. However, structural factors do not necessarily determine the outcomes, and the media can be agents of change, potentially contributing to police accountability in new democracies.

Did the Chilean media act as a mechanism of social accountability on protest policing during the 2006 student protest? I argue that in this instance the media did function in this capacity, but that their role was limited in three important ways. The three limitations pertain to self-censorship, provision of information, and inclusion—all of which reinforce a "law-and-order" frame for understanding the event. Rather than "proving" that this will be the media's reaction to all similar incidents in Chile or other new democracies, this case study aims to encourage studies of police reform in new democracies to consider further the impact of the media on such changes.

This study centers on the coverage of the student protest by the Chilean national newspaper *El Mercurio*. The focus on *El Mercurio* is important. Most scholars argue that the print media in Chile is very influential; more than other mediums it confers social prestige to those covered in its pages, and it is therefore argued to have a greater impact on public and political opinion.[14] *El Mercurio* in particular is widely considered the most important agenda-setting news media source in Chile.[15] Illustrating the power of the newspaper, Léon-Dermota explains that "no politician can survive without appearing on *El Mercurio*'s pages."[16]

The reach of *El Mercurio* and the *El Mercurio* media group is extensive. The newspaper group benefited tremendously from the Pinochet dictatorship (1973–90), under which it expanded to own 3 of the 5 daily Chilean national newspapers (of which *El Mercurio* is one) as well as 18 regional papers (covering 7 of Chile's 15 regions). It has also founded a digital radio network (Digital FM) with 33 stations between Arica and Punta Arenas, and hopes to enter television in the future.[17] In terms of the *El Mercurio* newspaper itself, almost all government offices and major businesses have subscriptions to *El Mercurio*, making it available for their employees to read, and almost all newspaper kiosks prominently display *El Mercurio*, allowing pedestrians to read the headlines as they walk by. Many morning television and radio shows summarize or even read major daily stories published in *El Mercurio*.

El Mercurio's relatively new and (arguably) equally conservative main competitor, *La Tercera* (published by Copesa media group), enjoys similar benefits. However, while *La Tercera*'s coverage of police repression of social protest is not substantially different in content than that of *El Mercurio*, it is often of a significantly lower quantity. There are also more critical media in Chile, such as the weekly political satire *The Clinic* or *Radio Bío Bío*, but the size of their audience does not match that of *El Mercurio*. What is written in *El Mercurio* is a significant part of what William A. Gamson and David Stuart call "symbolic contests" over how police reaction to social protest is to be perceived and whether or not accountability is deemed necessary.[18]

That being said, it is important to note that *El Mercurio*, the oldest newspaper in Chile, is a conservative newspaper that has traditionally supported the views of the landed elite. For example, it was actively involved in promoting the neoliberal ideas of the "Chicago Boys," as well as the 1973 military coup. In this sense, *El Mercurio* has historically supported police repression of social protest; it is not surprising that it continues to support similar action today. The analysis that follows reveals a debate within *El Mercurio* that is particularly significant given this context.

This analysis begins by placing the reaction of the Carabineros to the student protest within the history of police responses to earlier social protests in Chile. This is followed by an overview of all the articles published in *El Mercurio* addressing the 2006 police repression of student protesters (a total of thirty-five articles published from 30 May to 13 June 2006). Three questions will be asked for the purpose of assessing the degree of social accountability found in the articles. First, who is being shamed for wrongdoing? Second, what are they being shamed for? Third, what institutions of horizontal accountability are being called upon? In each section, competing frames for understanding the answer to these questions are highlighted and analyzed.

Police and Social Protest: The Chilean Context

Police violence in the face of social protest, especially in countries with an authoritarian past, is an area where agreement concerning police wrongdoing is not easily achieved. In Chile, the Carabineros have a long history of repressing social protest that predates the Pinochet regime. The period in which the Carabineros de Chile was established was characterized by high levels of social and political unrest. Thus, among the first roles assigned to the new police force was to control social protest. For example, under the leadership of Carlos Ibáñez del Campo (then minister of the interior), the Carabineros violently ended labor demonstrations in the port of Iquique in May and June 1925, and Carabineros were used again in 1931 to quell protest in reaction to unemployment, which led to the death of at least a dozen people.[19] The use of Carabineros to combat social protest continued after Ibáñez's first term as president (1927–31), especially between June and July 1934, when the Carabineros confronted a protest by evicted peasant squatters, killing hundreds of peasants. Again, in 1946, political instability led to strikes and demonstrations, which in turn prompted repression by the Carabineros.[20] Repression of social protest in an effort to control "subversion" eventually became a key function of the Carabineros.[21] This role was strengthened by the adoption of the Law of State Security in 1958, article 4 of which states that anyone who " 'in any form or by any means rises up against the constituted government or provokes a civil war' is committing a crime against state security."[22]

The use of the Carabineros and occasionally the military to repress social protest (especially in the copper mines) continued throughout the

1960s, when the Carabineros also became increasingly involved in land disputes. For example, "*Carabineros*, trying to evict some squatters from a plot of land at Pampa Irigoin, just outside of Puerto Montt, killed eight people and wounded fifty more" in 1969.[23] With the 1973 coup, the Carabineros became even more closely tied to the military, and was henceforth tightly integrated into the military government. Together, the Carabineros and the military participated in the killing of people opposed to the regime until DINA (the Pinochet regime's security agency) was officially created in June 1974.[24] With a deteriorating economy in the early 1980s, social protest became more common and police reaction was strong. Mass mobilizations sparked by the 1983 economic crisis exploded, leading to police repression that included "brutal sweeps through the shantytowns" between 1983 and 1986.[25] The Carabineros framed these protests as threats to the government and even the institution of the Carabineros itself. In 1985, *Revista de Carabineros* (*Carabineros Magazine*) explained, "The implicit objective of the mass movements is to gravely disturb the peace, which constitutes a direct and unrestrained attack on the system of government. . . . [The term "police brutality"] not only discredits the government but also the *Carabineros* and is an attempt to besmirch the moral authority of both."[26]

Incidents of police violence against social protest in Chile have continued since the return of electoral democracy in 1990. A review of Human Rights Watch, Amnesty International, and US State Department annual reports from 1990 to 2004 finds that during this period at least 138 protesters were injured and six killed as a result of the violence perpetrated by Carabineros against protesters. Because of missing data, these numbers do not include similar reports of "excessive use of force" by police that failed to specify the numbers of people injured or killed as a result.[27]

To be sure, the Carabineros have undergone some reform since the return of civilian government in 1990. For example, most criminal cases are now handled by civilian (not military) courts, a reform of the penal process law has placed checks on some traditional Carabineros practices, and a form of community policing has been implemented. However, none of these reforms have touched on the issue of police repression of social protest. Cases that involve a Carabinero harming a civilian or a civilian harming a *Carabinero* still go to military (not civilian) court. Between

1990 and 1997, 90 percent of the almost eight hundred cases brought to military courts by citizens alleging police violence were dismissed by judges.[28] Moreover, the reform of the penal process law applies only to civilian and not military courts, and community policing does not touch on the issue of protest.

Nevertheless, while the Carabineros have an important (and continuing) history of involvement in the repression of social protest, they have an equally important history of being well respected by large segments of the Chilean population as a disciplined police force that is free of corruption and dedicated to its defined community. In an issue of *Revista de Carabineros* from 1927, it is explained that the new police force, unlike those of the past, has a new role defined as "making the *Carabinero* into a true guide and teacher for the general public, someone who is their best friend, and their most loyal defender and counsellor, always effective in stopping anything that might disturb public order."[29] This framing of the role of the Carabineros continues in their promotional material today, and is exemplified by their current slogan, "Un amigo siempre" ("Always a friend"). As recently as 2016, public opinion polls have shown that a majority of Chileans trust the Carabineros (54 percent) compared to lower levels of trust in the judiciary (7 percent) or Congress (4 percent).[30] However, this level of support is much lower among the poor and youth, who are often targets of police violence, and it is very possible that the media play a role in shaping public opinion in support of police actions.[31]

Coverage of the 2006 Student Protest in *El Mercurio*: Assessing Social Accountability

While the media play an important role in framing debates, not everyone is included in these debates. Aside from editorializing journalists, a total of 22 people had their positions either quoted or summarized in articles discussing the incident of police "excesses" that transpired on 30 May. In contrast, the Argentine conservative national newspaper *La Nación* presented the positions of 50 different people in one week of coverage of an incident of excessive police violence in that country.[32] Of the 22 people whose positions on the event were made public through *El Mercurio*, the majority (12) were government officials or politicians and 4 were current

TABLE 4.1.

Categories of people referenced	Who is cited?	Who is to blame?	For what?	Mechanisms of accountability advocated?
Government officials or politicians	12	7	1. Government used police to silence protesters (1) 2. Government should have resolved conflict before it went to the streets (3)	Resignation of minister (1)
Current or past Carabineros	4	27	1. violated democratic norms (7) 2. bad apples (6)	Dismissal of individual officers (14)—8 in favor, 6 against. Judicial action (4) Institutional change (3)
Students/protesters	4	9	1. Violent protesters justify police action (5) 2. Protesters and police share blame (2)	Crackdown on street crime (2)
Journalists	n/a	1	1. Journalist who were injured did not follow procedures for covering protests (1) 2. Journalists made this a case of wrongdoing by framing it that way (2)	0
Other	2	0	0	0
Total	**22**	**44**	**27**	**24**

Source: *El Mercurio*'s coverage of the 2006 Chilean student protest, 30 May to 13 June 2006 (35 articles). Notes: The numbers provided in the table refer to the number of references made to a particular person (or group) (from one of the categories) or this person or group's position on the three issues. One reference indicates that in one article one person/group, or the position of one person/group, from the identified category was mentioned. A quote from the person/group may have been provided, their ideas may have been paraphrased, their action may have been noted (e.g., pursuing a court case) or, for references to journalists, the journalist may have editorialized on the topic.

or past members of the Carabineros. Of the remaining 6, 4 were spokespeople for the Coordinating Assembly of Secondary Students (the group leading the protests), but their positions were not given much coverage or weight. Indeed, one student leader (María Jesús Sanhueza) quoted as critical of the Carabineros' actions was described in *El Mercurio* as a disputed member of the student leadership who "unjustifiably missed more than half of her classes."[33]

The literature on protest policing suggests that the media's preference for approving police actions pushes the public to favor a "law-and-order" frame over a "civil rights" frame. At the very least, the social accountability provided by *El Mercurio* limits the voices of those framing the event as a wrongdoing requiring mechanisms of horizontal accountability to be activated. For clarity, a numeric summary of the positions found in the articles is shown in Table 4.1. The text that follows provides the nuance and analysis needed to better understand the numbers.

Who Should be Held Accountable?

There were 44 references to blame in the 25 *El Mercurio* articles that addressed police repression against the 2006 protesters. In total, the references identify 4 individuals or groups as responsible for what happened. Of the 3 most commonly identified wrongdoers, the Carabineros (as a whole, a group within the organization, or individual officers) were referred to in 27 references to blame. The second most common group identified as responsible for the police repression was the protesters themselves (or violent infiltrators). This was the case in 9 references. Third, 7 references saw the government (including President Michelle Bachelet and her ministers of the interior and education) as responsible. One person, the director general of the Carabineros, blamed journalists. It is interesting that many of these allegations of wrongdoing were offered cautiously, indicating a degree of self-censorship. For example, President Bachelet blamed the Carabineros, but her minister of the interior clarified that she meant only to reinforce the excesses recognized by the leadership of the Carabineros.[34]

There are a number of possible reasons for this self-censorship, including a legacy of recently derogated but persisting contempt-for-authority laws. Until not long ago, Chile had more contempt-for-authority laws than any other country in Latin America, and these laws were applied more frequently in Chile than elsewhere. In addition, the punishments for violating these laws were more excessive, including significant prison sentences for some transgressors.[35] However, the most serious and widely used contempt-for-authority law, section 6b of the Law of State Security, was derogated in 2001, and articles 263 and 264 of the Chilean Criminal Code were derogated in 2005. In spite of this, significant opposition by some authorities to the derogation of these laws led to articles 263 and 264 of the Criminal Code being replaced with article 264. Instead of punishing those who challenge the *honor* of authorities, article 264 seeks to punish those whose words are interpreted as a *threat* to upset order in the eyes of these same authorities.[36] The latter can be interpreted by judges in the same manner as the former, and violations remain criminal rather than civil offences. Articles 413 and 418 of the Criminal Code that address offence and slander (*injurias* and *calumnia*) have also been used more widely since 2005.[37] Article 417 of the Military Code of Justice continues to protect Carabineros against defamation; its only modification since the dictatorship has been a reduction (from ten to three years) in the prison sentence attached, and a shifting of these cases from military to civilian courts. Many authors contend that these laws have led to self-censorship by journalists and affects how they present the news.[38]

Many Chilean journalists and government communications officers I have spoken to argued that they did not perceive any legal limits to what they could say or write. Instead, the primary limit identified by the interviewees was their (or their employer's) desire not to offend the Carabineros for political or career reasons. Politically, interviewees argued that a principal concern of both the government and *El Mercurio* is "citizen security," defined as policy priorities aimed at combating common (particularly property) crime. The owner of *El Mercurio*, Agustín Edwards, founded and financially supported the Fundación Paz Ciudadana, an organization that has lobbied successfully for government money and attention to citizen security since 1992. In order to combat crime and achieve citizen security, the interviewees explained, it is important to maintain the support of the Carabineros; criticizing their actions would not be helpful in this regard. This is a position that was expressed by both government communications officers and journalists.[39]

Journalists in particular identified the career limitations of not supporting this political position. For example, critical police reporting can result in journalists not being invited by the Carabineros to press conferences, or not being offered exclusives. Given the focus of citizen security on crime, such an exclusion from the main sources of information on crime could force a police reporter to change their specialization or leave their newspaper altogether. Thus, whether for legal, political, or career reasons, it is likely that both journalists and politicians who are evasive in assigning blame for police repression of the student protest are engaging in self-censorship.

What Should They be Held Accountable For?

Of course, social accountability involves more than simply the naming of wrongdoers by the media. It also involves identifying the actions thought to constitute wrongdoing. This section will examine each of the groups blamed for the 2006 incident and assess the statements that indicate what they should be held accountable for. It is important to note that not all references to blame explain why the person identified is responsible for the police repression. For example, while most people quoted or referred to in *El Mercurio* (including members of the Carabineros themselves) agree that the Carabineros engaged in "excesses," not all of those quoted or referred to explain what specifically they should be held accountable for. Only thirteen of the twenty-seven references to Carabinero wrongdoing explain what they should be held accountable for. When explanations are provided, each group (the Carabineros, the protesters, the government, and journalists) is linked to the violence in a different manner. These links reveal a debate regarding the degree of wrongdoing committed, and the manner of determining why some actors are held to be more responsible than others.

First, the Carabineros are thought by some to be accountable for violating democratic norms. The Carabineros as an institution were reported to have admitted that "unjustified excesses" were used against the three journalists, but they rejected responsibility for harming students.[40] Two days later, perhaps following the lead of the Carabineros, President Bachelet gave a speech in which she denounced the police actions. While she described the "incidents" (*hechos*) against both the journalists and the students as "condemnable and unjustifiable," she elaborated significantly more on the violence against the journalists. She explained that she "condemns the events that took place yesterday (Tuesday) to representatives of the media. . . . For our government it is fundamental that there be complete freedom of expression and the possibility to exercise this work."[41] Later, Interior Minister Andrés Zaldívar clarified the president's comments, saying that "the declaration of the President was only in reaction to the excesses of the *Carabineros*, that which was recognized by their own High Command."[42]

It is important to note here that the term "excesses" is the same term used by the director general of the Carabineros, and while the term obfuscates what happened, it was quickly adopted by both politicians and *El Mercurio* journalists, likely for reasons of self-censorship explained in the previous section. Zaldívar also repeated the president's message that, according to democratic norms, "procedures should never lead to abuses or the exercise of force beyond what is assigned to the *Carabineros*. It is not within the role of the *Carabineros* to do what they did with the journalists or bring in a girl by pulling her by the hair."[43]

Other political leaders also emphasized that the Carabineros went beyond their acceptable role in a democracy, although the term "democracy" was rarely used explicitly. For example, the president of the Christian Democratic Party, Soledad Alvear, condemned the Carabineros for their "actions that were completely unmeasured. The *Carabinero*-citizen relationship should continue to perfect itself and events like what happened yesterday don't contribute to this direction."[44] Alluding to Chile's international reputation as a democracy, the president of the Socialist Party, Camilo Escalona, stated that the Carabineros were responsible for "embarrassing Chile in front of the world."[45] More provocatively, student leader María Jesús Sanhueza "qualified the action of the *Carabineros* as 'terrorist.' "[46] In total, seven of the thirteen explanations for why the Carabineros were responsible for what happened make implicit or explicit reference to the violation of democratic norms or the constitutional limits of the Carabineros' role.

The second explanation for Carabinero responsibility emphasizes the excesses of individual officers, and six of the thirteen references to

Carabinero responsibility take this position. For example, Interior Minister Andrés Zaldívar explicitly stated, "I . . . defend the *Carabineros*; one cannot disqualify the institution for the acts of a few."[47] His position is consistent with that of the Carabinero leadership, which, according to *El Mercurio*, "admitted that the Special Forces engaged in a procedure outside the bounds of regulated procedures when they attacked two cameramen and one photo-journalist meters from La Moneda [government house], as well as other events that made up the hard line anti-disturbance actions taken during the student protests."[48] Court cases also tend to individualize accountability. Thus, three references that focus on the wrongdoing of individual officers are references to court cases lodged by civil-society organizations against the Carabineros for specific incidents of violence.[49]

While the majority of quotes or references to blame identify the Carabineros as responsible, many articles imply that the actions of the Carabineros need to be considered in light of the actions of the protesters. During another student protest on 2 June (a few days after the 30 May protest), the Carabineros chose "cautious action" as a form of rebellion against the government's dismissal of some of their officers who were directly involved, and official condemnations of their previous "excesses."[50] Using two different frames, seven quotes or references address explicitly the relationship between Carabineros and the protesters, mostly in response to the "caution" of the Carabineros.

First, it is argued that the "excesses" of the Carabineros were justified considering the threat they faced. This position follows two lines of argument, the first being that the student protesters were infiltrated by violent groups and individuals. Immediately after the 30 May protest, an *El Mercurio* article explained that "infiltrating *encapuchados* [hooded people] and delinquents predominated in the conflicts that occurred yesterday. The students could not neutralize them."[51] The newspaper also blamed the protesters for some of the violence against journalists. A caption under one photograph states, "This is how a rock came from *encapuchados* and hit the head of *El Mercurio* journalist Francisco Aguila."[52] Similarly, Interior Minister Andrés Zaldívar stated in response to the Carabineros' later inaction that "one should not be weak with the *lumpen* who infiltrate movements, like that of the students."[53]

At first glance this argument appears to legitimize the protesters and distinguish them from the alleged infiltrators; however, the line between legitimate protesters and infiltrating delinquents is blurry. For example, it is not inconsequential that the student protesters were blamed for not "neutralizing" the infiltrators; in 2011 the Piñera government put forth a bill (rejected in 2013) that would have seen protest organizers held financially responsible for any damage caused by their protest, even if committed by "infiltrators." Moreover, the "infiltration" argument was used by those justifying police repression not only against shadowy infiltrators, but against the students and journalists who were the primary recipients of the repression as well. In this sense the response of the director general of the Carabineros is perhaps more honest. Summarizing his position, *El Mercurio* explained, "in terms of the student protest, he admits that there were political and delinquent infiltrators. But he clarified that students were involved in the aggressions against *Carabineros*."[54] The director general was quoted as saying, "[students] were involved in the aggressions against the *Carabineros*. It's a fact. The majority of those arrested were students."[55]

The second and less common frame is that the Carabineros and the protesters were both equally to blame. The interior minister maintained that both groups committed excesses and should be held accountable according to established democratic mechanisms. For example, he stated, "The civilian who attacks a *Carabinero*, throws rocks, breaks a public telephone, must be arrested and charged."[56] An *El Mercurio* editorial on 2 June placed this equal-blame perspective within a frame that emphasized the need for social order, rather than democratic mechanisms of accountability. As the article stated, "no less indignant, condemnable and unjustified are the destructive actions of the other protesters."[57] The author goes on to argue that President Bachelet's "unilateral" focus on the wrongdoing of the Carabineros could "lead the forces to self-inhibit their actions against those who commit violence. This, for its part, could be understood as an incentive for violent individuals to make their actions more extreme, with the peace of mind that the police will not put up major resistance for fear of sanctions and loss of their professional careers. This framework is dangerous for public security."[58] The term "public security" is often used in a manner that is interchangeable with "citizen security." Thus, it is possible that the equal-guilt position is taken so as to not offend the Carabineros and thereby avoid potential political or career consequences. Regardless, such a position implies that the actions of the Carabineros, while excessive, may have been justified considering the perceived threat they faced. The police in a democracy have the legitimate right to use violence against civilians when necessary; the question raised in this context is whether or not this protest was indeed a case of wrongdoing.

The third group identified as responsible for the police "excesses" against the protesters was the government. Very often police repression of social protest is thought to be a political decision taken by the government to silence opposition. Indeed, a number of people I interviewed, particularly (but not exclusively) those from human rights organizations, believe that the government supports the use of police repression against social protest. However, only one person in the *El Mercurio* coverage of the student protest was quoted as making this association, and that was student leader María Jesús Sanhueza. She stated, "The government is afraid of what the student organization has done and wants to stop it by whatever means necessary."[59] Most others hold the government responsible only for not resolving the conflict before it went to the streets, implying that the actions taken by the Carabineros were justified or predictable once the conflict erupted in the streets. For example, Congressman (*Diputado*) Alberto Cardemil (National Renewal Party) shamed the president for not resolving the conflict, implying that the police were just doing their job: "The dismissal of the police chief is the culmination of a succession of errors committed by La Moneda, because they left the political floor to the actions of the Carabineros in their control of public order. . . . If the President wants to get angry at someone she should get angry at her ministers who have still not resolved the education crisis"[60]

Finally, and focusing solely on the violence of the Carabineros against the journalists, only José Alejandro Bernales Ramírez, at the time the director general of the Carabineros, blamed journalists themselves for their injuries. When asked why the Carabineros "lost their patience" on 30 May, Bernales stated, "While I am not excusing anyone, I ask myself, why were none of the journalists (who suffered excesses) accredited in the police area? They know how the institution works and they know how to approach a group of Carabineros, and to never take photos in the middle of police action.... They were looking for proof of *Carabinero* excesses and, as well, that they lose patience. One in a hundred loses patience."[61] Supporting the guilt of journalists in another article portraying the Carabineros in a favorable light, an anonymous officer was quoted as asking, "What are you journalists looking for? What are you selling? When a *Carabinero* is hitting, they are responding to those who protest. You [journalists] look and look for the moment. Never when protesters hit a *Carabinero*. This isn't news."[62] In fact, *El Mercurio* published many pictures and much written text showing Carabineros being attacked by students, whereas relatively few examples were given of the opposite.[63]

Nevertheless, it is important to note that almost half (thirteen of twenty-seven) of those people quoted or referred to in *El Mercurio* who specified particular actions as wrongdoing identified the Carabineros as the wrongdoers in this incident of "excessive violence." Clearly the police force was being shamed for going beyond their proper role in a democracy. However, it is equally important to recognize that a majority (twenty of twenty-seven) of the total number of these quotes or references present justifications for the level of force used by the Carabineros. These justifications include: the excesses were those of individual officers; the level of force was proportionate to the threat faced; this was the inevitable result of the government not resolving the conflict before it went to the streets; those injured placed themselves in that position. Thus, while the Carabineros are identified as wrongdoers, competing frames question the significance of this wrongdoing.

Also worth noting is that few voices from civil society were included in this debate. We do not know the positions of the unions or university organizations that supported the high school students, and few of those present at the protests were asked their views. We also do not have the perspective of human rights organizations, even though the Human Rights Commission was noted to have been one of two organizations initiating a court case against the Carabineros. Insufficient information was provided to properly judge the level of violence used by police, or for human rights organizations to track such information.

How Should They be Held Accountable?

Finally, social accountability also involves media activating mechanisms of horizontal accountability. While there were 44 mentions of blame found in the articles analyzed, and 27 mentions of why this blame was assigned, in only 24 instances were particular mechanisms of accountability advocated, used, introduced, or rejected. These mechanisms included the dismissal of selected Carabineros or ministers deemed responsible (15), judicial action (4), a crackdown on street crime (2), and institutional change (3).

The most discussed mechanism of accountability was President Bachelet's decision to dismiss 10 Carabineros as well as the head of the Special Forces (the organization in charge of managing the protest) and his immediate subordinate. Of the 23 references to mechanisms of accountability, 14 focused on this issue. Members of Congress from left or left-of-center political parties (the Party for Democracy and the Christian Democrats) were quoted as supportive of the dismissals in 3 quotes and references.[64] In contrast, members of Congress from the opposition right and right-of-center parties (National Renewal and the Independent Democrat Union) disagreed with the dismissals in 3 quotes and references. For example, Senator (*Senador*) Alberto Espina (National Renewal) explained, "What needed to be done was to investigate the specific incidents of excesses, but not dismiss police personnel or remove police chiefs from their positions. With this type of action one ends up inhibiting the ability of the police to act."[65]

The position of the Carabineros themselves was mixed. Eight quotes or references reveal that the institution was upset enough with the dismissals to engage in the rebellious "caution action" in response to the student protest on 2 June. However, *El Mercurio* reported that there was disagreement within the Carabineros as to whether or not Colonel Osvaldo Ezequiel Jara, the head of the Special Forces, should have been dismissed. Some anonymous officers agreed with Jara's dismissal, arguing that his leadership supported the use of "iron fist" (*mano dura*) policing,[66] but others argued that neither Jara nor his superior, General (*General Inspector*) Jorge Acuña, should be associated with the excesses. Rather, those who should be held accountable were "those officials who really gave the orders that led to the excesses."[67] One anonymous officer saw Héctor Henríquez, the general chief of security and public order (*general inspector y director de orden y seguridad*), as responsible, qualifying Henríquez's decisions as more "political" since he has direct connections with the minister of the interior.[68] Going further, ex-director general Fernando Cordero of the Carabineros put forth the question, "Is the government going to face up [to their responsibility] and remove the minister that, with two months of leadership has had an awful management [record]?"[69] In contrast, when Director General José Alejandro Bernales Ramírez was asked why Colonel Jara's superiors had not been held responsible, he responded: "Because the person [Jara] who is on the street with the people, guiding and giving orders, is the prefect."[70]

The debate within the Carabineros appeared to be divided between blaming a few bad apples versus blaming the political leadership. In either case, it was not the institution of the Carabineros that needed to be reformed in order to ensure that such an action would not occur again. It is also interesting to note that within the debate over whether the dismissals constituted an appropriate mechanism of accountability, the perspectives of the Carabineros themselves were given more coverage than those of elected politicians. This may be the result of media bias or of civilians' fear of offending the Carabineros. Of course, missing completely is the perspective of civil-society organizations. Regardless, as the debate in *El Mercurio* reveals, dismissals are very political and may not actually change institutional practices.

Compared to the discussion around the dismissal of Carabinero officers, relatively little attention was given to the judiciary as a mechanism of accountability. Indeed, it was only mentioned in four instances. One politician was referred to as supporting judicial sanctions, and Party for Democracy senator Guido Giardi was said to have argued that judicial and not only administrative sanctions should have been applied.[71] The only other references to the need to involve the judiciary in addressing the wrongdoing were brief mentions of two court cases being put forth against Carabineros for particular instances of excessive violence. One case was presented to the military courts by the Chilean College of Journalists.[72] The other case was presented by the Human Rights Commission and the Teachers' College of Puente Alto.[73] There was no mention of a judicial investigation into the whole event, and the journalists at *El Mercurio* did not pursue the point raised by Giardi. It appears that judicial accountability was considered limited, and journalists failed to push for further activation.

Another form of accountability referred to in the articles stems in part from the belief that the protesters were to blame for the violence. For example, during the protests that followed the one on 30 May, *El Mercurio* reported that the government was taking steps to prevent other "days of violence" by increasing security. They explained, "A re-enforcement of police contingents in the principal streets of the capital has *Carabineros* prepared for today, with the goal of avoiding the excesses and conflict similar to what occurred last week during the student marches."[74] A couple of days later *El Mercurio* explained that the government further "prepared a new law that will be applied more rigorously against all those who are caught provoking disturbances in the street. According to high-level sources in the Interior Ministry, the initiative is due to the preoccupation of the executive with the almost zero percent of formal charges laid by the Public Ministry in relation to the number of people arrested."[75] There was no mention of the potential impact of this new law on the right to protest, and there was also no mention of new laws or regulations to assist in restricting future police "excesses."

However, three people were quoted as arguing in favor of the institutional changes that they felt would ensure that such incidents would not be repeated. One political leader simply argued that the Carabineros needed to rework how they deal with adolescents: "For the natural biology of youth, their expression, their movement, their speed, they are distinct to the conversations or maintenance of public order with workers or university students. . . . Maybe they [the Carabineros] have gotten out the habit of fighting with adolescents."[76] In contrast, other quotes demanded more substantial institutional changes. Both Alejandro Guillier, then president of the College of Journalists, and Camilo Escalona (president of the Socialist Party) argued in favor of creating a Ministry of Public Security and moving the Carabineros there from the Ministry of Defense, a move that would place the Carabineros under civilian rather than military control. Guillier argued that this needs to be done "in order to advance and develop methods of working that correspond with the rule of law and with a country with an advancing democracy."[77] Escalona argued that the creation of such a ministry was "urgent and indispensable."[78]

This goal of moving the Carabineros under the Interior Ministry was first laid out in the Program of Government of the Accord among Parties for Democracy, in place since 1990. Despite a long history of Carabineros subordination to the Interior Ministry between its creation in 1927 and the 1973 coup, the Carabineros successfully resisted attempts to restore that arrangement until 2011. The police have argued that the Interior Ministry has "a direct link to the government's political agenda," and thus they are more politically independent within the Ministry of Defense.[79] The government unsuccessfully attempted to move the Carabineros in 1989, 1991, 1992, 1993, and 2001.[80] However, in 1990 President Patricio Aylwin (1990–4) was successful in at least moving some domestic security issues away from the control of the military by establishing a Public Security Council (later Public Security and Information Office) within the Interior Ministry.[81]

The history of this proposal might lead one to expect that journalists would pursue the opinions of other public officials regarding the comments of Guillier and Escalona. This would have been an opportunity for journalists to test the water and see if there was more support than in the past for such a change. However, none of these calls for civilian control over the police were put into their historical context, nor did the journalists follow up with other public officials (let alone members of the public) about their perspectives on these proposals. The comments of Guillier and Escalona were not even the focus of their own articles; rather, they were slipped into an article that dealt more generally with political leaders' reactions to the dismissal of the Carabineros.

Conclusion

El Mercurio's coverage of police repression during the 2006 student protest did provide a degree of social accountability, and it revealed that support for police repression of social protest is not structurally determined by legacies of authoritarianism. Emphasizing this point, this study has focused on *El Mercurio*, the least likely of all Chilean newspapers to criticize police repression of social protest. From this perspective, the newspaper's overall reaction to the student protest was exceptionally supportive of the protesters and critical of Carabineros actions. Indeed, the significance of this media coverage in the Chilean context inspired two young Chilean journalists to produce a well-watched documentary film and accompanying book analyzing how the students were able to gain such positive media coverage and public support.[82] Relative to other protests in Chile, the 2006 student protest sparked a noteworthy debate in the media regarding police repression. Whether successful or not at achieving other forms of police accountability, media coverage of this event will act as a future reference point.

The *El Mercurio* articles covering this protest give weight to the view that the excessive violence by Carabineros violated democratic norms, and that they need to be held accountable as a result. The published quotes supporting this position came from influential figures, including President Michelle Bachelet, as well as the presidents of the Christian Democratic and Socialist Parties (both prominent parties within the governing coalition, the Concertación). This coverage is important in that it recognizes that police reaction to social protest within a democracy is qualitatively different than that which is acceptable under an authoritarian government. It also emphasizes that Chile is now a democracy, and that old repressive police practices will no longer be tolerated. Thus the media act as a mechanism of social accountability, shaming police for wrongdoing and challenging denials that such actions are wrong.

More broadly, the articles in *El Mercurio* also present competing views (or frames) regarding who is most responsible for committing wrongdoing, what type of wrongdoing they have committed, and how the wrongdoer(s) should be held accountable. The existence of this debate is an important aspect of social accountability as it provides the opportunity for actors included in the debate to challenge old frames that may have simply presented police repression as an unfortunate but acceptable or necessary fact of life.

However, the coverage of the event also reveals important limits to *El Mercurio*'s role as a mechanism of social accountability. That is, while police repression of social protest is not structurally determined, important obstacles do remain. First, many voices were excluded or dismissed within the debate, and only a very few members of civil-society organizations or the public in general were given a voice. In terms of the amount of coverage and the weight given, coverage favored political leaders and Carabineros whose views were least critical of the police institution. This exclusion or muffling of voices and perspectives might be attributable to media bias, self-censorship, or the efficiency with which journalists access public officials compared to civil-society actors.[83] Regardless, such an exclusion of voices from civil society and a reliance on official sources has been shown in previous research to contribute to greater police repression of social protests.[84]

Second, there is an undeniably important practice of self-censorship that constrains how journalists and public officials can hold the Carabineros accountable. If one cannot offend the Carabineros without legal, political, or career consequences (whether real or imagined), the criticisms that need to be expressed in order to shame wrongdoers, activate mechanisms of accountability, or challenge old frames for understanding wrongdoing will necessarily be limited or cautious. This limitation suggests that effective police reform might require a revision or reform of media laws or practices. Moreover, the priority placed on "citizen security" by the government and *El Mercurio* may also play a contributing role in media and political self-censorship, an issue well worth exploring in future research.

Third, while possibly a circular argument, the coverage in *El Mercurio* provides insufficient information regarding details of the tumult; they do not provide information regarding how many of the protesters and journalists were injured, nor do they explain the nature of their injuries. This information is important supporting evidence needed for the media to effectively shame wrongdoers and cause the public, politicians, and social movement organizations to activate mechanisms of accountability. The circular nature of this argument stems from the possibility that the media may not print this information because it is not collected by public institutions or social movement organizations. Regardless of the source of the problem, social accountability requires adequate information. Further research is needed to understand better why such information was not provided in this case.

Finally, the media may work as a more effective mechanism of social accountability when the wrongdoing is more widely accepted in the society as actual wrongdoing. For example, corrupt politicians who have accepted bribes in exchange for voting in a certain manner are more easily identified as wrongdoers.[85] The repression of social protest by police has a long history in Chile (as it does in many other countries in Latin America), and is intimately tied to the idea of public order. This history dates back to the creation of the current police forces and has persisted through both democratic and authoritarian governments. Thus, the acceptance of police repression of social protest as wrongdoing is not obvious. For example, many of those referred to in the *El Mercurio* articles analyzed here argued that the police "excesses" were justified, or that there was no need to apply mechanisms of accountability, or both. In the case of police repression of social protest, the media's role in presenting views that challenge accepted norms or frames becomes an important part of its role in social accountability. The exclusion of many voices from this debate in *El Mercurio* could be one of the most important limits of the paper's role as a mechanism of social accountability.

In conclusion, police repression of social protest continues to persist in new democracies throughout Latin America. While the levels of repression are certainly not as high as during previous authoritarian regimes, the continuation of this practice places important limits on freedom of expression. The public relies on the media to let it know what has happened and who is responsible. Differentiating police repression of social protest under an authoritarian regime, in a democracy the public also expects the media to tell them how wrongdoers are going to be held accountable for their actions. If they are not going to be held accountable, the media provides a forum for wrongdoers or public authorities to explain why this is so. This is what Andres Schedler calls "answerability."[86] Such media accountability of protest policing is not speculative; rather, it has been shown in the literature on protest policing in established democracies to impact levels of repression depending on the frame used by the media to present such incidents. High levels of police repression of social protest are not simply structurally determined; they are in part contingent on media coverage. The media are an important mechanism of social accountability thus far understudied in new democracies, especially as a forum for reframing police violence. Understanding the limits and strengths of the media in this role calls for more research.

Notes

1. Reprinted from *Policing Protest in Argentina and Chile* by Michelle D. Bonner. Copyright © 2014 by Lynne Rienner Publishers, Inc. Used with permission.
2. F. Aguila and R. Olivares, "Vuelta a la violencia empañó paro," *El Mercurio*, 31 May 2006.
3. P. Lezaeta, "Carabineros admite 'excesos injustificables,' " *El Mercurio*, 31 May 2006.
4. R. Olivares and D. Muñoz, "Nuevos incidentes marcados por la cautela en el accionar policial," *El Mercurio*, 1 June 2006.
5. For examples see Dominique Wisler and Marco Giugni, "Under the Spotlight: The Impact of Media Attention on Protest Policing," *Mobilization: An International Journal* 4, no. 2 (1999): 172 and 184; William A. Gamson, *Strategy of Social Protest*, 2nd ed. (Belmont, CA: Wadsworth, 1990); Roger Geary, *Policing Industrial Disputes: 1893 to 1985* (Cambridge: Cambridge University Press, 1985), 128–30; Jennifer Earl, Sarah A. Soule, and John D. McCarthy, "Protest under Fire? Explaining the Policing of Protest," *American Sociological Review* 68, no. 4 (2003): 584; Donatella della Porta and Herbert Reiter, eds., introduction to *Policing Protest: The Control of Mass Demonstrations in Western Democracies* (Minneapolis: University of Minnesota Press. 1998), 18.
6. See Enrique Peruzzotti and Catalina Smulovitz, eds., introduction to *Enforcing the Rule of Law: Social Accountability in the New Latin American Democracies* (Pittsburgh, PA: University of Pittsburgh Press, 2006), 3–33. Peruzzotti and Smulovitz define social accountability as a form of vertical accountability that, like elections, is used to hold public officials accountable. Social accountability is non-electoral and involves the activities of civil society and the media.
7. Andreas Schedler, "Conceptualizing Accountability," in *The Self-Restraining State: Power and Accountability in New Democracies*, ed. Andreas Schedler, Larry Diamond, and Marc F. Plattner, 13–28 (Boulder, CO: Lynne Riener Publishers, 1999).
8. Schedler, "Conceptualizing Accountability," 13–28.
9. See Donatella della Porta, "Police Knowledge and Protest Policing: Some Reflections on the Italian Case," in *Policing Protest: The Control of Mass Demonstrations in Western Democracies*, ed. Donatella della Porta and Herbert Reiter (Minneapolis: University of Minnesota Press, 1998), 247–8; Wisler and Giugni, "Under the Spotlight," 172–3; Dominique Wisler and Marco Tackenberg, "The Role of the Police: Image or Reality?" in *Patterns of Provocation: Police and Public Disorder*, ed. Richard Bessel and Clive Emsley (New York: Berghahn Books, 2000), 122.
10. Wisler and Giugni, "Under the Spotlight," 173.
11. Wisler and Giugni, "Under the Spotlight," 173; see also Wisler and Tackenberg, "The Role of Police," 122; della Porta and Reiter, introduction to *Policing Protest*, 19.
12. Wisler and Giugni, "Under the Spotlight," 178–81, 184; della Porta and Reiter, introduction to *Policing Protest*, 19; Geary, *Policing Industrial Disputes*, 131.
13. della Porta and Reiter, introduction to *Policing Protest*, 19.

14   Maria Aparecida Ferrari, "Public Relations in Chile: Searching for Identity amid Imported Models," in *The Global Public Relations Handbook: Theory, Research, and Practice*, ed. Krishnamurthy Sriramesh and Dejan Verčič (Mahwah, NJ: Lawrence Erlbaum Associates, 2003), 389; see also Ken Léon-Dermota, *And Well Tied Down: Chile's Press Under Democracy* (Westport, CT: Praeger, 2003), 147.

15   See Human Rights Watch, *The Limits of Tolerance: Freedom of Expression and the Public Debate in Chile* (New York: Human Rights Watch, 1998), 22; Guillermo Sunkel, "Introducción: La investigación sobre la prensa en Chile," in *Investigación Sobre la Prensa en Chile (1974–1984)*, ed. Fernando Reyes Matta, Carlos Ruiz S., Guillermo Sunkel, and José Joaquín Brunner (Santiago de Chile: Estudios ILET, 1986), 99, 102, 104; Léon-Dermota, *And Well Tied Down*, 130; Claudio Durán and Arnold Rockman, "Analisis Psico-Historico de la Propaganda de Agitación del diario El Mercurio en Chile 1972–1973," in *Investigación Sobre la Prensa en Chile*, 29; see also author's interviews, Santiago, Chile, 8 June–15 July 2009.

16   Léon-Dermota, *And Well Tied Down*, 138.

17   Walter Krohne, *Las dos caras de la libertad de expresión en Chile* (Santiago: Universidad Academia de Humanismo Cristiano, 2005), 92, 333–4.

18   William A. Gamson and David Stuart, "Media Discourse as a Symbolic Contest: The Bomb in Political Cartoons," *Sociological Forum* 7, no. 1 (1992): 55–86.

19   Anthony W. Pereira, *Political (In)Justice: Authoritarianism and the Rule of Law in Brazil, Chile and Argentina* (Pittsburgh, PA: University of Pittsburgh Press, 2005), 49; Simon Collier and William F. Sater, *A History of Chile, 1808–2002* (New York: Cambridge University Press, 2004), 222.

20   Collier and Sater, *A History of Chile*, 228 and 245.

21   Azun Candina, "The Institutional Identity of the Carabineros de Chile," in *Public Security and Police Reform in the Americas*, ed. John Bailey and Lucía Dammert (Pittsburgh, PA: University of Pittsburgh Press, 2006), 82.

22   Quoted in Pereira, *Political (In)Justice*, 50–1.

23   Collier and Sater, *A History of Chile*, 325.

24   Pereira, *Political (In)Justice*, 25.

25   Collier and Sater, *A History of Chile*, 377.

26   Quoted in Candina, "The Institutional Identity of the Carabineros de Chile," 84.

27   For an example, see Amnesty International, *Amnesty International Report 2002*, https://www.amnesty.org/en/documents/pol10/0001/2002/en/.

28   Claudio Fuentes, "Violent Police, Passive Citizens: The Failure of Social Accountability in Chile," in *Enforcing the Rule of Law: Social Accountability in the New Latin American Democracies*, ed. Enrique Peruzzotti and Catalina Smulovitz (Pittsburgh, PA: University of Pittsburgh Press, 2006), 161.

29   Quoted in Candina, "The Institutional Identity of the Carabineros de Chile," 81.

30 CEP (Centro de Estudios Públicos), *Estudio Nacional de Opinión Pública No. 79* (abril-mayo 2017), https://www.cepchile.cl/cep/site/artic/20170601/asocfile/20170601155007/encuestacep_abr_may2017.pdf. Owing to a corruption scandal in the Carabineros in 2017, confidence in the institution decreased to 37 percent that year. However, of the institutions surveyed, the Carabineros were still ranked second in public confidence, tied with the investigative police force, the PDI. Ranked first were the armed forces at 40 percent.

31 Claudio A. Fuentes, *Contesting the Iron Fist: Advocacy Networks and Police Violence in Democratic Argentina and Chile* (New York: Routledge, 2005), 64.

32 Michelle D. Bonner, "Media as Social Accountability: The Case of Police Violence in Argentina," *International Journal of Press/Politics* 14, no. 3 (2009): 296–312.

33 Otón Gutiérrez and Rodrigo Cerda, "María Jesús Sanhueza es cuestionada por su liceo," *El Mercurio*, 6 June 2006.

34 P. Molina, "Zaldívar reivindica rol de Carabineros," *El Mercurio*, 2 June 2006.

35 Human Rights Watch, "Progress Stalled: Setbacks in Freedom of Expression Reform," *Chile* (report) 13, no. 1 (B) (2001): 20.

36 Facultad de Derecho, Universidad Diego Portales, *Informe Anual Sobre Derechos Humanos en Chile: Hechos de 2006* (Santiago: Universidad Diego Portales, 2007), 79.

37 Facultad de Derecho, *Informe Anual*, 79.

38 Rosalind Bresnahan, "The Media and the Neoliberal Transition in Chile: Democratic Promise Unfulfilled," *Latin American Perspectives* 30, no. 6 (November 2003): 45; Krohne, *Las dos caras*, 192; Aparecida Ferrari, "Public Relations in Chile," 388; CODEPU, *Informe de Derechos Humanos 1990–2000* (Santiago: CODEPU, 2001), 134.

39 Part of this analysis is drawn from forty-five interviews conducted by the author in Santiago, Chile, between 8 June and 15 July 2009, as well as preliminary research conducted in Santiago, Chile in June 2006. The author's interviews were with journalists, NGOs, government ministries, and the police.

40 P. Lezaeta, "Carabineros admite 'excesos injustificables'," *El Mercurio*, 31 May 2006.

41 N. Yanez, "Bachelet interviene para criticar acción policial," *El Mercurio*, 31 May 2006.

42 P. Molina, "Zaldívar reivindica rol de Carabineros," *El Mercurio*, 2 June 2006.

43 Raquel Correa, "Los debores policiales," *El Mercurio*, 4 June 2006.

44 "Decisión de remover a jefes policiales no logran unanimidad en el mundo político," *El Mercurio*, 1 June 2006.

45 "Decisión de remover a jefes policiales no logran unanimidad en el mundo político," *El Mercurio*, 1 June 2006.

46 M. Hüne, "Casi 800 mil escolares pararon en todo Chile," *El Mercurio*, 31 May 2006.

47 Correa, "Los debores policiales."

48 Lezaeta, "Carabineros admite 'excesos injustificables.' "

49 Lezaeta, "Carabineros admite 'excesos injustificables' "; "Denuncia de periodistas," *El Mercurio*, 2 June 2006; René Olivares and David Muñoz, "Nuevos incidentes marcados por la cautela en el accionar policial," *El Mercurio*, 1 June 2006.

50 P. Lezaeta, "Jefes de Fuerzas Especiales caen por excesos," *El Mercurio*, 1 June 2006.

51 Olivares and Muñoz, "Nuevos incidentes."

52 "Lesionado periodista de 'El Mercurio,' " *El Mercurio*, 1 June 2006.

53 "Zaldívar: El Gobierno no claudicará ante el vandalismo," *El Mercurio*, 2 June 2006.

54 Pilar Molina Armas, "General Director de Carabineros: 'Hubo cautela, no repliegue'," *El Mercurio*, 10 June 2006.

55 Armas, "General Director de Carabineros: 'Hubo cautela, no repliegue.' "

56 Correa, "Los debores policiales."

57 "Fuerza pública y vandalismo," *El Mercurio*, 2 June 2006.

58 *El Mercurio*, "Fuerza pública y vandalismo."

59 Hüne, "Casi 800 mil escolares."

60 *El Mercurio*, "Decisión de remover a jefes policiales." For a similar quote by other congressman, see P. M. Chadwick, " 'El miércoles fue la huelga de la policía,' " *El Mercurio*, 2 June 2006.

61 Molina Armas, "General Director de Carabineros."

62 Beatriz Undurraga, "Cabo relata el rigor del trabajo en Fuerzas Especiales," *El Mercurio*, 2 June 2006.

63 See, for example, the photo linked with the article: "Gobierno cedió ante categorical presión de alumnus secundarios," *El Mercurio*, 4 June 2006.

64 *El Mercurio*, "Decisión de remover a jefes policiales."

65 *El Mercurio*, "Decisión de remover a jefes policiales."

66 P. Lezaeta, "Los roces internos por las destituciones," *El Mercurio*, 1 June 2006.

67 P. Lezeata, "Remociones generan puntos de vista en mandos de Carabineros," *El Mercurio*, 2 June 2006.

68 P. Lezeata, "Remociones generan puntos de vista en mandos de Carabineros."

69 *El Mercurio*, "Decisión de remover a jefes policiales."

70 Molina Armas, "General Director de Carabineros."

71 *El Mercurio*, "Decisión de remover a jefes policiales."

72 N. Yanez, "Bachelet interviene para criticar acción policial," *El Mercurio*, 31 May 2006; "Denuncia de periodistas," *El Mercurio*, 2 June 2006.

73 Olivares and Muñoz, "Nuevos incidentes."

74 Francisco Aguila, "250 carabineros más a la Alameda," *El Mercurio*, 5 June 2006.

75 Rodrigo Vergara and Francisco Águila, "Gobierno prepara dura ley contra violentistas," *El Mercurio*, 7 June 2006.

76 *El Mercurio*, "Decisión de remover a jefes policiales."

77 Yanez, "Bachelet interviene."

78 *El Mercurio*, "Decisión de remover a jefes policiales."

79 Lucía Dammert, "From Public Security to Citizen Security in Chile," in *Public Security and Police Reform in the Americas*, ed. John Bailey and Lucía Dammert (Pittsburgh, PA: University of Pittsburgh Press, 2006), 70.

80 Candina, "The Institutional Identity of the Carabineros de Chile," 86; see also Gregory Weeks, *The Military and Politics in Postauthoritarian Chile* (Tuscaloosa: University of Alabama Press, 2003), 54 and 79.

81 Dammert, "From Public Security," 63. In 2011 a law was finally passed to move the Carabineros from the Ministry of Defense to the Ministry of the Interior. The transfer took place in 2012. However, cases of Carabineros harming civilians or civilians harming Carabineros continue to be tried in military courts.

82 Andrea Domedel and Macarena Peña Y Lillo, *El Mayo de Los Pingüinos* (Santiago: Radio Universidad de Chile, 2008).

83 Robert M. Entman, for example, argues that "the least expensive way to satisfy mass audiences is to rely upon legitimate political elites for most information." See Entman *Democracy Without Citizens: Media and the Decay of American Politics* (New York: Oxford University Press, 1989), 18. Public officials are seen as legitimate; they supply facts and journalists have regular and relatively easy access to them. Moreover, the media's tendency to privilege public officials as sources may have been further reinforced in Chile during the Pinochet government, when for almost two decades public officials were the *only* approved source of information for journalists.

84 della Porta and Reiter, introduction to *Policing Protest*, 19.

85 See Enrique Peruzzotti, "Media Scandals and Social Accountability: Assessing the Role of the Senate Scandal in Argentina," in *Enforcing the Rule of Law: Social Accountability in the New Latin American Democracies*, ed. Enrique Peruzzotti and Catalina Smulovitz, 249–71 (Pittsburgh, PA: University of Pittsburgh Press, 2006).

86 Schedler, "Conceptualizing Accountability."

5

The Police Ombudsman in Brazil as a Potential Mechanism to Reduce Violence

Anthony W. Pereira

As was stated in the introduction to this volume, Latin America is the most violent region on the planet. A look at recent data on homicide, a relatively reliable indicator, reveals that in 2015 the region recorded more than a third of the world's homicides, while containing less than 10 percent of the world's population. Roughly 140,000 Latin Americans are murdered each year.[1] A "top ten" of countries with the highest murder rates in the world in recent years contains seven countries from Latin America and the Caribbean, and is headed by Honduras and Venezuela.[2] This gruesome pandemic of everyday violence remains underexamined and largely unexplained.

Is this violence inevitable, the inescapable result of centuries of inequality and oppression? As Pablo Policzer argues in the introduction to this volume, a certain type of structural explanation (although not all structural accounts) would suggest that the answer is yes. Scholars on the right have tended to identify Iberian culture and institutions as the root cause of contemporary violence.[3] On the left, the tendency is to argue that violence is an inevitable byproduct of Latin America's subordinate position in the global economy and political system.[4] While both of these "deep structural" positions are less appealing than they used to be, they are still influential, and still tempt analysts into questionable, strongly dichotomous generalizations. In the words of Stanford historian Niall

Ferguson, for example, "North America was better off than South America purely and simply because the British model of widely distributed property rights and democracy worked better than the Spanish model of concentrated wealth and authoritarianism." In another passage the same author asserts, "The newly independent [Latin American] states began their lives without a tradition of representative government, with a profoundly unequal distribution of land and with racial cleavages that closely approximated to that economic inequality. The result was a cycle of revolution and counter-revolution, coup and counter-coup."[5] In such a view, Latin America *is* doomed because of the original sin of an inadequate "model" of economic and political development.

There are reasons to believe that such accounts are oversimplified. First, a focus on alleged deep structures ignores the high degree of variation in Latin America's violence. On the one hand, countries such as Argentina, Chile, and Uruguay have homicide rates closer to those of Western Europe than the rest of Latin America, and (in the case of the first two countries) lower than that of the United States.[6] On the other hand, relatively high rates of violence characterize nations such as Honduras, El Salvador, Venezuela, Belize, Colombia, Jamaica, Guatemala, Mexico, and Brazil. Second, rates of violence in Latin America have changed considerably over time. As Pablo Piccato points out in his chapter in this volume, the long-term trend for homicide rates in Mexico since the nineteenth century has been a steady decline. Despite recent surges in violence in Central America and the Caribbean since 1995, the long-term trend in many other Latin American and Caribbean countries is also one of decline.[7] According to Steven Pinker, this trend is a universal one, brought about by an increase in state capacity and the spread of progressive ideas.[8] Given that, how can the constants of prior colonial rule, inequality, and oppression adequately account for rates of violence in Latin America? It seems probable that other variables, more conjunctural and interactive, would be part of an adequate explanation of the pattern of change and variation in Latin American violence.

The homicide rate has more than doubled in Brazil since 1980.[9] The scale of this killing makes Brazilian violence one of the most serious political and social problems in the region. While Brazil's per capita homicide rate puts it roughly in the middle of the regional rankings, its absolute number of homicide victims—61,283 in 2016—was the largest in Latin America and the Caribbean, representing over 40 percent of the regional total, and making Brazil the country with the largest absolute number of murder victims in the world in that year.[10]

The police in Brazil both reflect and contribute to the problem of violence in the country. The Brazilian police have gained notoriety for inefficiency, the widespread use of force (especially torture and summary executions), and corruption. In the words of one specialist, "an antagonistic relationship between the police and the population at large is an almost universal problem in Latin America . . . [but of] the Southern Cone countries, the crime and policing situation in Brazil is by far the most extreme."[11] As another observer writes, "Brazil's police are among the world's most violent and corrupt, and human rights, particularly those of socially marginalized groups, are violated with impunity on a massive scale."[12] In 2016, 4,222 people, or 7 percent of all homicide victims, were killed by the police, with 925 killed in the state of Rio de Janeiro and 856 in São Paulo.[13] Another study of the police in Rio de Janeiro found that roughly 10 percent of the manslaughters in one year were committed by the police, and that over ten civilian suspects were killed for each police officer killed in alleged confrontations.[14]

Demands for police reform have risen to the top of the political agenda in Brazil as violent crime has escalated. These demands are mixed. Some are simply for the police to do a better job at providing security, even if that involves being more, rather than less, violent. But others come from civil-society organizations that seek increased democratic control over the police and a strengthening of the police forces' commitment to human rights. Some of these organizations have argued that police inefficiency and violence are part of the same problem, and that only by reducing its violence can the police become a more effective force for preventing and investigating crime.

Reforms reflecting the latter assumption have been enacted over the last twenty years at different times and in different ways in the patchwork quilt of Brazil's twenty-six states and federal district. This chapter looks at one such measure: the creation of police ombudsmen. It first contrasts structural and contingent approaches to explaining violence in Latin America, and discusses the notion of mechanisms for reducing violence.

The second section presents some information on the police ombudsmen in Brazil, with special reference to the experience in two states. Finally, the conclusion assesses the potential of the ombudsmen as a mechanism for reducing violence.

Structural and Contingent Perspectives on Violence in Latin America

When US president Barack Obama met Venezuelan president Hugo Chávez before the opening ceremony of the Fifth Summit of the Americas in Port of Spain, Trinidad, on 17 April 2009, Chávez gave Obama a copy of Eduardo Galeano's *The Open Veins of Latin America*.[15] Galeano's well-known book describes a history of exploitative violence against Latin America's workers, *campesinos*, and Indigenous people by Europeans, Americans, and Latin America's own oligarchs and state officials. These acts are depicted as fundamental to the formation and subsequent development of Latin America. While the insight that violence has been a major factor in Latin America's history is not controversial, it is debatable whether or not this history and its structural legacies are responsible for condemning the region to high levels of violence in perpetuity; perhaps much of this violence is actually contingent and therefore susceptible to mitigation in the short to medium term. As Pablo Policzer writes in the introduction to this volume, "shining a light on the contingent and not just the structural opens up new possibilities and solutions."

We can accept that some causes of violence might be contingent without negating the importance of structural factors. One statistical study, for example, found that increases in income inequality are correlated with rises in crime rates.[16] This finding has important implications for Latin America, the region of the world distinguished by the highest levels of income inequality, but such findings need not rule out the search for more contingent factors that can account for variation and change in violence in the region. Another claim is that Latin America's urban population grew in recent decades much faster than those of other regions such as Asia and Africa, and that this rapid urbanization is linked to the rise in homicides. This is because urbanization elevated factors linked to violence, such as "inequality, unemployed young men, dislocated families, poor government services, [and] easily available firearms."[17]

Accepting contingency involves shifting from an emphasis on invariant structures and process, or laws, to a focus on mechanisms, as Pablo Policzer points out in his introduction to this volume. According to Charles Tilly, "in actual social life invariant structures and processes are rare or non-existent."[18] For Jon Elster, laws usually entail inappropriate claims to generality; however, mechanisms are more modest than laws, as they are "frequently occurring and easily recognizable causal patterns that are triggered under generally unknown conditions or with indeterminate consequences."[19] Mechanisms allow explanation but not prediction; in Tilly's words, explanations involving mechanisms "reject covering-law regularities for large structures.... Instead, they lend themselves to 'local theory,' in which the explanatory mechanisms and processes operate quite broadly but combine locally as a function of initial conditions and adjacent processes to produce distinctive trajectories and outcomes."[20]

If we accept these claims, we can try to identify mechanisms that appear to have reduced violence in Latin America. These include certain forms of civil-society mobilization and public policies. Two relatively recent and widely noticed examples deserve mention. In Bogotá, Colombia the homicide rate fell from around 80 per 100,000 in 1993 to 21 in 2004. Some analysts attribute this drop to an integrated municipal program that included public health interventions, the reclaiming of public space, criminal justice reform, the improvement of crime and violence information systems, control of public alcohol consumption, and assistance to "at-risk" youth.[21] Similarly, intentional homicides in the city of São Paulo, Brazil fell by almost 70 percent between 1999 and 2006. Policies that had been previously introduced included dry-laws, voluntary disarmament initiatives, social programs, increased incarceration, and reforms in police organization and procedures.[22]

The causal significance of any alleged mechanism is likely to be contested, as indeed those mentioned above are. One potential difficulty for analysis is that many violence-reduction measures are likely to be what Elster calls "Type B" mechanisms. These are mechanisms that can affect the dependent variable, or the outcome the analyst is attempting to explain, in opposite directions, making it unknown a priori what the net effect is likely to be. The example Elster gives for this is an alcoholic environment for children: some children in such an environment grow up to be alcoholics, while others reject alcohol as adults.[23] There is also no reason that the range of possible outcomes of Type B mechanisms is limited to two. For the purposes of this discussion, the enactment of the same policies, or the creation of organizations with the same formal design, may produce different outcomes in different environments; that is, they might reduce violence in one place, while failing to reduce it in another. Brinks, for example, finds that variations in the institutional design of the judiciary and prosecutors' office had little impact on the differences between legal responses to police killings in five Latin American cities. The key factor in his study is the socioeconomic status of the claimants; higher-status claimants were better able to obtain an effective judicial response after their family member had been victimized by the police.[24]

One important recent (2009) attempt to explain violence consistent with the approach espoused here is Violence and Social Orders: A Conceptual Framework for Interpreting Recorded Human History by Douglass North, Joseph Wallis, and Barry Weingast. The authors begin by complaining that there is a "lack of systematic thinking about the central problem of violence in human societies," and proceed to argue that "how societies solve the ubiquitous threat of violence shapes and constrains the forms that human interaction can take, including the form of political and economic systems."[25] They then contrast what they call "natural states" with "open access societies."

The core difference between these two types of societies is how they control violence. In natural states, "access to violence is open to anyone strong enough and well-organized enough to use it. The natural state coordinates these individuals and groups through an interlocking set of rent-creating arrangements that limit access throughout the rest of society."[26] The political management of violence is based on "the manipulation of economic privileges."[27] Despite the label, open access societies actually limit access to the means of coercion, and thus violence; they base the management of violence on impersonal rules and organizations. Formal institutions, including the judiciary, embody agreements about how and when violence can legitimately be used, and hem in specialized military and police forces. These institutions and agreements regulate the formal authority granted to the military and police to intervene in private interactions. According to North, Wallis, and Weingast, "The resulting rules governing the use of violence in open access orders must be impersonal; that is, the agreements must be independent of the identity of the individual member of the military or police force and, equally important, independent of the identity of the political officials. If the rules do not apply impersonally, the society is a natural state."[28]

For North and his collaborators, the transition from a natural state to an open access society involves the attainment of three conditions: the rule of law for elites; the recognition of "perpetually-lived organizations" (such as corporations) in the public and private spheres; and the "consolidated" control of the military.[29] This last condition, the most difficult to achieve in the authors' judgment, means that "nonmilitary elite groups and organizations must be capable of disciplining the military force through nonmilitary means."[30]

Some questions could be raised about *Violence and Social Orders*. The binary categories of these two forms of society place a rather tight straightjacket on contemporary societies and world history, blurring other important distinctions that could be made. The description of open access societies is also rather lyrical. These are societies with widely held beliefs about the importance of inclusion and equality for all citizens; they display a lack of barriers to entry into economic, political, religious, and educational activities; they offer deep support for organizational forms, such as contractual enforcement, that are open to all; they are places characterized by an impartially enforced rule of law that applies to all citizens and state officials. One wonders how much this description is ideological rather than empirically based. Furthermore, the authors' claim that only twenty-five countries and 15 percent of the world's population presently meet their criteria for open access societies excludes Latin America from the promised land entirely—an act of exclusion that might not be justified.

Nevertheless, the book's framework provides several useful insights for the analysis of Latin American violence. These are:

1. Societies with high levels of violence are not dysfunctional or "sick." They are not imperfect approximations of societies with lower levels of

violence. They have their own logic. For example, violence can be a way of controlling access to, and maintaining, economic privileges. For this and other reasons, elites may have little incentive to attempt to diminish violence.

2. Institutions created to diminish violence are likely to produce different results in different contexts.

3. Institutions created to diminish violence (including the police ombudsman, discussed below) often embody attempts to subject the wielders of coercion to impersonal rules, thus creating movement towards the open access society described above.

With these considerations in mind, the following section will describe a new organization designed to diminish police violence in Brazil.

Police Ombudsmen in Brazil

Brazil's police forces have a checkered history. The police forces of São Paulo and Rio de Janeiro were organized in 1831, two years after Robert Peel created the Metropolitan Police Force in London.[31] In Rio, one of the police force's main functions was to recapture escaped slaves and to whip slaves for a fee, at the request of the slave owners. The state thus provided a disciplinary service paid for by private interests. Whipping slaves was vital to the maintenance of the broader socioeconomic system, because slavery was so central to economic relations and the class structure.[32] Police violence therefore has deep historical roots in Brazil and has long been part of a system of class domination and social exclusion. At the same time, criticism of police violence and the gradual expansion of citizenship are also part of the country's history.[33]

The uniformed military police, responsible for patrolling on the streets, became powerful armies that served provincial governors in the Old Republic (1898–1930). They were subjected to increasing control by the federal state, and especially the army, during the first presidency of

Getúlio Vargas (1930–45). The plainclothes civil police, responsible for criminal investigations, grew out of judicial investigators attached to the crown in the nineteenth century; their main instrument, the police inquiry (*inquérito policial*), has existed in Brazil since 1841. Both forces were modified under the 1964–85 military dictatorship. The military police were put under army control and deployed in the repression of political opponents and dissidents, while the civil police lost much of their investigative capacity.[34]

The end of the dictatorship saw the above-mentioned development of pressures to reform public security. By the 1990s, many political actors on different sides of the ideological conflicts of the 1960s and '70s had come together to analyze and propose ways to curb increasing violence, especially in Brazil's cities. Out of these proposals came several new accountability mechanisms, as well as the reinforcement of existing accountability mechanisms (see Table 5.1). In addition, civil-society organizations such as the São Paulo Institute Against Violence (Instituto São Paulo Contra Violência) and Viva Rio—funded by donations from businesses—established partnerships with state agencies aimed at improving policing.[35]

In universities, academics and policy analysts founded new centers that combined traditional preoccupations with human rights with a focus on policing and ways to improve it. These include the Centre for Studies of Criminality and Public Security (Centro de Estudos de Criminalidade e Segurança Pública, or CRISP) at the Federal University of Minas Gerais in Belo Horizonte; the Centre for Studies of Security and Citizenship (Centro de Estudos de Segurança e Cidadania, or CESeC) at the Candido Mendes University in Rio de Janeiro; the Centre for the Study of Violence (Núcleo de Estudos da Violência, or NEV) at the University of São Paulo; and the Centre for the Study of Coercive Institutions (Núcleo de Estudo das Instituições Coercitivas, or NIC) at the Federal University of Pernambuco.

It was in this context that police ombudsman's offices were established. "Ombudsman" is a Swedish word meaning "a representative or agent of the people." The first ombudsman was an officer appointed by the Swedish legislature in 1809 to investigate administrative and judicial complaints.[36] In the twentieth century, the concept travelled widely and moved well beyond the original institutional design limiting the ombudsman to the legislature. A survey analyzed Latin American ombudsman's offices, some

TABLE 5.1
Advantages and Disadvantages of Various Accountability Mechanisms in Brazilian Public Security

Mechanism	Advantages	Disadvantages
Voting	Broad participation; median voter theory; elections with broad suffrage should increase production of public goods, including security	Inadequate voter information; lack of candidate/party differentiation; escalating superficial "tough on crime" rhetoric; lack of executive branch control over police
Ombudsman	Independent entity to receive complaints about police corruption and violence	No independent investigative capacity; lack of visibility; police resistance
Community councils	Local participation and influence	May not be representative; police may not respond to demands (consultation rather than binding decision-making); lack of resources
Civil-society foundations (e.g., Instituto São Paulo Contra a Violência, ISPCV)	Partnership between broad civil-society group and government to improve policing	May privilege business interests over others
Disque-denúncia	Collects information while preserving anonymity of informants	May not overcome mistrust of police
Ministério Público	Independent, meritocratic recruitment and high-quality staff	May be more interested in investigation than punishment; reluctance to interfere in police investigations; overwhelming number of cases; police resistance
Mainstream media	Broad audiences; competition produces watchdog effect and "societal accountability"	Sensationalism (the "politics of fear"); short attention span—problems identified but coverage later dropped; bias: media conglomerates have their own economic and political interests

Mechanism	Advantages	Disadvantages
Corregedoria (police internal affairs)	Ready access to information; knowledge of police procedures	may lack independence; corporatist attitudes—reluctance to convict police for crimes against civilians
Courts (military and civil)	Can guarantee procedural rights for defendants	Slow; Inegalitarian—defendants with resources are less likely to be punished; in military justice, corporatist attitudes—reluctance to convict police for crimes against civilians
Written codes of police conduct	Can create transparency by codifying acceptable behavior for citizens and police	Police resistance
SENASP (Secretaria Nacional de Segurança Pública)	Articulates a vision of progressive national public security policy at the federal level	Few resources; unstable politically—staffed by political appointees; reluctant to require reform as a condition of the granting of its resources to the states
International human rights institutions (e.g., Inter-American Court for Human Rights)	Subjects national and local politics to international human rights norms	Highly selective (few cases) and slow; hard to enforce judgments
Contentious action (e.g., marches, demonstrations, petitions, etc.)	Allows for multiple expressions of grievances; flexible, democratic, diverse; can be strengthened by strategic use of social media (for example, videos of police violence uploaded to Facebook or circulated via Twitter, WhatsApp, or other apps)	Subject to collective action problems; civil society often fragmented, with partial views of the problem; no obligation for authorities to respond—demands often not institutionalized
Vigilantism	Can conform to local conceptions of justice	Violates rule of law (no procedural rights for the accused)

of them quite powerful, in Guatemala, Honduras, El Salvador, Colombia, Peru, and Bolivia.[37]

The first police ombudsman's office in Brazil was created in São Paulo in 1995, with a national forum of police ombudsmen being set up in 1999. Since then, the institution has proliferated, and twenty-one of Brazil's twenty-six states now have one.[38] This proliferation was a two-step process. São Paulo was the site of strong resistance to the military regime, especially in the 1970s and early '80s, with the endogenous creation of strong civil-society organizations in the area of human rights. These organizations focused on issues such as the abuse of political prisoners' human rights, amnesty for those convicted of political crimes, and the dismantling of the exceptional decrees and laws, especially the National Security Law, which gave the executive branch almost unlimited power vis-à-vis legislatures and the judiciary. In the 1990s, after the end of military rule, the human rights movement addressed other problems, such as the treatment of ordinary criminal suspects by the police, the judiciary, and the prison system, and it was in that context that the police ombudsman was created.

In other parts of Brazil in subsequent years, the creation of police ombudsmen had a somewhat more exogenous character. After the Secretariat for Public Security (Secretaria Nacional de Segurança Pública, or SENASP) was created in 1998, it began to condition its transfer of funds to states on the existence of a police ombudsman.[39] In addition, there was strong international support for the initiative, most notably from Canada and the European Union. The European Union, for example, provided roughly 6.5 million euros and technical assistance to the Special Secretariat for Human Rights for the creation and support of police ombudsmen from 2005 to 2008.[40] The EU lent considerable technical expertise to the project as well. This initiative gave an incentive to states that had not yet created a police ombudsman to do so, for the new agencies would then be eligible for the EU money.

The ombudsman is supposed to register public complaints about the police and facilitate the investigation of these complaints by the internal affairs unit of the state civil and military police forces. These complaints are registered anonymously and can be made in person, over the telephone, or via the Internet. Priority is usually given to allegations of lethal violence by the police. Observers argue that the ombudsmen provide an important feedback function, making police misbehavior more transparent and establishing the right of the public to oversee and control the state's use of force.[41] The police ombudsmen, at least potentially, establishes a new accountability mechanism in Brazilian public security consisting of at least three stages: information, justification, and (at least in some cases) punishment and/or compensation. It is a form of "horizontal" accountability (one police department being made accountable to another agency within the state), but at the same time it is also a form of "vertical" accountability (police are required to respond to citizen complaints).[42] The ombudsman could also create a fourth stage of accountability: proactive reform or changes in policing that diminish the problems that citizens complain about.

This initiative has received substantial international support as well. Multilateral agencies have supported the creation of ombudsman's offices throughout Latin America over the last three decades. According to one European observer, the "Latin American ombudsman . . . has become one of the region's quintessential democratic institutional innovations over the past twenty years, offering citizens an additional channel of institutionalized participation and oversight beyond the ballot box."[43] The ombudsman has also been described as "a permanent judicial and democratic voice of conscience within the state."[44] The ombudsmen provide an important feedback function, making police misbehavior potentially more transparent and establishing the right of the public to oversee and control the state's use of force.[45]

The origin of the institution lies in Europe, and considerable support for the Brazilian experiment has come from the EU, but there are other international actors in Brazil's police ombudsman story as well. The Canadian government has offered considerable bilateral support for the creation of various types of ombudsmen in the public sector.

A review of fourteen police ombudsman offices in various Brazilian states, conducted in 2008, found a wide variety of institutional designs among them. Their legal status differed: some were created by law, others by executive decree, and yet others by both law and decree. Some ombudsmen were appointed directly by state governors, with no fixed mandates; others were appointed by state secretaries of public security; and in some states, a council that included civil-society actors played a part in the selection process. Staffing levels and the degree of infrastructural support varied sharply. Some ombudsmen provided a free telephone service (an 0-800 number) to complainants; others did not.[46] The implications of these and other variations for the performance of the police ombudsman's offices has been underexplored in the literature. The section that follows is an attempt to begin such an examination, exploring two case studies, and applying some insights of historical institutionalism to them. Historical institutionalism emphasizes sequences, the interaction between social mobilization and the institutional development of the state, and long causal chains leading to particular patterns of policy change.[47]

The police ombudsman in São Paulo—Brazil's wealthiest, most industrialized, and most populated state, with roughly 45 million people—is probably the most professional, effective, and transparent office of its kind in Brazil. It grew out of the State Council for the Defense of the Human Person (Conselho Estadual de Defesa de Pessoa Humana, or CEDPH), a part of the State Secretariat of Justice, in which 80 percent of the members are representatives of civil-society organizations. The council did not have the ability to investigate complaints of human rights abuses, and the idea of an ombudsman grew from that. The São Paulo police ombudsman has considerable independence. The ombudsman is appointed by the state governor from a list of three candidates drawn up by the CEDPH. He or she has a fixed two-year term that can be renewed once.[48] The office of the ombudsman exists in an office building far from the Secretariat of Public Security, symbolizing its independence.

The São Paulo police ombudsman is backed up by a solid institutional infrastructure and enjoys administrative and financial autonomy from the secretary of public security and the police. The ombudsman presides over a consultative council made up of eleven members; the other ten members are chosen by the secretary of public security from a list provided by the state's general ombudsman (*ouvidor geral*). Its staff consists of a technical support team and an administrative support team. These teams include five advisors and ten assistants, all of whom are required to have university degrees, as well as two police investigators, ten policemen seconded to the office, and interns. The ombudsman staff produces abundant, up-to-date information about the complaints the office received and—more importantly—their resolution. This includes the suspension and firing of police officers for proven violations of human rights.[49] While the investigations are conducted by police internal affairs, and the punishments carried out by internal disciplinary panels and courts (both military and civilian), the ombudsman's office works with the police to track the final disposition of all cases, and thus the state's response to complaints. The police ombudsman's office in São Paulo also has considerable financial autonomy. When the office was created by the administration of Governor Mario Covas in 1997, a dedicated budget for the agency was specified in the authorizing legislation.[50] This practice, in which the executive branch directly allocates resources to the ombudsman, rather than routing it through the Secretariat of Public Security, has continued.

São Paulo's high degree of capacity and autonomy is reflected in its performance. In a study of fourteen police ombudsmen commissioned by the federal Special Secretariat for Human Rights, São Paulo was one of only three states (along with Pará and Rio Grande do Norte) that was identified as regularly tracking the outcomes of investigations of police killings of citizens.[51] In 2007, 11 percent of all complaints received by the São Paulo police ombudsman's office were allegations of police homicide.[52]

The situation in São Paulo is in stark contrast to the conditions of the police ombudsman in Pernambuco, a small state with a population of roughly 9 million in the impoverished northeastern region of the country. In Pernambuco, the police ombudsman has little political independence and little capacity, such that it was described by the São Paulo police ombudsman in 2008 as "an ombudsman without an ombudsman's office" (um ouvidor sem uma ouvidoria).[53] It is located across the street from and is administratively part of the Secretariat of Social Defense—a problematic physical and organizational location for an institution that is supposed to be independent of the police.[54] Its budget is determined on a discretionary basis by the secretary of social defense. As in São Paulo, the ombudsman in Pernambuco does not carry out his own investigations, but rather feeds information to the police internal affairs office (or corregedoria).[55] In the mid-2000s, the office received an average of about forty complaints a month.[56] Abuse of police authority is the most common allegation, brought typically by males aged thirty-five to forty-five who reside in poor neighborhoods. When the ombudsman's office records these complaints and turns them over to internal affairs, the *corregedoria* can then decide to open an investigation into the alleged police misconduct and, if evidence of wrongdoing is uncovered, recommend to the secretary of social defense that a range of remedies be applied, such as disciplinary action or dismissal. Investigations can also result in cases in state courts, both military and civilian, depending on the nature of the crime.[57]

However, unlike in São Paulo, basic information about the results of complaints brought to police ombudsman in Pernambuco—the first element of accountability—does not exist.[58] The ombudsman does not publish a report for the public, and the semesterly reports she prepares for the governor contain only complaints, not the final disposition of complaints.[59] Unlike its São Paulo counterpart, the Pernambuco police ombudsman's office does not post the outcomes of its cases on a website. Whereas the web page of the São Paulo office contains voluminous information on complaints and the results of those complaints, its counterpart in Pernambuco consists of a single page containing a complaint form.[60] Furthermore, the ombudsman has no fixed mandate as in São Paulo. The ombudsman is appointed by the governor, serving at the governor's pleasure, limiting her ability to take on politically sensitive cases. Furthermore, with a small staff of four, the office lacks effective capacity.[61]

These limitations of capacity and autonomy seem to influence the Pernambuco police ombudsman's performance. A sample of cases from 2005, 2006, and 2007 revealed that only 0.2 percent of complaints were related to police homicide, a striking difference from the 11 percent of all cases registered in São Paulo in 2007. It is unlikely that this is due to a lack of police homicides in Pernambuco; a great deal of anecdotal information circulates in the state about the existence of police death squads, for example. Instead, it seems to indicate a greater fear on the part of the public in Pernambuco to bring these cases to the ombudsman, and/or a lower degree of confidence that such cases will be dealt with discreetly and effectively.

The Pernambuco sample referred to above, of 419 cases in the 2005–7 period, provides a window into the workings of the police ombudsman. The sample represents 41.5 percent, 31.3 percent, and 27.2 percent of all the cases brought to the police ombudsman in those years, respectively. Close to a majority of the complainants (47.5 percent) are between the ages of twenty-five and forty-four, and the corporation most frequently complained about is the military police (42.7 percent). The most common complaints are abuse of authority (46.1 percent), physical aggression (16.9 percent), bad service (*mau atendimento*) (10.7 percent), verbal aggression (6.2 percent), and a lack of police presence (4.1 percent). A startlingly large proportion of these cases did not result in disciplinary action within the police force. More than two-thirds of the complaints (68.5 percent) resulted in "no response" from the *corregedoria*, while 29.4 percent were "archived" or shelved. Only 0.5 percent of cases went to a civilian court, while another 0.5 percent triggered an internal disciplinary hearing (*sindicância*).

In contrast to the police ombudsman, the Pernambuco *corregedoria* is staffed by 172 members drawn from the police forces.[62] Because in many instances the *corregedoria* staff will go back to work in other departments within the police, it cannot accurately be described as a mechanism of external control, nor does it have complete independence to rigorously investigate allegations of police misconduct. Further, police who are perceived to stay too long in internal affairs may see their careers suffer.[63] The lack of external control in the way internal affairs conducts its investigations can be seen by the fact that, as a first step in handling a complaint, the internal affairs investigator goes to the commander in charge of the police accused of wrongdoing to hold a *sindicância*. Furthermore, the *corregedoria* is bound by strict time limits in discharging its disciplinary duties, resulting in the frequent suspension of administrative punishments of police officials. Interestingly, the *corregedoria* has no fixed time limit for the investigation of complaints brought to it by the ombudsman, nor does it have adequate information-management systems to monitor these cases. Human rights organizations complain that punishments of the police as a result of *corregedoria* investigations tend to be rare.[64] This seems to be especially true in the case of high-ranking police officials.[65]

In Pernambuco, the internal affairs staff alleges that the reports received from the ombudsman are often insufficient to facilitate an adequate investigation. The ombudsman's staff, for their part, tend to see the *corregedoria* as a corporatist agency more interested in protecting its own than uncovering wrongdoing. The ombudsman does not have high visibility in Pernambuco, and almost never appears in the press. Dr. Luiz Guerra de Morais, ombudsman from 2003 until 2007, generally took a nonconfrontational line towards the police. Nevertheless, he stated in public in 2006 that "in my judgment, the system does not work."[66]

Although information is lacking for a thorough evaluation of the police ombudsman's office in Pernambuco, there are strong reasons to conclude that it has not been particularly successful.[67] One reason for this might be the design of the institution.[68] As noted, the police ombudsman in Recife, the capital of the state of Pernambuco, serves at the pleasure of the governor, whereas her São Paulo counterpart is nominated by an organization dominated by civil-society representatives, and serves for a fixed term.[69] There is also evidence that many of the police ombudsmen in Brazil share the limitations of the Pernambuco office, and have not attained the degree of independence of the São Paulo police ombudsman. In a study of five police ombudsman's offices, for example, Lembruger found that 85 to 93 percent of complaints did not result in any punishment of the accused.[70]

Differences between the way the São Paulo and Pernambuco police ombudsman's offices operate may also be due to contextual and informal factors rather than just institutional design. As in São Paulo, many of the formal attributes of Pernambuco's police ombudsman's office embody the principles of accountability and transparency in that they establish the public's right to complain about the police. However, in establishing a working relationship with police internal affairs, the Pernambuco office does not monitor the results of complaints as the office in São Paulo does. This means that a fundamental aspect of accountability—adequate information—is not being provided in Pernambuco. Such information could be provided without the creation of any new legislation or regulations; all that would be required would be for the ombudsman herself to insist on such a supervisory role, with the work done either by *corregedoria* staff or new personnel in the ombudsman's office. Yet this has not been done. The working relationship that has been established between the ombudsman and internal affairs is that the former is a passive appendage of the latter. Table 5.2 summarizes the difference between the police ombudsmen in São Paulo and Pernambuco, indicating that the former benefits from both a more optimal institutional design and political will.

The Pernambuco police ombudsman's office seems to illustrate Philippe Schmitter's comment that accountability only becomes apparent

TABLE 5.2
Differences between São Paulo and Pernambuco Police Ombudsmen

Institutional design that strengthens ombudsman independence and capacity		São Paulo
Institutional design that weakens ombudsman independence and capacity	Pernambuco	
	Low political will for an effective ombudsman	High political will for an effective ombudsman

when it is defective, and it may well be that many of the other similar institutions in Brazil bear a closer resemblance to the Pernambuco case than the São Paulo organization.[71] In the opinion of one specialist, for example, few ombudsmen "enjoy effective autonomy,"[72] and Comparato even shows that in some states the police ombudsmen are police officials, thereby compromising the independence essential to the ombudsman ideal.[73]

In a comparative study of ombudsmen in Bolivia, Colombia, El Salvador, Guatemala, Honduras, and Peru, Uggla concludes, "the influence of the ombudsman can hardly be deduced from the formal, legal dispositions regarding the institution. Indeed, the strength and autonomy of the institution are generated by a process that is primarily political."[74] In the Pernambuco case, the political process seems to have resulted in a police ombudsman with a low degree of independence and capacity in comparison with her São Paulo counterpart. The most striking evidence of this is the abundance of publicly available information about the final disposition of complaints in São Paulo, and the absolute lack of equivalent information in Pernambuco. Despite this clear difference of outcomes, however, it should be emphasized that the present analysis is not definitive. We have not been able to carry out the kind of detailed analysis of cases that might clarify the apparent variation between the two institutions. Most importantly, the impact of the ombudsman on levels of police violence has not been established in either case. But this study could provide the beginnings of a more systematic comparison that might shed light on those issues.

It should be added that the office of police ombudsman is an "embedded" institution; it works only in conjunction with other institutions, especially police internal affairs. In principal-agent terms, the situation of the police ombudsman is complex. She or he is an agent of the public, who bring complaints to it. But the office of ombudsman is also a principal vis-à-vis police internal affairs, because it can induce investigations that otherwise might not have taken place, and it is supposed to monitor the outcomes of those investigations. Similarly, in a specific case it could also become the agent of the governor or another member of the executive branch, a member of the legislature, or even (depending on the circumstances) a prosecutor in the Public Ministry. Its effectiveness is thus highly dependent on the effectiveness of other organizations in the state, as well as civil-society associations.

An intriguing possibility is that in Pernambuco the police ombudsman is a "sleeper" institution—dormant and ineffective at first, but energized and effective later, when the right combination of factors occurs (such as a committed governor, strong pressure from civil-society organizations, and so on).[75] Only further monitoring of the performance of these agencies in Pernambuco and other Brazilian states will reveal whether this potential is realized.

"Sleeper" institutions are not new. Rothstein, for example, argues that the Swedish institutions of horizontal accountability established in the early nineteenth century, of which the ombudsman's office was one, did not work particularly well in the first decades of their existence. Corruption, nepotism, cronyism, and inefficiency were apparently rife in the Swedish civil service. But according to Rothstein, an existential crisis brought about by defeat in war created the conditions in which the institutions gained autonomy and effectiveness, boosting horizontal accountability and improving the performance of the state bureaucracies.[76]

In Rothstein's words, "generalized trust, understood as the belief that you live in a society . . . where the moral standards of the other agents in general are high, leads to a decrease in transaction costs." For Rothstein, the existence of efficient institutions—those that provide public goods in a relatively impartial manner—are key to generating trust. In his view, "efficient institutions change agents' choice of strategy by increasing the likelihood that they will believe most other agents cooperate honestly, which in turn makes it more rational for the individual agent to reciprocate benevolently."[77]

Conclusion

There are good reasons to believe that violence in Latin America is not the inevitable byproduct of a colonial and postcolonial past in which inequality, social exclusion, poverty, and class oppression were the norm. It is at least partially contingent. Contingent violence can be curbed through specific mechanisms; the most promising of these involve new public policies, civil-society mobilization, or (usually) some combination of the two. This applies to police violence as well as other forms of violence. Brazil's police violence is arguably the worst in the region, given the sheer scale of the killing, especially in large cities such as São Paulo and Rio de Janeiro.

An important recent reform that could affect levels of police violence is the establishment of the ombudsman's offices. These institutions are part of a larger trend towards ombudsmen in Latin America. Ombudsmen are, at least in principle, independent authorities who can channel public demands into the state apparatus, making citizens' political participation meaningful and inducing both retroactive and proactive forms of accountability.

At present, more is unknown than known about the impact of ombudsmen on levels of police violence in Brazil. The institution is recent, the first established less than fifteen years ago, and most created in the last few years. The potential of the ombudsmen is that of a new accountability mechanism—a feedback loop that channels public complaints about police misconduct to political authorities who not only can authorize the investigation and punishment of wrongdoers among the police, but also initiate reforms that make such wrongdoing less likely in the future.

The new institutions offer much promise. At best they can serve to democratize and demilitarize policing. At worst, however it may be nothing more than facades, mere "suggestion boxes" that lead to no substantive action, or (in extreme cases) police reactions that endanger complainants. The initial comparison of São Paulo and Pernambuco offered here suggests that the police ombudsmen in these two states differ significantly in terms of the formal design of the institutions and the informal political environment in which they operate. São Paulo provides more information than does Pernambuco on the outcome of the investigations triggered by the complaints it receives, resulting in a much greater level of transparency. So far we lack the evidence, however, to conclude that the São Paulo police ombudsman's greater effectiveness includes an increased ability to reduce police violence. Only further in-depth research will answer some of the questions raised in this chapter.

Notes

The author would like to thank members of the workshop (Hendrik Kraay, Raul Molina, Jean Daudelin, Michelle Bonner, J. Patrice McSherry, Jorge Zaverucha, Andreas Feldmann, Pablo Policzer, and Francisco Gutiérrez Sanín), as well as two anonymous reviewers, for comments on earlier drafts of this chapter. The author would also like to acknowledge the support of the British Academy for a small research grant (SG-48381 of 1 January–31 August 2008) that facilitated research for this chapter.

1   The data is from the United Nations Office on Drugs and Crime (UNODC), "Intentional Homicide Victims 2012–2016," https://dataunodc.un.org/crime/intentional-homicide-victims (accessed 8 July 2018). The total number of homicides for Latin America and the Caribbean was 139,466, with all countries reporting data from 2015 except Venezuela, which reported data for 2016. See also Mark Ungar, *Policing Democracy: Overcoming Obstacles to Citizen Security in Latin America* (Washington, DC: Johns Hopkins University Press, 2011), 2, and "Shining light on Latin America's homicide epidemic," *Economist*, 5 April 2018, https://www.economist.com/briefing/2018/04/05/shining-light-on-latin-americas-homicide-epidemic.

2   The top ten in 2018 were Honduras, Venezuela, Belize, El Salvador, Guatemala, Jamaica, Lesotho, Swaziland, Saint Kitts and Nevis, and South Africa. From Petr H., "25 Countries with the Highest Murder Rates in the World," *List25*, 19 February 2018, https://list25.com/25-countries-with-the-highest-murder-rates-in-the-world/5/.

3   For an example of this approach, see Howard Wiarda, *Corporatism and National Development in Latin America* (Boulder, CO: Westview, 1981).

4   For a review of these approaches, see William L. Canak, "The Peripheral State Debate," *Latin American Research Review* 19, no. 1 (1984): 3–36.

5   Niall Ferguson, *Civilization* (London: Penguin, 2011). The first quote is from p. 138, while the second is from 127.

6   From UNODC, "Intentional Homicide Victims 2012–2016."

7   Data from Mexico show that its homicide rate rose from 8.7 per 100,000 in 2004 to 19.3 in 2016, more than doubling in twelve years. While I do not disagree with Picatto's generalization that there has been a long-term decline in homicide rates in Mexico,

spikes such as the one described above give some substance to public fear of violence. From UNODC, "Intentional Homicide Victims 2012–2016."

8   Steven Pinker, *The Better Angels of Our Nature: The Decline of Violence in History and Its Causes* (London: Allen Lane, 2011), see especially 49–59.

9   See, for example, Alba Zaluar, "The Paradoxes of Democratization and Violence in Brazil" (paper presented at the International Conference Latin America, Brazil and the European Union Extended, Federal University of Rio de Janeiro, 2004), http://www.brasiluniaoeuropeia.ufrj.br/en/pdfs/the_paradoxes_of_democratization_and_violence_in_brazil.pdf. The country's homicide rate increased from 11.7 per 100,000 in 1980 to 28.4 in 2015. From UNODC, "Intentional Homicide Victims 2012–2016."

10 From Marcos Augusto Gonçalves, "E agora, Brasil? Segurança Pública," *Folha de São Paulo*, 21 April 2018, special supplement, 1.

11 Mercedes Hinton, *The State on the Streets: Police and Politics in Argentina and Brazil* (Boulder: Lynne Rienner, 2006), 8.

12 Frances Hagopian, "Brazil and Chile," in *Assessing the Quality of Democracy*, ed. Larry Diamond and Leonardo Morlino (Baltimore, MD: Johns Hopkins University Press, 2005), 128–9. Hagopian is quoting from a 2003 Freedom House report.

13 From Igor Mello and Daniel Salgado, "62,517 mortes violentas," *O Globo* (Rio de Janeiro), 6 June 2018, A3.

14 Julita Lembruger, *Civilian Oversight of the Police in Brazil: The Case of the Ombudsman's Offices* (Rio de Janeiro: University Candido Mendes Center for Studies on Public Security and Citizenship, 2002), 5.

15 See "Obama, Venezuela's Chavez Shake Hands at Summit," *Reuters UK*, 18 April 2009, http://uk.reuters.com/article/2009/04/17/summit-obama-chavez-idUKN1736198420090417.

16 Pablo Fajnzylber, Daniel Lederman, and Norman Loayza, "What Causes Violent Crime?" *European Economic Review* 46 (2002): 1323–57. Another study attributes Latin America's high rate of violent crime to high income inequality, low incarceration rates, and small police forces. See Rodrigo Soares and Joana Naritomi, "Understanding High Crime Rates in Latin America: The Role of Social and Policy Factors," (paper prepared for the conference Confronting Crime and Violence in Latin America: Crafting a Public Policy Agenda, John F. Kennedy School of Government, Harvard University, July 2007).

17 The Economist, "Shining light on Latin America's homicide epidemic."

18 Charles Tilly, *Explaining Social Processes* (Boulder, CO: Paradigm Publishers, 2008), 121.

19 Jon Elster, "A Plea for Mechanisms," in *Social Mechanisms: An Analytical Approach to Social Theory*, ed. Peter Hedström and Richard Swedborg (Cambridge: Cambridge University Press, 1998), 45.

20 Tilly, *Explaining Social Processes*, 9.

21 Soares and Naritomi, "Understanding High Crime Rates," 23.

22 Soares and Naritomi, "Understanding High Crime Rates," 23.

23   Elster, "A Plea for Mechanisms," 45.

24   See Daniel Brinks, *The Judicial Response to Police Killings in Latin America: Inequality and the Rule of Law* (Cambridge: Cambridge University Press, 2007).

25   Douglass North, Joseph Wallis, and Barry Weingast, *Violence and Social Orders: A Conceptual Framework for Interpreting Recorded Human History* (Cambridge: Cambridge University Press, 2009), xi.

26   North, Wallis, and Weingast, *Violence,* 121.

27   North, Wallis, and Weingast, 122.

28   North, Wallis, and Weingast, 121.

29   North, Wallis, and Weingast, 151.

30   North, Wallis, and Weingast, 170.

31   José Vicente da Silva Filho and Norman Gall, "A Polícia: Incentivos Perversos e Segurança Pública" in *Insegurança Pública: Reflexões Sobre a Criminalidade e a Violência Urbana*, ed. Nilson Vieira Oliveira (São Paulo: Nova Alexandria/Instituto Braudel, 2002), 205.

32   da Silva Filho and Gall, "A Polícia," 205.

33   I thank Hendrik Kraay for making this observation.

34   Hinton, *The State on the Streets*, 101.

35   See Paulo Mesquita Neto, "Public-Private Partnership for Police Reform in Brazil" in *Public Security and Police Reform in the Americas*, ed. John Bailey and Lucía Dammert, 44–57 (Pittsburgh, PA: University of Pittsburgh Press, 2006). See also Fiona Macaulay, "Knowledge Production, Framing and Criminal Justice Reform in Latin America," *Journal of Latin American Studies* 39 (2007): 628.

36   See Donald C. Rowat, "The Suitability of the Ombudsman Plan for Developing Countries," *International Review of Administrative Sciences* 50, no. 3 (1984): 207–11, and Anand Satyanand, "Growth of the Ombudsman Concept" *Journal of South Pacific Law* 3 (1999): 1–12.

37   Uggla, Fredrik, "The Ombudsman in Latin America," *Journal of Latin American Studies* 36 (2004): 423–50.

38   See Bruno Kondor Comparato, "As Ouvidorias de Polícia no Brasil: Controle e Participação" (paper prepared for the annual ANPOCS conference, Caxambu, Minas Gerias, 24–8 October 2006), and Rubens Pinto Lyra, "A Atuação dos Conselhos e Ouvidorias na Área de Segurança e Justiça," *Lusotopie* (2003): 383–96. See also, "Ouvidorias Estaduais e Distrital," Ministério dos Direitos Humanos, www.mdh.gov.br/informacao-ao-cidadao/participacao-social/forum-nacional-de-ouvidores-de-policia-fnop/quais-estados-fazem-parte-do-fnop-1 (accessed 8 July 2018).

39   More recently, in February 2018, the executive created a Ministry of Public Security at the federal level. SENASP, as well as the Federal Police and the Federal Highway Police are part of this new ministry. At the time of writing it is too early to tell what impact the new ministry will have on public security policy in Brazil. See Luciana Amaral,

"Governo anuncia criação do Ministério de Segurança Pública e confirma Jungmann como titular," *UOL Notícias*, 26 February 2018, https://noticias.uol.com.br/politica/ultimas-noticias/2018/02/26/governo-anuncia-criacao-do-ministerio-da-seguranca-publica-e-confirma-jungmann-como-titular.htm.

40 "Ouvidorias de Polícia e Policiamento Comunitário," Special Secretariat of Human Rights, Ministry of Justice, http://www.dhnet.org.br/dados/cartilhas/a_pdf_dh/cartilha_conte_ouvidoria.pdf (accessed 19 March 2007).

41 See for example Fiona Macaulay, "Problems of Police Oversight in Brazil," *Working Paper 33-02* (Oxford: University of Oxford Centre for Brazilian Studies, 2002), 14.

42 These distinctions between types of accountability come from Larry Diamond and Leonardo Morlino, eds., *Assessing the Quality of Democracy* (Baltimore, MD: Johns Hopkins University Press, 2005), xix–xxv.

43 Thomas Pegram, "The Peruvian Ombudsman: The Last Bastion of Universality?" (paper presented at the Annual Conference of the Society for Latin American Studies, University of Newcastle, Newcastle, 13–15 April 2007), 1.

44 Pegram, "The Peruvian Ombudsman," 6. Pegram is quoting from the Defensoría del Pueblo, *Primer Informe del Defensor del Pueblo al Congreso de la República 1996-1998* (Lima, 1998), 19.

45 Macaulay, "Problems of Police Oversight in Brazil," 14.

46 From Vivane Cubas, *Panorama Geral das Ouvidorias de Polícia* (São Paulo: Núcleo de Estudos da Violência, University of São Paulo, unpublished report, 2008).

47 Elizabeth Sanders, "Historical Institutionalism," in *The Oxford Handbook of Political Institutions*, ed. R. Rhodes, S. Binder, and B. Rockman (Oxford: Oxford University Press, 2008), 39–55.

48 Comparato writes that in only six Brazilian states does a fixed mandate for the police ombudsman exist. See Comparato, "As Ouvidorias de Polícia no Brasil," 8. For more on the police ombudsman's office in Minas Gerais, see Governo do Estado de Minas Gerais, *A Ouvidoria Agora Vai Falar* (Belo Horizonte: Del Rey, 2004), Governo do Estado de Minas Gerais, *A Ouvidoria de Polícia de Minas Gerais Mostra o Que Faz* (Belo Horizonte: Artes Gráficas Formato, 2004), and Governo do Estado de Minas Gerais, *Ouvir Para Fazer Melhor: Ações da Ouvidoria de Polícia em 2005* (Belo Horizonte: Del Rey, 2005).

49 The information in these two paragraphs comes from Antônio Funari Filho, police ombudsman in São Paulo from 2005 to 2009, as well as from http://observatoriodeseguranca.org/relatorios/ouvidoria, which contains reports from 2004 to 2012.

50 From "Lei Complentar no. 826," police ombudsman of São Paulo, 20 June 1997, http://www.observatoriodeseguranca.org/dados/estrutura/ouvidoria.

51 From Vinicius Boreki, "Ouvidoria de polícia só escuta, mas não reage," *Gazeta do Povo* (Curitiba), 22 August 2009, http://www.gazetadopovo.com.br/vida-e-cidadania/ouvidoria-de-policia-so-escuta-mas-nao-reage-bshs4bcdstxk5vpdm55jyf7ta. The study was carried out by Viviane de Oliveira Cubas of the Nucleus for the Study of

Violence at the University of São Paulo. It is worth noting that effectiveness in tracking investigations of lethal police violence is not directly correlated with the wealth of the states. Pará and Rio Grande do Norte, the other two mentioned as doing a good job in this area, are poor northeastern states.

52 "Relatório Anual de 2007, Tabela Geral de Denúncias por Departamento," police mobudsman of São Paulo, http://www.ouvidoria-policia.sp.gov.br/pages/RelatAnual2007.htm (accessed 30 September 2009).

53 Antônio Funari Filho, then São Paulo police ombudsman, "Police Ombudsmen: How to Perfect Their Mechanisms of Accountability?" (presentation in a workshop at Federal University of Pernambuco, Recife, 16 June 2008).

54 The ombudsman's office was originally located in a small building around the corner from the police internal affairs headquarters. In August 2007, it was moved into an unmarked former hotel, making it very hard to find. Many people on the street outside the building were unaware that the police ombudsman's office was there, and the ombudsman at that time told me that complaints had dropped off since the relocation. The presence of two armed military policemen outside the building was also potentially intimidating. In 2008, the office was moved again to its present location across the street from the headquarters of the Secretariat of Social Defense.

55 The *corregedoria* in Pernambuco is unusual in Brazil because it is integrated, combining the civil police, military police, prison employees, and fireman. Previously, each branch of the police had its own internal affairs department. The integration was carried out in 2000, becoming operational in 2001. José Luiz de Oliveira, Corregedor da Secretaria de Defesa Social de Pernambuco, interview with the author, 22 August 2006.

56 Governo do Estado de Pernambuco, "Ouvidoria: Relatório Semestral Referente ao 2º Semestre 2005 (Julho a Dezembro de 2005)," Secretaria de Defesa Social, Recife, 2005.

57 Daniel Brinks, "Leviathan Unleashed: State Killings and Impunity in Buenos Aires and São Paulo in the 1990s" (paper presented at the XXIII International Congress of the Latin American Studies Association, Washington, DC, 6–9 September 2001).

58 The formal name of the ombudsman's office in Pernambuco is the Ombudsman of the Secretariat of Social Defense. I refer to it here as a police ombudsman for the sake of simplicity.

59 The author obtained a copy of the Pernambuco police ombudsman's first semester report from 2005 by requesting it by email from the ombudsman himself, receiving a copy as an email attachment. However, it is not clear how many members of the public request copies of the reports, either by email or other means. Comparato notes that most police ombudsmen in Brazil nominally make their reports public, but only three (those in Rio de Janeiro, São Paulo, and Minas Gerais) put the reports on their websites. The police ombudsman's office in Bahia told Comparato that it did not release its reports to the public and only sent them to the relevant authorities (secretary of public security, state governor, heads of the military and civil police, and the Ministry of Justice). See Comparato, "As Ouvidorias de Polícia no Brasil," 9.

60 Go to the website (www.sds.pe.gov.br/) and then click on "serviços" [services]; "denúncias" [complaints]; "ouvidoria—fale com a ouvidoria" [ombudsman—speak to

the ombudsman]; and "registrar manifestação" [make a report]. In addition to filing a report electronically, members of the public can telephone the ombudsman, send them a message on WhatsApp, write a letter, or complain in person.

61 For an analysis of the limitations of the Pernambuco police ombudsman's institutional design and capacity, see Jorge Zaverucha, "O Papel da Ouvidoria de Polícia," *Sociologias* 10, no. 20 (2008): 224–35.

62 José Luiz de Oliveira, Corregedor da Secretaria de Defesa Social de Pernambuco, interview with the author, 22 August 2006.

63 One civil police *delegado* said that she had worked in internal affairs for eight years, and had never been promoted beyond the rank of *delegado* 1. Police *delegado*, Corregedoria, Recife, interview with the author, 7 July 2006.

64 In the *Third National Report on Human Rights in Brazil*, the authors write, "Complaints against the police for violence and corruption are registered by the police ombudsmen in São Paulo, Rio de Janeiro, Minas Gerais, and Rio Grande do Sul, but the internal investigations [*sindicâncias*] and administrative processes, criminal investigations and trials rarely lead to the verification of responsibility and the punishment of the guilty." See Paulo Mesquita and B. S. A. Affonso, *Terceiro Relatório Nacional sobre os Direitos Humanos no Brasil* (São Paulo: Núcleo de Estudos da Violência da Universidade de São Paulo [NEV-USP] e a Comissão Teotônio Vilela do Direitos Humanos [CTV], 2007), 13.

65 Preliminary data from 2005 obtained from the Pernambuco *corregedoria geral* shows that 4 members of the civil police and 26 members of the military police were fired for disciplinary reasons in that year, following a *corregedoria* investigation. In the civil police, this was 3 *agentes* and 1 technical support person; no *delegados* were fired. In the military police, 1 captain was fired, but most (21 of 26) were of the lowest rank (*soldados*) and aside from the captain, no officers were dismissed. From Pesquisa realizada em atendimento ao requerido no Protocolo No. 2010/2007-Cor. Ger., August 2007.

66 Dr. Luiz Guerra de Morais (then the police ombudsman of Pernambuco), speaking at a conference, "Live Citizenship: The Role of Police Ombudsmen," Hotel Best Western Manibu, Boa Viagem, Recife, 25 May 2006. His words were "Em meu entender, o sistema é falha."

67 An important study of the police ombudsmen in São Paulo, Pará, Minas Gerais, Rio de Janeiro, and Rio Grande do Sul confirmed this conclusion, finding that 85 to 93 percent of the complaints to the five ombudsman's offices did not result in any type of punishment of the accused. See Lembruger, *Civilian Oversight of the Police in Brazil*, 22.

68 See Zaverucha, "O Papel da Ouvidoria de Polícia."

69 The human rights ombudsman in Peru described by Thomas Pegram also serves for a fixed term. See Pegram, "The Peruvian Ombudsman."

70 Lembruger, *Civilian Oversight of the Police in Brazil*, 22.

71 Philippe Schmitter, "The Ambiguous Virtue of Accountability," in *Assessing the Quality of Democracy*, ed. Larry Diamond and Leonardo Morlino (Baltimore, MD: Johns Hopkins University Press, 2005), 26.

72 Lyra, "A Atuação dos Conselhos e Ouvidorias," 384.

73 Comparato, "As Ouvidorias de Polícia no Brasil," 7.

74 Frederick Uggla, "The Ombudsman in Latin America," *Journal of Latin American Studies* 36 (2004): 448.

75 I thank Jean Daudelin for raising this possibility.

76 Bo Rothstein, *The Quality of Government* (Chicago: University of Chicago Press, 2011).

77 Rothstein, *The Quality of Government*, 214–15.

6

Democracy, Threat, and Repression: Kidnapping and Repressive Dynamics during the Colombian Conflict

Francisco Gutiérrez Sanín

In Colombia, democracy has long coexisted with civil war, criminal violence, brutal repression, and major state fractures. From 1980 onwards, until recently,[1] Colombia simultaneously witnessed a substantial increase in different types of crimes and violence—including kidnapping, the focus of this chapter—along with a substantial degree of institutional opening and democratization (including a remarkably open new constitution in 1991). This presents a puzzle. On the one hand, violent attacks against elites should at some point destabilize democracy. On the other, one of the main promises of democratic institutions is that, within certain time horizons, they are able to tame violence. Why did neither happen in Colombia? Why did violence fail to destabilize democracy or trigger a substantial regime closure? In this chapter, I focus on the specific problem of kidnapping, and ask why elites did not respond to the threat of kidnapping by escalating repression.

Any reader familiar with the Colombian situation might think that repressive escalation did indeed take place, in the context of a sham democracy. Colombia's repressive record is extraordinarily brutal and massive.[2] But, as we will see, the state's *institutional* response to kidnapping was rather weak, despite the efforts of several actors to strengthen the design and operation of repressive institutions. One of the outstanding features of the story is the failure of projects oriented in this direction. How can this failure be explained? Noting the very high levels of repression in Colombia does not answer the set of questions posed in the previous paragraph; it only transforms them. If, for example, kidnapping at least partly explains the expansion of paramilitary groups in the country, then the question remains as to why repressors opted for illegal actions. Were they too tightly constrained by liberal checks and balances? In this case, democracy and democratization would be the culprits of a substantial portion of the extreme violence that Colombia has witnessed in recent decades. If the system had allowed for some kind of repressive stiffening against kidnappers, then the outcome might not have been so destructive. Note, however, that this counterfactual would only be true if paramilitary and institutional solutions are perfect substitutes for each other, which they are not. Or was it too little liberalism, because the regime was essentially closed? But then it would have been easy to adopt the radical and open repressive measures that a substantial part of the elite was proposing. Note that both answers are based on the so-called threat theory (TT) of repression,[3] which proposes that the degree of repression is proportional to the "intensity" (measured in some abstract way) of the threat.

By evaluating the repertoire of different actors' responses to kidnapping, along with the outcomes in terms of institutional designs and repressive activity,[4] I identify some of the effects of kidnapping on Colombia's political regime and, at the same time, the meaning and limits of TT when applied to this and analogous cases. I find that despite their power, connections, and mobilization capacity, the politicians that strived for a stiffening of kidnapping legislation failed miserably. Other, more general, legal and institutional repressive efforts also came to a standstill. Politicians with repressive leanings enjoyed support but were unable to orient themselves within the democratic maze of checks and balances, which sits rather well with standard democratic theory. What the latter does not capture, however, was the ability of very specific repressive coalitions to "open back doors" that institutionally improved the position of illegal, murderous, and repressive activities. However, legal and illegal modes of repression were *not* perfect substitutes because their costs and benefits were different,⁵ they were related to different operational logics, and they addressed different sectors and coalitions.⁶

How can all of this be translated in terms of claims about the explanatory power of TT? On one hand, TT's core notion—that there is some kind of link between threats to elites and repression—holds, which is not terribly surprising. However, the kidnapping narrative presented here suggests that TT is poorly specified, and illustrates some of its shortcomings. First, not all elites responded in the same way to kidnapping, nor did they face the same level of threat. Second, those who were clearly in favor of repressive solutions faced severe collective action problems. Third, because of the chronic fracture of the state and the political system, in addition to the collective action problems that elites face, the unitary actor model of the state cannot be applied to this particular problem, as TT routinely assumes. Fourth, the proposition of a direct link from threat to repressive response faces serious aggregation problems. It is difficult to compare across threats—or repressive practices, for that matter—because repertoires of violence are complex and multidimensional. A further analytical insight is related to the way in which rationalistic and structural explanations interact. If threats and the responses to them are structurally determined, then class structures and conflicts should shed light on the incentives and proclivities for coalition formation and violence repertoire adoption. "Rationalism" and "structuralism" are thus not necessarily in competition. Both face an analogous methodological challenge: that of specifying the resolution level at which agency will be defined.

In the first section of this chapter, I provide the basic context regarding both institutional developments and the trajectory of kidnapping in the country. The second section explains why guerrillas would indulge in massive kidnappings and why democratic politicians cared about this. The third section focuses on the efforts of politicians to face kidnapping by toughening up the system. This is basically a history of failure. In the fourth section I examine "success": the way in which pro-repressive actors were able to create institutional designs favorable to their purposes. I focus on the semilegal status that the paramilitary enjoyed during almost half of their formal existence (eight out of twenty years). The fifth section discusses the possible relationships between lethal repression and kidnapping in Colombia. In the conclusion, I discuss the limits of extant threat theories and suggest avenues to better specify the relationship between threat and repression. Throughout the discussion I rely, in addition to the relevant literature, on several sources: the press, a database of judicial procedures related to kidnapping, and in-depth interviews.

A Natural History of Kidnapping in Colombia

After the long and traumatic cycle of internal conflict known as *La Violencia* (from approximately the mid-1940s to the early 1960s), the main Colombian political parties signed a consociational agreement—the *Frente Nacional*—that limited political competition in order to stabilize the country (but also to exclude the opposition). By the 1960s, there were already high-profile abductions, along with debates about how to deal with them, and by the 1970s, kidnapping had become a serious problem. In the 1980s, guerrillas—along with imitators and competitors—began to practice kidnapping on a massive scale, in what observers increasingly referred to as "the industrialization of kidnapping." The main targets of the "classical" rural guerrillas—such as the ELN (*Ejército de Liberación Nacional*) and the FARC (*Fuerzas Armadas Revolucionarias de Colombia*)—were cattle ranchers and large landowners. An essentially urban guerrilla—the M-19 (*Movimiento 19 de Abril*)—used kidnapping as a tool to advance high-profile campaigns against the system.

In the 1970s, at least three M-19 acts made a big impact on public opinion. The first was the abduction and assassination of trade union leader José Raquel Mercado, under the accusation that he was a traitor to the working class. The M-19 posed a set of demands that would have to be met in order to spare Mercado's life. It also launched a plebiscite in the streets inviting citizens to express their preferred outcome (the killing or the liberation of the hostage). It declared that, in this way, it expected to create a wedge between the government and the "yellow" trade unions it was denouncing. This at least it partially obtained; the worker confederation headed by Mercado denounced the government's indifference to the fate of its leader. In the end, the government did not cede, and Mercado was assassinated.

The second significant M-19 act was the takeover of the embassy of the Dominican Republic, from February to April 1980. The hostages included the ambassadors of fifteen countries, including the United States, along with numerous other diplomats. The M-19's demands were both political and economic: releasing M-19 political prisoners, publishing the movement's communiqué, and paying a large sum of money. The government staunchly refused to yield to the M-19's demands, at least publicly. And third, the M-19 supported a strike in a major agro-industrial enterprise, along with the kidnapping of one of its owners.

Operations like the takeover of the Dominican embassy involved not only prolonged and very detailed preparation, but also a wealth of technical skills, which were a scarce resource, especially for the fairly small groups that were the guerrillas in the 1970s. This explains why it was not the "spectacular mode," which would prove to be more important in the long run, but the more silent although much more massive "rural mode." In 1980, the justice minister stated that there had been 1,722 "crimes against individual liberty" in Colombia, the bulk of which, according to journalist Enrique Santos Calderón, were kidnappings. According to the same source, there had already been 2,924 in 1981.[7] Kidnapping was acquiring what the press already called "industrial proportions." It became one of the two major sources of funding for Colombia's guerrillas—the other being the drug trade.

In 1982, the M-19 held Marta Nieves Ochoa, the niece of a narcotrafficker, for ransom. The crime syndicates responded swiftly and decisively. They created a death squad, *Muerte a Secuestradores* (Death to Kidnappers—MAS for its acronym in Spanish), which rescued Ms. Nieves quickly after killing, torturing, and maiming several of the guerrillas' alleged civilian supporters. The MAS also went public, arguing that it made no sense to combat kidnappers within the bounds of law: "They shouldn't have expected that in response to their crimes we answered in the style of the Gray Ladies."[8] Gray Ladies they were not, and their example served as the inspiration for several illegal or semilegal paramilitary rural alliances. Some paramilitary leaders suggested that state agencies or a closed group of entrepreneurs might have coordinated the paramilitary initiatives to some extent.[9] But the interaction between paramilitaries and intra-systemic actors (state agencies and entrepreneurs) became more widespread because it was easily reproduced and it appealed to actors with a narrow and highly localized worldview.

In 1982, President Belisario Betancur initiated a peace process with the M-19, the EPL (Ejército Popular de Liberación), and the FARC. The next brilliant idea of an ELN dissident was to kidnap the brother of the president as a way of denouncing the collusion between the not-militant-enough guerrillas and the government. Even relatively balanced observers reacted with anger to this act.[10] For its part, the FARC committed itself to ending kidnapping, but apparently did not keep its promise.[11] Soon, opponents of the peace process were claiming that it had continued to kidnap through intermediaries. The peace process eventually broke down, and kidnapping reached new heights.

The Virgilio Barco administration (1986–90) faced an armed conflict on two fronts: the drug lords declared a war on the state—opposing the extradition treaty between Colombia and the United States—while the insurgents continued waging theirs. In the meantime, paramilitary groups spread to all regions of the country and started to kidnap. In 1988, Barco issued Decree 180, also known as the Statute for the Defense of Democracy, or the Anti-Terrorist Statute, which over time increased the penalty for kidnapping, from twenty-five to sixty years.

In the midst of a deep institutional crisis, a sector of the political elites adopted the idea of convening a constitutional assembly to reinvent the country's institutional framework. The 1991 Constitution was the result of a broad civil pact, but also of a series of peace accords that achieved the return to civilian life of several insurgent factions (among which were the M-19 and the EPL). But the number of kidnappings *grew* in the 1990s, and quite dramatically at that. There may have been many reasons behind this. The paramilitaries had started as an anti-kidnapping squad, but they eventually discovered the efficacy of the practice and were soon claiming their (minority) share of the abduction "market." The FARC, the ELN, and the paramilitaries, who kept on fighting, took control of the areas that the demobilized guerrillas abandoned. The remaining guerrillas also chose to target new sectors in the population. In the beginning, the potential victims had been mostly the rural rich, foreigners, large entrepreneurs—especially those involved in some type of scandal—and prominent politicians. But later they substantially broadened their targets. The Colombian state, which was going through a process of decentralization since 1986, had given local governments more fiscal and political autonomy. Mayors and members of municipal councils started to be systematically abducted.

The guerrillas also developed a new technique (the so-called *pescas milagrosas*, or "miraculous catches"), based on the sudden installation of a road checkpoint, followed by a more or less random capture of two or three people. The guerillas rapidly incorporated the practice as an important part of their repertoire.

Additionally, common criminals entered the fray and started kidnapping. There were three direct links between criminal and political kidnappings. First, criminals could use the political practice of kidnapping as a smoke screen to cover their own abductions—for example by attributing their acts to the guerrillas. In other words, by becoming the main kidnappers, the guerrillas reduced the costs—and thus lowered barriers to entry—for other actors. Second, criminals could sell their victims to the guerrillas, securing a basic income and saving themselves the trouble of building the relatively sophisticated organizational apparatus that having many hostages requires. Lastly, big-time criminals—mainly the Medellín Cartel—also performed political abductions to influence public opinion and to wreak havoc within the system.

In sum, kidnapping began to affect people of all social strata. A similar process had been taking place in the rural areas, where the guerrillas were influential. Because there are only a few very rich, their carrying capacity—even if they are kidnapped several times, which indeed happened—is small. Furthermore, they have resources to flee or fight back. The guerrillas searched for ever-new targets, but this increased the political costs of kidnapping.

It is not surprising, then, that the proverbial straw that broke the back of yet another peace process with the guerrillas—the one launched by the government of César Gaviria (1990-94)—was the kidnapping and assassination of a politician. The following administration (Ernesto Samper, 1994-98) suffered a number of military defeats against the FARC, after which the latter captured a number of military personnel. While the government claimed that this was a massive kidnapping, the guerrillas maintained that the soldiers were "war prisoners" who would be returned only in exchange for the FARC members captured by the state. Andrés Pastrana (1998-2002) was elected with one key program: to achieve a negotiated peace with the FARC. His four years in office were extremely turbulent, and marked by instability. It would not be an exaggeration to say that kidnapping was a central protagonist of the period. The FARC seemed more interested in exchanging its militants for soldiers than in striking a long-lasting pact. Moreover, the FARC persisted in its kidnapping activity, and may even have increased it. There was substantial evidence that the FARC was using the huge demilitarized area that the president conceded to it to hide its hostages. With every day, the pressure mounted against the peace process. But the FARC was not the only problem. The ELN, believing that it had been marginalized, organized a large-scale operation to demand governmental attention: a collective kidnapping in a church in Cali and the hijacking of a plane in the north of the country. The paramilitaries followed suit, focusing on public figures that they considered too dovish with regard to the FARC.[12] At the end of the Pastrana administration, nobody believed that the process could succeed, and yet another spectacular kidnapping—this time of a prominent Congress member—served as a pretext to terminate it.

In the 2002 elections, a presidential candidate, Íngrid Betancourt, tried to proselytize in a FARC region and was kidnapped.[13] This triggered an international wave of solidarity with her, but also pressure in favor of a "humanitarian exchange" (*intercambio humanitario*) between the FARC and the state. Alvaro Uribe's government (2002–10) had a much more hawkish stance than its predecessor, and at first it denied such a possibility. It is worth mentioning that Uribe's father had been abducted, and eventually assassinated, by the FARC.[14] However, a combination of circumstances—for example, the government attempted to rescue the governor of one of the main departments; the operation failed, and the governor was killed—allowed for a gradual opening of a window of opportunity for the exchange of prisoners, with successive new closures and reopenings taking place according to the conjuncture. In the meantime, Uribe was able to claim to have radically reduced kidnapping.

This seemed to close the whole chapter—at least in the view of the government, the bulk of opinion makers, and the increasingly despondent relatives of the victims. But the kidnapping (hi)story was just beginning. A set of national and international circumstances converged to give the issue prominence. First was the coming to power of leftist governments in neighboring countries. The new leaderships in Venezuela, Bolivia, and Ecuador had ideological, national, and strategic reasons to promote a peaceful solution to the Colombian conflict. Second, Europe was interested in the issue for several reasons, including the fact that Íngrid Betancourt, the most prominent guerrilla hostage at the time, was a French citizen. Third, the actions of the victims' relatives had a highly symbolic impact, which the media covered in very broad and emotional terms. The Uribe administration probably expected that all of this would have a very strong anti-guerrilla effect, and it was partially right. The widespread coverage of the plight of the victims and the mobilizations against kidnapping also put quite a bit of pressure on the government itself. The support for some kind of agreement between the guerrillas and the state grew rapidly, both in Colombia and abroad.

To diffuse the pressure, Uribe not only produced some spectacular unilateral acquittals of FARC prisoners—something totally at odds with his hawkish posture toward the internal conflict—but also proposed that Hugo Chávez, Venezuela's president, act as a mediator to produce a "humanitarian accord" (*acuerdo humanitario*). This proved to be a huge miscalculation. In effect, Uribe discovered too late that the primary actors in the conflict had different priorities. For the government, the objective was to denounce and fight the guerrillas. For the relatives of the victims, the objective was to liberate their loved ones. For potential mediators from the international community, it was to put the government and the guerrillas at the same table and thus take the first step towards a full-fledged peace process. When Chávez began to speak of his strategy with respect to the Colombian conflict—which contradicted Uribe's—in increasingly open terms, and he was not disavowed either by the Europeans or by fellow Latin American governments,[15] he was brusquely dismissed as mediator. This step created serious repercussions for relations between Bogotá and Caracas. In the midst of an increasingly shrill confrontation between Colombia and its neighbors about these and other hot issues, the *acuerdo humanitario* came to a standstill. This was followed by a spectacular governmental success—a military operation in 2008 that liberated Íngrid Betancourt and other FARC hostages—which triggered a wave of national euphoria. Even while Uribe and Pastrana had different approaches to the problem of violence, kidnapping had played a central role in each president's administration.

Complex Rationales

From the point of view of the guerrillas, it is easy to understand why the creation of a "kidnapping industry" would make sense. First, it is an extraordinarily attractive source of income. Families can pay huge ransoms. The typical victim—for example, a cattle rancher—is a fixed target in a broad expanse of land where state and police control are weak or simply nonexistent.[16] Mobile guerrillas have overwhelming operational superiority over such a victim. Second, kidnapping allows the insurgents to coordinate political and economic activities. Indeed, it is not clear how political objectives interact with economic ones in every case. For example, in the 1980s, the M-19 presented the kidnapping of Camila Michelsen, the daughter of a banker, as retribution for the fraudulent bankruptcy of her father, which had hurt thousands of customers' savings. But the M-19 eventually collected a huge ransom. In this case, the political dimension seems to have been parasitic and opportunistic. But political grievances are not a simple whitewash for economic greed, and this is particularly the case in very confusing and messy contexts. While demanding the initiation of a peace process, the ELN presented its massive kidnapping in Cali as purely "political" (as a way to force the government to pay attention to the ELN), but then it surfaced that the relatives of the hostages owed substantial ransoms. The incident is even more complex, though, because it is hard to doubt that the ELN wanted to achieve the political objectives it claimed to be pursuing. What eventually surfaced was probably the result of the following sequence: a) the political kidnapping took place; b) the demands were forwarded and the negotiations started; c) in the meantime, the relatives contacted the ELN; d) in the process, the ELN discovered that this was a good opportunity to obtain economic dividends. All in all, though, kidnapping is exceptional in that it is an act that captures rents and at the same time hits the class enemy. There are few violent activities that are simultaneously so clearly political and a substantial source of income. Third, kidnapping can wreak havoc among the ranks of the system, as the standard literature about terrorism asserts.[17] By targeting specific sectors and behaviors, insurgents can trigger severe collective action problems among systemic actors.

Last but not least, and related to the previous point, kidnapping can be used as a policing mechanism. In this context, extortion and kidnapping are conceived of as instruments to force a potential defector to be loyal. In the rough hierarchy of punishments that the guerrillas use to establish social control,[18] kidnapping is an intermediate step between warning and killing, which can be used to discipline the economic elites and keep them at bay (the downsides of which will be explored below). Those who abided by the rules of the group were "untouchable" and, at least in theory, enjoyed a kind of insurance. Since the credible threat of kidnapping is so intimately related to extortion, it was a means to force uncooperative actors to accept insurgent territorial control, or at least territorial relevance. Extortive quotas became semi-taxes, as the FARC's communiqué 002 of 1998 revealed.[19] The paramilitaries were also conscious of the implications of extortion and kidnapping for social/territorial control: "What we really cared about was not the money but to have control over the merchants, because we knew that they would not be able to pay both the guerrilla and us."[20] In highly contested territories, who pays whom has crucial strategic implications.

Now let us consider why it may be worthwhile for a politician to become an anti-kidnapping activist. An initial and obvious reason is that politicians themselves were commonly kidnapped, especially after decentralization, as noted in the previous section.[21] Politicians follow not only the proverbial Schumpeterian "animal instincts," in this case getting elected, or ideological concerns; they are also marked by crucial experiences in their lives, and kidnapping is likely to become one. As the practice of kidnapping spreads, it becomes a credible threat even against politicians who have not been victimized. Kidnapping limits, territorially and otherwise, the range of activity on offer to practical politicians, as the case of Íngrid Betancourt dramatically shows: by the threat of abduction, the guerrillas and other actors are able to forbid the entry of unwanted politicians into large swaths of the territory.

Additionally, kidnapping is a hate-sowing crime. It triggers virulent passions, which give strong incentives for politicians to try to use these passions to their advantage. There are several reasons that make kidnapping a hate-sowing offence. First, victims are put in a condition of sheer helplessness in which they suffer the full commoditization of their lives.

But this does not allow us to present kidnapping simply, or wholly, in terms of a "market." Actually, one of the worst things about kidnapping—at least in the Colombian context—is that it did not constitute a genuine market, with prices and more-or-less clear rules of the game. Victims cannot follow an algorithm of the type, "if I adopt behavior X [for example, not telling the police] and pay above Y [say, 50 percent of what the kidnapper demands], then no blood will be spilled." Ransoms vary wildly according to haphazard and idiosyncratic factors, such as the malevolence or benevolence of the group's main negotiators, the military and political conjuncture, etc.

Furthermore, kidnappers frequently break their promises. In the case of Camila Michelsen—the daughter of a financial tycoon—the press revealed that the M-19 had collected the ransom but failed to liberate her. This is not uncommon,[22] and it is probably "structural." The structural nature of cheating comes from two sources. First, the guerrillas have to be unpredictable; otherwise, victims will learn how to react, and the rate of success (the number of ransoms paid) will fall. If they become predictable, this allows the family—and eventually the authorities—to develop a defensive script and/or to prolong talks, with the corresponding sharp increase in the probability of capture of the offender. Second, when the victim's family comes to an agreement, it is settling the issue *and at the same time* signaling its vulnerability (and its possession of resources). If a family pays a ransom punctually, this may give the perpetrators reasons to abduct additional members of the same family instead of trying their hand with new (and possibly tougher) victims. So the dilemma is to pay easy and fast and expose yourself to a continuous and ruinous milking, or hold tight and risk the life of a close relative (father, mother, brother). Guerrilla negotiators could be brutal and aggressive, and change their demands and conditions abruptly.[23] Cheating, killing hostages whose ransoms had been paid, and demanding ransoms for the bodies of victims who had died while in captivity were all functional for the sake of maintaining unpredictability.

But this "structural" arbitrariness acquired extremely odious idiosyncratic expressions, which inflamed victims, their relatives, and their social networks. As the initial population of well-to-do adult males was depleted, the guerrillas focused on ever-new populations, breaking widely shared social norms and, at the same time, promoting non-class-based solidarity between the victims.[24] Furthermore, the continued practice of kidnapping contributed to the delegitimization of the guerrillas, a process in which a politician could be interested for ideological, instrumental, or "vital" reasons. Such delegitimization can be observed at both the regional and national levels. In the Magdalena Medio region, a string of "good" FARC commanders had coexisted with the cattle ranching elite for years. However, a "bad" commander started to overburden the population with exactions—probably trying to fulfill quotas established by the FARC leadership—and started to kidnap those who did not pay, which created the conditions for a virulent anti-insurgent reaction.[25] At the national level, the combination of economic and political objectives further undermined the guerrillas' claim to moral superiority over the system.[26] Since kidnappings, to be effective, had to target influential people—the rural rich and active politicians—it eventually created a critical mass of decision-makers viscerally opposed to the guerrillas.[27]

In short, guerrillas may have had good reasons to initiate the so-called kidnapping industry. Through kidnapping they could gain rapid access to large-scale rents, promote their political agenda, and control broad sectors of the population both in relatively safe as well as in contested territories. However, the political costs of kidnapping were potentially high for several reasons: kidnapping triggered virulent passions against the guerrillas, creating a critical mass strongly opposed to and delegitimizing them, and giving politicians strong incentives to mobilize anti-kidnapping constituencies. Politicians got interested in kidnapping as actual or potential victims. They could also try to champion the cause of the victims for purely electoral reasons. Given that kidnapping—even after becoming an "industry"—maintained a class bias throughout,[28] one would expect that anti-kidnapping leadership would enjoy a high probability of success. But in Colombia things turned out differently.

Repressive Failures

Politicians and state officials (especially from the security sector) attempted three formal institutional responses to kidnapping: disciplining, upgrading, and untying. By "disciplining," I mean efforts directly oriented at preventing the "shirking" of the families of the victims and thus solving collective action problems among them. "Upgrading" implies stiffening the punishments against kidnappers and their accomplices. "Untying" is the loosening of the checks and controls on the behavior of authorities in charge of the repression of the insurgents and their purported civilian supporters (see below for details). All of them were inspired by the need to respond to the threat with a collective and long-term solution. All disregarded basic liberal criteria. All had limited effects, because they triggered collective action problems.[29] In this section, I sketch their trajectory and review some of the public discussions they elicited.

I start with disciplining. Concerning kidnapping, the need to discipline the victims was more or less conventional wisdom among the Colombian political elites already in the 1970s. As shown above, it is difficult to find an event in which the government yielded (at least publicly and explicitly) to any of the political demands that the guerrillas issued as a condition to free a hostage. But political and other elites soon came to understand that it was not sufficient for the state to behave sternly, as the victims and society faced a social dilemma with respect to their behavior toward the offence. Precisely because of this, some argued, those who paid the ransom that the kidnappers demanded opened the gates of the fortress to the enemy. The solution was for the state to enforce the collectively better—but potentially costly for the individual—nonpayment strategy. In the words of one writer for Bogotá's *El Tiempo*,

> This means that [ours is] a society that acts as if it had completely surrendered to the bandits and that seems ready to pay a ransom in the form and quantity it is demanded. . . . Well: this is the first instinct the government has to defeat. It should not fear that by taking the normal course of action—the more energetic the better—some lives are lost, because what is being lost by the other system is much more serious: you are compromising a whole society when you meekly give it up to terror, and you kindly impede the government from intervening and chasing the delinquents. This is the highest level of moral disorder, and we cannot permit it to continue. Some say that if things are not done

> like that [cautiously] the . . . hostages will be assassinated. And—inspired by the very individualist and Hispanic criterion that we Colombians have in front of the law—every . . . person declares that what is really important is his/her particular case, that ransom is paid and lives saved. The government cannot, must not accept, this situation under any circumstance, and should warn the country that from now on it will implacably persecute [kidnappers], and that it will prosecute as well those who engage in commerce with the bandits because technically they are intimidated and, involuntarily, accomplices. This is hard, but it is harder to allow that society dissolves, victim as it is of extortion and blackmail.[30]

The borderline murderous tone and content of such a declaration—which picks up all three motives: discipline, untie, and upgrade—are in no way exceptional. It took a long time, though, for these kinds of demands to come to fruition. In September 1992, a group of Congress members presented the Proyecto de Ley No. 46 "Por el cual se dictan Medidas para la Erradicación del Secuestro." The bill empowered the general prosecutor to sequester the assets of the hostages and their relatives and to investigate the movements of their bank accounts above the sum of sixteen minimum salaries. They also wanted to establish an obligation to denounce the abduction, as the majority of families preferred to negotiate directly with the group without informing the authorities.

By then, the victims of kidnapping had organized, and they had created an NGO, *País Libre*,[31] which succeeded in using one of the new mechanisms for popular participation from the 1991 Constitution: legislative initiative. Citizens could present a bill to the Congress if more than 1 percent of voters supported it. This gave rise to the Anti-Kidnapping Law or *Ley Antisecuestro* 40 of 1993 (henceforth LAS), the only successful use of this participation mechanism in the Constitution. This is in no way unintentional. In both the 1990s and the 2000s, the state, the media, and political/economic actors promoted massive mobilizations against kidnapping. No other offence triggered such a massive repudiation.

The LAS not only transformed the payment of ransoms into a criminal offence, but also allowed the office of the prosecutor to control the assets of the victim and his or her family to ensure that no large transactions would take place. Despite being inspired by previous Italian legislation, the Colombian Constitutional Court ruled that paying a ransom for a loved one was not only a right, but also a duty (related to solidarity, a basic constitutional tenet since 1991), and that collective needs could not overrule basic individual rights. Only some technical aspects of the LAS (such as the creation of new anti-kidnapping security bodies) were not struck down. The critics of the court's decision protested bitterly: rebuking the LAS would offer incentives to the terrorists ("to multiply the payments is to multiply the kidnappings") and would run counter to the international experience—which showed, they argued, that standing fast against terrorism was the best way to face it. However, contrary to many other situations in the 1990s, there was no serious and sustained opposition to the court when it issued its final decision. Members of Congress had already expressed their concern that the LAS would violate the rights of the victims. Hundreds of people probably breathed a discreet sigh of relief.

Now let us now consider upgrading. Although several crimes have prompted repressive proposals, none have played such a crucial role in stimulating "repressive imagination" as kidnapping. In the 1970s, the basic reflex was to put kidnapping under the jurisdiction of military justice. Stiffening the punishment has also been a typical response to the threat. As mentioned previously, the idea that kidnapping was such a serious offence that it could not be pardoned has appeared at critical junctures, and it became an issue during the peace processes of several administrations. Both Bill 46 of 1992 and the LAS prohibited offering amnesties to kidnappers, but this was also found to be unconstitutional. As also mentioned previously, during Barco's administration, the punishment against kidnappers was severely increased. In 2002, the government pushed through the [anti-terrorist] Law 733, which increased the penalty for kidnapping so much that it became greater than the punishment for homicide. The Supreme Court decided that this was unconstitutional, as it was absurd for the state to protect freedom more than life.[32]

Kidnapping has also inspired on a cyclical basis proposals for the reintroduction of the death penalty in Colombia. An early commentator presented the idea as a way of preserving democracy. He claimed that if the authorities let the situation get out of hand, the country would face the danger of a coup, "like in Chile, Argentina, or Uruguay."[33] Despite these solemn admonitions, the specter of a coup never became too scary, and subsequent pledges for the reintroduction of the death penalty were based on the rationalist argument that increasing the costs of committing the offence would diminish its occurrence.[34] The idea reappeared from time to time whenever an especially notorious incident took place.

But the notion that more severe punishments were a better policy was also contested, and not only by the leftist opposition. For example, Fernando Cepeda—a well-known political scientist and cadre of the Liberal Party—asserted that there were two great anti-terrorist strategies, the German dovish and the American hawkish ones. A paper by the RAND Corporation had presented the following "statistical evidence: in Germany there had been no kidnapping [between 1970 and 1975], and in the United States 21." How could a lack of dissuasion be successful? Terrorists, said Cepeda, had many objectives, not only collecting a ransom. They wanted to promote armed propaganda, demoralize the elites, and polarize society, and they could fulfill all of these objectives regardless of whether the state agreed to negotiate with them.[35] Thus, simpleminded dissuasion crashed against a wall.

However, leaders from the security sector were not convinced by such nuances. For example, the director of the police during the Samper government seemed particularly fond of the idea of punishing kidnappers with death, and he proposed it several times. Samper—who was facing a huge corruption scandal—eventually warmed to the idea. He probably calculated that it would provide him with desperately needed support. Samper's kidnapping czar was also in favor of it because, he said, it would express neither the incapacity of the state nor the inefficacy of the previous anti-kidnapping policy, but rather "the indignation of the government and the whole country" in front of that crime.[36] However, the proposal did not arouse much attention. It was considered, reasonably enough, a smokescreen. Some observed caustically that the challenge for Colombia was not to reintroduce, but rather to ban, capital punishment.[37] Once again, they had a point. Others offered some purely operational reasons that prevented the country from making such a move: international commitments and legitimacy. The proposal was silently put on the shelf. In recent years, other authors have argued that, Colombian justice being so imperfect, instituting the death penalty would cause irreparable errors.[38] But this is not the last word. For example, Senator Jairo Clopatofsky created a web page dedicated to reinstalling the death penalty for "crimes against humanity" such as terrorism, homicide, and especially "that most detestable of offences, kidnapping, that not only acts against the victim but also against its social and familial entourage."[39] He presented two core arguments. First, his own version of the dissuasion theory: "The death penalty creates a reverential fear among the citizens, which pushes them in the direction of complying with the law." Second, the international environment was then favorable to iron-fisted measures. For example, the Organization of American States' Resolution 837 of 2003 established that it was necessary to reform traditional penal policies to face terrorism.[40] The debate remained open, and only the reduction in kidnapping rates deflated it.

The third type of response to kidnapping was to untie: to weaken checks and balances in order to allow for unobstructed repression. Mainstream journalists spilled liters of ink in the 1980s against the "attorney's syndrome" (*síndrome de la procuraduría*)—i.e., the negative effects of judicial control of the military. In essence, they supposed that it weakened the army's combat capacity. The reaction against the syndrome was motivated only partially by kidnapping and was part of a much wider anti-subversive mood. However, when untying was defended as an anti-kidnapping device, the language escalated very rapidly and could take clearly homicidal modulations. Repressing kidnapping was not a political but a medical task —independently of the motivations of the act. "The authorities deserve and need the most absolute backing without apologies when they have to act heavy handedly [*con mano fuerte*]," claimed one editorial in *El Tiempo*, the country's main newspaper. "It should not be forgotten that delinquents of this type [kidnappers] are fanatics moved by politics or by greed, that they do not respect life, and are exemplars of a pest that must be extirpated. Action must be taken."[41]

The untying drive has bogged down the development of adequate control institutions and has facilitated several murderous outcomes. At the same time, the overall institutional trajectory went (until 2002) in the opposite direction: the strengthening of the institutional controls on the executive, especially in the 1991 Constitution. Even after 2002, the anti-control instincts of a broad sector of politicians, security leaders, and opinion leaders seemed to have an upper hand. The Uribe administration strongly defended the need to both upgrade and untie.[42] His vice-president expressed the operation in terms of a tradeoff between liberty and security: the latter was the fundamental good and a precondition for the former. Sacrifices in liberty (and in liberalism) were thus necessary. A sector of the press responded to these reflections with alacrity. Untying the state and tying (controlling) the citizens would solve the security problems. Law 733 of 2002 was quite draconian, but in the process of debate in Congress it was watered down.[43]

In sum: with respect to all three institutional procedures, the use of kidnapping as a reason to weaken the liberal guarantees of the regime was moot at best. Disciplining basically failed. The LAS received support from a broad swathe of society, but it was an extremely short-lived effort. Collective action problems between the elites, and between elites and the victims of kidnapping, eventually stifled disciplining efforts.[44] The upgrading of the penalties was partially successful. But (formal) capital punishment has not yet had a real chance of being approved, and during the peace processes several governments managed to propose and pass through amnesties to kidnappers. By and large, the untying strategy has had the best record. For example, the military, which has been accused of committing—or enabling—atrocities, has enjoyed widespread impunity. Yet the opposition to the *síndrome de la procuraduría* in the 1980s did not, in the end, have too many results to show; and the 1991 Constitution strengthened the checks and balances on the regime and the controls on the states of exception.

Repressive Successes: Opening Institutional Back Doors

In the previous section, I showed how the checks and balances on the Colombian political regime limited disciplining, escalation, and untying. A standard argument in favor of repression was that democratic checks and balances were the trigger for the most murderous and destructive dynamics. Had the system allowed a stiffening of repressive designs, the latter would not have been necessary. The proposition corresponds to a very popular hydraulic mental model, according to which accumulating too much pressure below the surface is likely to cause an explosion.

The model fails on two accounts, however. First, regarding the "big" landscape—e.g., those institutions directly related to the nature of the political regime—it can reasonably be argued that the Colombian regime was not only fairly open but also underwent a serious process of improvement. Yet at the level of "small" institutional arrays things are much fuzzier (and uglier). In particular, paramilitary groups enjoyed a semilegal status during half of their bloody saga. In effect, they appeared in 1982 and started conversations with the government in 2002. They could claim a legal status during eight of these twenty years. Between 1965 and 1968, under the logic of national security, the state legalized the creation and promotion of self-defense.[45] This legislation was scrapped in 1989, but it was reintroduced in 1994. Through Decree 356 of 1994, the Gaviria administration created private security cooperatives, though during a short period they remained mainly inactive. The Samper administration activated them, through the *Superintendencia de Vigilancia y Seguridad Privada*'s *Resolución No. 368*, passed on 27 April 1995.[46] The *resolución* also gave them broader attributions, permitting them to carry combat weapons (*armas largas*) and communication devices. Public opinion came to know them by the Orwellian name of *Convivir* (which in Spanish means "to coexist or to tolerate"). On paper, the objective of the *Convivir* was to foster cooperation between civilians and the army in the struggle against illegal groups. In practice, they became an instrument of the paramilitaries, both for their territorial expansion and for cementing alliances with broad social sectors in the territories under their influence. It was not only the patina of legality that the *Convivir* gave the paramilitaries, but also the signal that they enjoyed official support, which made the paramilitaries important.[47]

The *Convivir* experience shows the second problem of the hydraulic model: the actors, coalitions, measures, and responses that played a key role in the semilegalization of the paramilitaries were very specific and are not necessarily present in other scenarios. In other words, different modalities of repression are not necessarily substitutes for one another. For example, the cattle ranchers' association, along with leaders of the security sector—which were operationally related to the dynamics of kidnapping—strongly promoted the institutional model of the *Convivir*.

During a strongly contested campaign, Samper's defense ministry promised to activate the *Convivir* at the twenty-fourth cattle ranchers' congress. The response was enthusiastic.[48] Actually, when the government seemed to get cold feet about the *Convivir* project, the cattle ranchers' association strongly expressed its dismay. Since, by then, the president was already under heavy fire from both the public and the US government because of the money that narcotraffickers funneled into his campaign, he was not in a position to open another battle front. As he declared, to remain in power he had to coordinate the demands of the very powerful. Both cattle ranchers and high-ranking officers were extremely active in the defense of the cooperatives, and they were therefore able to simultaneously signal their support to the cooperatives and to suggest that any opposition to the project was likely to have high costs (among them were Jorge Visbal Martelo, cattle ranchers' association president, and high-ranking officials such as Interior Minister Carlos Holmes Trujillo; Defense Minister Gilberto Echeverri Mejía; General Luis Enrique Montenegro, the director of the Presidential Security Agency, or DAS; General Víctor Julio Álvarez Vargas, commander of the army's First Division; Superintendent of Security Germán Arias; and Álvaro Uribe Velez, Antioquia governor and future president of the country). For the cattle ranchers, the *Convivir* was literally a matter of life and death. As one of the group's leaders underscored, delinquency and subversion cost nearly 40 percent of the cattle production.[49] The same leader argued that the *Convivir* should have sophisticated weaponry, as shotguns were no match for the guerrillas.[50] He also demanded that membership in the *Convivir* be mandatory, as many multinational firms were funding the guerrillas.[51] The cattle ranchers actually described the *Convivir* as both an expression of the right to self-defense and a way to link the population to the anti-subversive strategy of the army. In this vein, the cattle ranchers' association not only promoted the *Convivir*, but also suggested the creation of national militias supported by "civil society."[52] The association's leaders and their allies proclaimed that, in the face of the systematic "absence of the state," self-defense was a right. Private violence would also be a bargaining chip in an eventual negotiation with the guerrillas. A ranchers' association leader wrote to the president that "the guerrillas want to dismantle all the controls that the state has to defend society and advance the conflict without security, without paramilitarism, without the *Convivir*, without public order decrees."[53] This is as eloquent a declaration as one can find of the feeling that privatized violence and the state were part of the same cause.[54] State spokespersons had a similar view. For example, for General Enrique Montenegro, by then the director of the DAS, "the suppression of the *Convivir* instead of discouraging the phenomenon of self-defenses [the paramilitaries] would promote it, because it would close the door to the legal organization of the population under the vigilance of the state. . . . If the door is closed to the *Convivir*, there is no alternative to a paramilitarism run amok [*incontrolado*]."[55] In this characteristic endorsement of the hydraulic model, it apparently did not occur to General Montenegro that the state also could, and should, fight against the paramilitaries. The only alternatives were to tolerate them or to offer an acceptable substitute. This view was widely shared within the security sector.

Very soon, the *Convivir* became the thinly-veiled, legal version of the paramilitaries in several regions. A development that could have been easily predicted, but that went against the hydraulic model and General Montenegro's expectations, was that the *Convivir* and paramilitarism were complements, not substitutes. The *Convivir* eventually played a crucial role in a further wave of paramilitary expansion. Typically, a group of notables in a given municipality, with the support of the main local military or police figure, created the *Convivir* and used it as a cover to invite paramilitary henchmen.[56] The *Convivir* was also used as a tool to funnel funds to the paramilitaries and as a very strong link between major economic agents—multinationals, cattle ranchers, agro-industrialists—and the paramilitary project. They also became the portent of things to come for extremist politicians—notably, but not only, Álvaro Uribe, by then governor of Antioquia and a strong partisan of the *Convivir* cause[57]—and a focal point for the convergence of diverse illegal actors linked directly or indirectly with the paramilitaries. Indeed, the idea of launching the *Convivir*-like private security efforts resurfaced cyclically during the Uribe administrations, sometimes by governmental initiative, sometimes by the initiative of cattle ranchers[58]—among other reasons, to substitute the paramilitaries that had returned to civil life.[59]

Conclusions

What were the effects of massive kidnapping on the Colombian political regime? If guerrilla myopia is assumed, rationalist explanations can account for their indulgence in massive kidnapping over a long period to coordinate key objectives such as funding via ransoms or extortions, social control (policing), and political pressure. However, the political costs were enormous. To be viable, kidnapping had to be hate-sowing. Massive kidnapping activated very radical anti-guerrilla constituencies, both at a general level (public opinion, etc.) and at a specific one (social groups that felt the brunt of the guerrilla attacks and pressure). Here, "rationalism" and "structuralism" seem to be cooperative strands of reflection; we need both to understand why an actor decided to initiate a dynamic and how this created a specific constellation of social forces.

All of this suggests that to understand the consequences of kidnapping for the political regime, it is necessary to consider the concrete coalitions that formed as a response to its "industrialization." Kidnapping was an offence that had "preferred" victims—people who were particularly vulnerable *and* attackable—and this produced specific forms of mobilization among them. Furthermore, as shown above, collective action problems were endemic when systemic actors tried to divine a response to the challenge of kidnapping. No reasonable model can omit this key aspect of the dynamics considered here, and thus no model can reasonably assume that the state or the system is a unitary actor.

Another problem for TT is to capture the specific role of different threats that fed repressive responses. For example, the paramilitaries expressed a variety of concerns and demands. Can a specific weight be attributed to kidnapping?[60] And how great was this threat compared to others? This question seems particularly difficult to answer from a comparative perspective. Last but not least, I believe the narrative described above suggests that the study of repression might be enriched by looking both "above" the political regime (state failures) and "below" (small institutional designs that become very central at specific conjunctures).

Notes

1. This chapter considers the problem of kidnapping until the beginning of the first Uribe administration, in 2010, when kidnapping rates began to drop. I do not consider here policies against kidnapping in general; only those that involved a change in the repressive activities of the state. I also do not consider the rich literature that has been published on kidnapping in recent years, which is essentially descriptive, and does not discuss as yet its impact on the political regime. Sometimes I use the present tense, but the peace agreement between the state and the FARC (achieved in 2016) made of kidnapping—which had already been falling during the Uribe years—a very marginal phenomenon.

2. Francisco Gutiérrez Sanín, *El orangután con sacoleva. Cien años de democracia y represión en Colombia* (Bogotá: Random House-Mondadori, 2014).

3. Or "threat-response theory"; see, for example, Jenifer Earle, Sarah Soule, and John McCarthy, "Policing Under Fire," *American Sociological Review* 68 (2003): 581–606.

4. Elisabeth Wood, "Variation in Sexual Violence during War," *Politics and Society* 34, no. 3 (2006): 307–42.

5. James Ron, *Frontiers and Ghettos: State Violence in Serbia and Israel* (Berkeley: University of California Press, 2003).

6. I write in the past tense because my narrative ends in 2010, not because I am so overly optimistic as to assume that the phenomena described here cannot appear again.

7. These figures were calculated by contemporaries, and there is no good reason to doubt them. However, there is quite a large mismatch with the ones provided by the two main "official" sources, the National Department of Planning and the NGO against kidnapping, País Libre. In their account, there were forty-four events in 1980, and it was only in the late 1990s that the number exceeded two thousand. Perhaps different counting criteria explain the difference.

8. Gutiérrez Sanín, *El orangután con sacoleva.*

9. See Mauricio Aranguren, *Mi confesión: Carlos Castaño revela sus secretos* (Bogotá: Oveja Negra, 2001).

10. Abdón Espinosa Valderrama, "Contra el terrorismo," *Espuma de los acontecimientos* (1 December 1983), 5A.

11. Centro Nacional de Memoria Histórica, *Una sociedad secuestrada* (Bogotá: Imprenta Nacional, 2013), 170.

12. The public figures they kidnapped, the peasants they massacred.

13. She was rescued in July 2008.

14. Several ministers of his administration were in a similar situation. For example: Francisco Santos, vice-president, was kidnapped; Cecilia María Vélez, education minister, had several relatives abducted and killed.

15. And not even by the United States, which was interested in obtaining the liberation of three of its nationals in the hands of the FARC.

16   And since labor relations in certain rural contexts can be strongly "personal" and adversarial, it is relatively easy to gather information about the rural rich; see Barrington Moore, *Social Origins of Dictatorship and Democracy: Lord and Peasant in the Making of the Modern World* (Boston: Beacon Press, 1966).

17   See for example Albert J. Bergesen and Omar Lizardo, "International Terrorism and the World-System," *Sociological Theory* 22, no. 1, Theories of Terrorism: A Symposium (March 2004): 38–52.

18   For details, see Mario Aguilera, "Justicia guerrillera y población civil 1964–1999," in *El caleidoscopio de las justicias en Colombia*, ed. Boaventura de Sousa Santos and Mauricio García, 389–422 (Bogotá: CES-Universidad de los Andes—Ican—Siglo 21, 2001).

19   Centro Nacional de Memoria Histórica, *Una sociedad secuestrada*.

20   Proceso 1589, Delito: Concierto para Delinquir Cuaderno Copia No. 6, Folios 86–172 (Bogotá: Secreto—Departamento Administrativo de Seguridad, 16 March 1989).

21   Centro Nacional de Memoria Histórica, *Una sociedad secuestrada*.

22   For an early event, see "La historia de un secuestro bien denunciado," *Editorial* (8 August 1984), 4A.

23   For a good example of unpredictability, see Herbert Braun, *Our Guerrillas, Our Sidewalks: A Journey into the Violence of Colombia* (Lanham, MD: Rowman and Littlefield, 2003).

24   Mejía, Hernán Vallejo, "Oración por la paz y contra la extorsión y el secuestro," *El Tiempo*, 21 February 1985, 5A.

25   Francisco Gutiérrez, "Clausewitz Vindicated? Economics and Politics in the Colombian War," in *Order, Conflict and Violence*, ed. Stathis Kalyvas, Ian Shapiro, and Tarek Masoud (Cambridge: Cambridge University Press, 2008), 219–41.

26   And since the guerrillas lowered the barriers to entry for other purely economic actors, they were acting on a deeply criminalized landscape with which they interacted very actively (for example, common criminals sold hostages to the guerrilla according to the press).

27   For example, between 2002 and 2010, the president's father was killed after a kidnapping, and at least four ministers had been abducted or had suffered an abduction of a close relative.

28   The rich are more likely to be victimized than the poor. This is probabilistic, not deterministic. Hundreds, perhaps thousands, of poor civilians were being abducted by the guerrillas—for example, during the *pescas milagrosas*. Furthermore, by scaring away investment, kidnapping might have hit the poor in indirect ways. However, by the very logic of the crime, it became the only conflict-related offence that directly hit the well-to-do harder.

29   Recall Eckstein's conceptualization of the political consequences of certain forms of violence: when they work, they are able to produce severe problems of collective action within the incumbent coalition.

30   "Negocios y delitos," *El Tiempo*, 29 January 1973, 4A.

31 See Fundación País Libre's website at http://www.paislibre.org/site/.
32 Centro Nacional de Memoria Histórica, *Una sociedad secuestrada*.
33 Alejandro González, "Una dolorosa lección," *El Tiempo*, 3 March 1980, 5A.
34 See, for example, José Ignacio Vives's argument for the necessity of the Proyecto de Acto Legislativo No. 1 de 1985, "Por medio del cual se autoriza la implantación de la pena de muerte para los delitos de secuestro."
35 Fernando Cepeda Ulloa, "La meta de los terroristas," *El Tiempo*, 2 March 1980, 4A.
36 "Samper propone la pena de muerte," *El Tiempo*, 22 February 1996, 8A.
37 Javier Giraldo S.J., "Samper y la pena de muerte," 1996, http://www.javiergiraldo.org/spip.php?article11 (accessed 19 April 2015).
38 "Pena de muerte: ¿serviría?" *Revista Semana*, 9 November 1992, http://www.semana.com/especiales/articulo/pena-de-muerte-serviria/18576-3 (accessed 19 April 2015).
39 Jairo Clopatofsky, "La Pena de Muerte en Colombia: Una Reflexión posible para la consecución de la seguridad Democrática," Proyecto de Acto Legislativo por medio del cual se Reforma o Modifica el Artículo 11 de la Constitución Política de Colombia (2003).
40 Clopatofsky, "La Pena de Muerte."
41 "¿Secuestro político?," *Cosas del día*, 21 August 1977, 4A.
42 The debates surrounding Law 733 of 2002, an anti-terrorist bill, had clearly anti-liberal overtones.
43 Despite the government enjoying overwhelming majorities.
44 These reappeared cyclically but always created a serious divide between the victims and the government. The basic agenda of the victims (if one includes in this category the host and his immediate family) was to pressure the government to obtain fast and risk-free releases. But this went directly against the disciplining agenda, which consisted of putting the long-term interests of the state above any personal consideration.
45 Gutiérrez, *El orangután con sacoleva*.
46 The *superintendencia* is the governmental entity that was supposed to regulate the provision of private security in the country.
47 Gutiérrez, *El orangután con sacoleva*.
48 *Carta Fedegan*, no. 32 (Bogotá: Federación Colombiana de Ganaderos, January–February 1995), 15–16.
49 Jorge Visbal Martelo, "Convivir o no convivir," *El Tiempo*, 27 August 1997. Visbal is presently being judged under the accusation of having links with paramilitary group.
50 Visbal Martelo, "Convivir o no convivir."
51 In this context, he also demanded the death penalty for kidnappers; see "Instaurar la pena de muerte pide FEDEGÁN," *El Tiempo*, 26 October 1996, http://www.eltiempo.com/archivo/documento/MAM-558957 (accessed 19 April 2015).

52 *Carta Fedegan*, no. 32.

53 Gutiérrez, *El orangután con sacoleva*.

54 But it went only a little bit further from the official point of view expressed by the leader of the cattle ranchers' association, Visbal, who predicted that dismantling the *Convivir* would produce an expansion of paramilitary groups; see "Aquí hay legislar para frenar la guerra," *El Tiempo*, 11 August 1997, 2B.

55 Visbal Martelo, "Convivir o no convivir."

56 Francisco Gutiérrez Sanín and Mauricio Barón, "Restating the State: Paramilitary Territorial Control and Political Order in Colombia (1978–2004)," *Crisis States Research Centre Working Papers Series* 1 (London: London School of Economics and Political Science, 2005), 66.

57 "Uribe inicia debate internacional de convivir," *El Tiempo*, 24 July 1997.

58 "¿Farc avanza hacia zonas 'paras'?," *El Tiempo*, 14 February 2006, 1–4.

59 "¿Volver a las Convivir?," *El Espectador*, 12 March 2005, 4A.

60 In certain contexts, the answer is "yes." For example, I found recently that both large-scale cattle ranching and kidnapping were associated with massacres during the 1990s. By the way, this highlights the importance of identifying coalitions behind repressive responses. However, this is an exception. In general, I believe that the problems of aggregation are too severe for TT to cope with.

To End the War in Colombia: *Conversatorios* among Security Forces, Ex-Guerrillas, and Political Elites, and Ceasefire Seminars-Workshops for the Technical Sub-Commission

Jennifer Schirmer

> *I have been carefully listening to everyone these last two days in this Conversatorio, and I find I have a question to ask ourselves here at the table: If the government wants peace, if the armed forces want peace, if the guerrillas want peace, if the international community wants us to want peace, then where lies the problem?*
>
> —Air force colonel, participant in the *Conversatorio* "Conflict, Negotiations and Post-Conflict in El Salvador: Lessons for Colombia," 2006

In this chapter, I describe a low-profile project called Skilling for Peace, which I quietly began in 2000 to constructively engage the security forces in dialogues with former guerrillas, political representatives, journalists, and other members of Colombian civil society at the height of a crisis in the peace talks. These dialogues, known as *Conversatorios*, served as precursors to the more formal peace negotiations that later took place in Havana between the Colombian government and the Revolutionary Armed Forces of Colombia (FARC). All of the police and military officers who sat at the table in Havana passed through these dialogues during their Course on Strategic Studies (Curso de Altos Estudios Estratégicos) at the War College (Escuela Superior de Guerra) on their way to being promoted to generals and admirals. They were the *crème de la crème* of the officer corps. The *Conversatorios* featured more than fifty-two structured dialogues, which sought to develop constructive perspectives on peace negotiations with both the FARC and the National Liberation Army (ELN) insurgencies among the armed forces and members of the police, former guerrillas, and political elites. Based on a dozen years of building trust, by 2012, when the peace talks began under President Santos, the Joint Chiefs of Staff and the delegation of government negotiators requested that more than twenty Ceasefire Seminars-Workshops be organized over three years to prepare a delegation of nineteen civilian and military advisors. Later, an additional five active-duty generals and admirals worked jointly with members of the FARC leadership in Havana in formulating a ceasefire and disarmament and demobilization design as well as a tripartite mechanism for monitoring and verification with the United Nations, all suited to the particularities of the conflict in Colombia.

Many analyses emphasize what is intractable about a conflict and its spoilers, but in this project I sought to discover and act on that which could be identified as entry points to dialogue and changes in perspective. Such an approach did not presume the future to be inescapably violent. Rather, it rested on the assumption that it is imperative to parse the mindsets of actors on both sides of the conflict—especially the "skeptical spoilers" who have felt excluded from processes in the past or mistreated after the failure of previous peace talks—in order to better understand how to engage them directly in peace. For we can be reasonably certain that if these armed actors continue to be ignored, negotiations are doomed to failure.

This chapter reveals that in some instances, an openness to different perspectives can occur among some military officers on one side of the conflict and some former and current guerrillas on the other, both of whom are more than aware of the need to adapt to changing circumstances during a conflict. This project thus runs counter to the assertion that political violence among state and nonstate armed actors is endemic and intractable in Latin America, and particularly within Colombia.

The following analysis is presented in three parts. The first is devoted to the history of spoilers in peace processes in Colombia over the past three decades. The second focuses on the political background to the dialogues, including the nature of Colombian society and the social barriers to dialogue that Colombians needed to overcome if the security forces were to engage positively with peace negotiations. Finally, I discuss the *Conversatorios* and Ceasefire Seminars-Workshops central to the Skilling for Peace Project.

Spoilers and Attempts at Peace in Colombia

Since the late 1940s, according to Carlo Nasi, "spoilers have threatened to derail every single peace process" in Colombia. These have included "guerrilla groups (or their splinter factions), the armed forces, the Colombian Congress, drug-traffickers, entrepreneurs, rightwing paramilitary groups and even the U.S. government."[1] Because these groups all firmly believed that peace emerging from negotiations "threaten[ed] their power, worldview, and interests,"[2] they used violence and nonviolent sabotage and influence to undermine attempts to achieve it. One of the only peace processes during this period—initiated by President Virgilio Barco (1986–90) and continued by César Gaviria (1990–4)—was a result, according to Nasi, of the government's two "spoiler management techniques."[3] These techniques included the assurance to the armed forces that peace agreements with various guerrilla groups[4] did not entail institutional transformations of the army, coupled with the peace commissioner's request that the armed forces participate in "crafting a road-map in the Initiative for Peace." These measures of engagement were meant to secure, in particular, the army's compliance. Nevertheless, cooperation between the armed forces and the government remained deeply problematic, as one retired-colonel-turned-analyst recounts:

> Without being able to specify if it were for lack of communication, disagreement of visions, the lack of definition of

the truce, or all three, the government's peace efforts were not sufficiently well-received by the armed forces.[5]

The Barco and Gaviria governments also offered, in turn, some form of protection to demobilized guerrillas "to contain the potential damage caused by the spoilers."[6] There were two major spoilers at this time: on the one hand, the right-wing paramilitaries, sometimes in collusion with the army, assassinated over three thousand members of the FARC's political party, the Unión Patriota. On the other hand, the FARC assassinated some four hundred members of the demobilized Maoist guerrilla group the Popular Liberation Army. These spoilers threatened but ultimately failed to derail the peace process. Yet because the violence continued, observers consider this particular peace process to be only partially successful. Later attempts by President César Gaviria to negotiate with the FARC and the ELN yielded no results, and the armed conflict continued to escalate.[7]

Hence the opposition by the army to the Barco government's peace efforts did indeed diminish, especially in comparison to the resistance seen during the earlier tenure of President Betancur (1982–6). It was maintained, however, sotto voce, owing not so much to differences in strategy over how to address the "guerrilla problem," but "because officers did not feel committed to it and . . . because some of their members were involved with or believed in the 'dirty war.'"[8]

President Samper (1994–8) attempted to set up a demilitarized municipality of La Uribe to reinitiate peace dialogues with the FARC. But given that Samper's campaign had purportedly received money from the Cali Cartel, this attempt was roundly rejected by the commander of the army, General Bedoya, with many other commanders refusing to accept orders from a president with "ethical" issues.[9] During this period, the military regained its autonomy over security matters and conjured a dismissive attitude toward peace.[10] The FARC also took full advantage of this delegitimization of the presidency, initiating twenty-six simultaneous attacks throughout the country.

By 1997, citizens had deposited over 10 million symbolic votes in favor of "finding a negotiated solution to the Colombian armed conflict."[11] War fatigue brought Andrés Pastrana, with a conservative Nueva Fuerza Democrática platform for peace, into the presidency in May 1998.

However, with 450 members of the military and police held by the FARC as "prisoners of war," there was serious demoralization among the armed forces.[12] At this time the commander general of the armed forces, General Tapias, informed newly elected President Pastrana that "the democracy is in danger and the armed forces are in intensive care."[13] Nonetheless, Pastrana pressed forward with his platform, declaring peace negotiations with the FARC and the ELN to be a priority of his new administration. He proposed a "mini-Marshall Plan," referred to as Plan Colombia, which began as an economic blueprint for peace, offering alternative crops to small coca farmers. But lacking funding, the plan was completely rewritten in English by the US State Department with an antidrug focus. With 9/11 and a change of regime in the United States, aid that would amount to over $10 billion over the next ten years was primarily reserved for security forces' attacks against the guerrillas, in alignment with Washington's new priorities.[14]

Background to the Project

The *Conversatorios* project emerged from these efforts at peace between 2000 and 2002. During this period, there was little communication between President Pastrana and his peace commissioner and the High Command. A small advisory group of retired generals was created, but it had little influence (*muy al lado*).[15] This lack of dialogue would prove to be a serious error on the president's part.

Discontent among officers developed after the sacking of two generals by President Pastrana under pressure from the United States for having connections to paramilitaries. This was especially delicate as many officers interpreted this action to be the result of indirect pressure from the FARC, which was implied in the group's criticisms of paramilitary activities. Within a matter of days, the situation worsened: without an initial briefing to the armed forces by the executive office or peace commissioner, the president announced an indefinite extension of the demilitarized zone (*zona de despeje*). This resulted in a full-blown crisis, with twelve generals and twenty colonels offering their resignation in solidarity with Defense Minister Rodrigo Lloreda, who resigned after publicly stating that he did not believe the FARC were interested in negotiating. Emergency meetings with the generals limiting the *despeje* to a time period of six months temporarily resolved the crisis. Tension within military circles throughout the Pastrana government nonetheless continued: heavy military surveillance of both peace commissioners, Víctor Ricardo and Camilo Gómez; a press conference with the commander of the army, General Mora, railing against the prisoner exchange; and finally, a threat by the head of the air force to shoot down the plane of Peace Commissioner Gómez, then on his way to negotiate with the FARC.[16] Ultimately, the negotiations failed as a result of the FARC's hijacking of a commercial jet on 20 February 2002. That night, President Pastrana announced the suspension of the peace talks and authorized the remilitarization of the *zona de despeje*.[17]

The ELN talks in Geneva from 25 to 27 July 2000 were also thrown into crisis in the middle of the second meeting between Peace Commissioner Gomez and the ELN delegation when news arrived that paramilitaries led by Carlos Castaño were attacking the ELN's principal encampments in the province of Sur de Bolívar.[18] ELN commander Antonio García temporarily suspended the talks, noting that the paramilitary attacks "with the collaboration of the armed forces" were a provocation to impede the talks, and subsequent negotiations did not materialize.[19]

The paramilitary spoiler—with its military nexus—was extremely problematic, as Nasi points out. "In some regions, the military turned a blind eye to (and sometimes collaborated with) the activities" of these groups, with the claim they were unable to fight so many irregulars simultaneously. But after Plan Colombia strengthened the security forces, Nasi asks, "How could the military look the other way when the AUC [United Self-Defenders of Colombia] carried out massacres and extra-judicial killings?"[20]

Curiously, with the talks with the FARC and the ELN failing once again, the High Command believed there was nonetheless progress. Some of the officers who had previously opposed negotiations began to reconsider, as General Tapias recounted in a 2009 interview:

> In the beginning, [the officers] didn't understand. . . . Whatever kind of negotiations with illegal groups they always understand as a concession of the state, as a weakness of the state. . . . That was a difficult period, I won't deny it . . .

terribly traumatic, and one encountered direct opposition from some commanders.

But, General Tapias goes on, officers began to realize they needed to rethink *la estrategia* and bring the other officers on board for negotiations:

> It was a labor of persuasion, of conviction. Besides, there was no other alternative as it was a popular mandate with an elected president, with all the presidential candidates having committed themselves to a [*zona de*] *despeje*. . . . But little by little, they began to see our reasoning about what it was that was being done, when it was presented in the larger context. . . . At the end of it all, [President Pastrana's talks at el Caguán] were a failure due to the total lack of willingness by the FARC [to negotiate], but the realists made us realize that this was a necessary stage that had to be gone through in order to explore if the FARC were willing or not [to negotiate] in order to begin the following stage, which was to impose the force of the state on these [insurgent] groups.[21]

For the Skilling for Peace Project, the history of the Colombian military's role as spoiler of and antagonist to peace raised the larger question of how to include militaries in peace processes. Extrapolating from the history of spoilers in Colombia, I came to ask how it is that commanders are willing and able to create conditions within their institution to work in alliance with a president's peace efforts. Must there always be an incoherence between what is considered "the political" and "the military," leading military commanders to view negotiations as merely an extension of the battlefield, or worse, an extension of the privileges of a political elite that might, in a peace process, "sell out" the military's prerogatives?[22]

Over the following years, an increasingly precise bombing campaign, begun in 2002 but escalating in 2007, took its toll on the FARC. When President Santos reentered talks with the FARC in 2012, the military's newly minted strategy, supported by Plan Colombia, had indeed solidified, indicating to the political and economic elites (*los cacaos*) that military force was central to bringing the guerrillas to the negotiating table, and that the military's institutional interests and future needed to be considered if peace was to be realized. This called for a gradual acceptance of a combined strategy of "negotiating in the midst of the conflict" (negociar en medio del conflicto) with no ceasefire in place.[23] General Tapias explained:

> You have to understand that the term "negotiation" without disarmament and without demobilization has been so discredited in so many processes in Colombia. . . . Nevertheless, if you are one of those officers who still perceive of negotiations as implying military defeat, then clearly you will not support it. But if you see it as a form of achieving victory with fewer deaths and less suffering, then you will.[24]

Over time, in the *Conversatorios*, negotiations with the insurgency became increasingly acceptable to officers under these conditions. But early on, what the dialogue project was able to discern was that with this initial rethinking of military strategy came the need for a forum in which officers could express their uncertainties and anxieties about what peace negotiations might mean for them and their careers as well as their institution. This was an anxiety prompted by a perceived, and at times real, marginalization of the military by the governing elite (the president and his advisors), especially during past peace negotiations. (As we shall see, General Tapias's remarks also help explain why ceasefire and a disarmament and demobilization [DDR] program became for both sides such central elements in the creation of an architecture for peace under President Santos.)

    Hence, despite their proven legacy as spoilers, in my initial conversations with many high- and middle-ranking military and police officers, along with political elites and former guerrillas, during the 2000–2 period, I discovered a rather different set of wishes on the part of the armed forces. When I asked what I could proffer that would not duplicate other donors' efforts, there was a strong interest in establishing off-the-record, low-profile dialogues with those elite sectors in Colombian society to which officers normally did not have access. They were also keen to learn about "international options" in ending armed conflicts. Officers were interested in learning how to negotiate with the guerrillas at the same time as the military buildup was getting underway. This indicated three things. First, they believed that the correlation of forces "from the qualitative angle" between the FARC and the armed forces was at the time—2000—entirely "disadvantageous" for the state forces. This realization required, in their minds, a *delay but not a total rupture* in the possibility for negotiations with the FARC until a more coherent political-military strategy designed to equilibrate this correlation could be achieved in favor of the government, in order to increase its strength at the negotiating table. Hence the earlier negative reaction of many officers to President Pastrana's lack of time limits for the demilitarized zone demanded by the FARC.[25] They believed the zone provided a military advantage to the FARC, and that the guerrillas were merely utilizing the negotiations to gain time for a new redeployment of its forces rather than a sincere willingness for peace (we will return to this concern below).

Second, this indicates what was clear in all the *Conversatorios* since this initial period: officers believed that the Colombian conflict with the FARC had to end at a table of negotiations. Many maintained, though, the common view among armed actors in conflicts: that there was a need for a military campaign to "weaken" the enemy and establish respect for military strength was the only avenue to force the enemy to the negotiating table. By 2011, after close to a dozen years of a US-financed military campaign, the FARC and the ELN had been "very weakened but not totally weakened,"[26] and as a result, fewer and fewer military officers came to believe in the possibility for a complete military victory. As one colonel put it, "only the civilians who don't have to fight the war believe this." This officer made it clear, sotto voce, that he was including in this grouping President Uribe, known for his demands for "body counts."[27]

A third element was the recognition that the guerrillas had decades of experience in negotiating: the ELN in numerous attempts since 1991,[28] and the FARC, who had negotiated with several governments since 1984.[29] Many officers were extremely cognizant of the military's lack of experience in this regard, putting the armed forces at a distinct disadvantage. As one officer who characterized himself as "hardline but pragmatic" argued, "we don't have the years and years of training in negotiations as do the ELN or FARC. Will we be taken advantage of at the table *by all sides*?"[30] As we shall see, this fear became paramount in 2015 when military advisors, as part of the Technical Sub-Commission, journeyed to Havana to negotiate a ceasefire with the FARC.

While the prospect of having to reach political accommodation with the guerrillas was still met with much suspicion and ambivalence, the recognition of the need to draw the FARC into the political arena, where they were perceived to be most vulnerable, gained increasing legitimacy among the officers. As was discussed in the *Conversatorios*, broad electoral participation would likely debilitate the FARC and "dissolve" them as a political movement in very little time.[31] This recognition of the guerrillas' *political* fragility was the lesson from the Pastrana government, as some officers slowly came to realize:

> In a few years' time, Pastrana will be the hero of Colombian politics because he was able to foresee that the only way to defeat the guerrilla was to bring them into the political arena, and that this military campaign against them was all for naught at great cost.[32]

These new perspectives on negotiations and political fragility, I found, reflected a growing unease among some of the more moderate officers with the absolutist and triumphalist narratives so prevalent throughout the Uribe period (2002–10)—that of *"el fin del fin y no el comienzo del fin"* (the end of the end and not the beginning of the end of the guerrilla) proclaimed by the president and a number of officers in the High Command.

The Dialogues Project

In 2000 and 2001, serious concerns were raised about how to manage the armed forces and prepare officers for potential peace talks in the future. At this time, I was asked by both the High Command and Defense Minister/Vice-President Gustavo Bell to speak with the director of the Escuela Superior de Guerra, General Medina—who was keen to modernize CAEM officers' education—about organizing events to engage them in peacebuilding. With my academic background as an anthropologist, and my status as a neutral party who stood outside daily Colombian polemics, it was suggested that I could move easily among sectors and facilitate dialogue between the armed forces and civilian sectors, listening equally to all participants. After months of discussions with the military, the police, academics, journalists, as well as International Red Cross representatives in Bogotá, I organized a 26–28 March 2001 Seminar entitled "Military Operations within the Framework of the Respect and Defense of Human Rights and International Humanitarian Law" at a hotel in Bogotá at which the director of the War College and the commander of the armed forces, as well as international invitees, spoke to 320 officers (colonels and majors). The opportunity also arose (as had been planned) for these officers to speak directly with President Pastrana's peace commissioner, Camilo Gómez, in a respectful environment. This discussion lasted two long hours, with many difficult questions for the commissioner. This was his first opportunity to meet with officers, he admitted, and he vowed to meet with them more regularly in the future.

To build on the success of this initial event I was subsequently asked by General Medina to establish, with the approximately twenty-five colonels and navy captains who would be promoted to the rank of general and admiral each year, a long-term series of dialogues (three per year), referred to as *Conversatorios*. Over the thirteen years of the project, I would invite, in consultation with my two Colombian associates on the project,[33] three to four Colombian parliamentarians, academics, businessmen, journalists, and former guerrillas, among many others, for each event. Themes discussed ranged from the roots of the conflict, agrarian reform, the political participation of members from the previously disarmed and demobilized guerrilla groups, paramilitarism, as well as lessons learned from other peace processes.[34] As my associates would continually remind me, the multiple meetings I held with individual participants to prepare them for each event, especially with the officers of the High Command and government officials, were not so easily done by fellow Colombians. My status as a neutral academic and outsider who could foster trust as director of the project, I was assured repeatedly, was essential. It may also have helped that as a woman I was seen as a careful listener and circumspect interlocutor.

The Uribe Presidency

Adamantly opposed to the Pastrana-FARC talks, Álvaro Uribe won the elections in May 2002 (and again in 2006) by practically declaring war on the FARC, arguing that he and the armed forces would *exterminar la guerrilla* to uphold his Democratic Security Policy. He presented his Plan Patriota as an all-out attack on two fronts: drugs and the FARC. There would be no negotiation in the midst of the conflict. During Uribe's tenure, the FARC remain designated as terrorists on the US State Department list of Foreign Terrorist Organizations (FTOs) (since 1997). The DEA also called for extradition to the United States of the entire FARC Secretariat on the basis of drug trafficking.

Uribe eagerly assumed his role as commander of the armed forces on 7 August 2002, directly giving orders to mid-level commanders, especially during his first term.[35] Often, each commander attending a *Conversatorio* would receive a call on his cellphone from the president late in the evening, asking how many *bajas* ("kills" of FARC members) he had achieved that day. This provoked some notable responses: many were bothered by this micromanagement by the executive, which they saw as undercutting, indeed at times entirely marginalizing, the military High Command. They were also deeply concerned about Uribe's fanatical focus on body counts "rather than focusing on strategy," as one officer complained sotto voce. [36] And when the president attempted to change the Constitution so that he could run for a third term, a number of officers were furious, stating quite openly that "he is being absolutely undemocratic."

During Uribe's eight-year tenure, there was a 50 percent increase in the presence of armed forces and police in the more rural areas, and a battle strategy was implemented that had troops hold their ground and stay in place, which meant the FARC lost control of considerable territory. By 2007, and throughout the rest of the Uribe government (as well as the rest of the *Conversatorios*, which lasted until early 2014), with the direct access of multiple US advisors to seven major bases, there was a guaranteed influx of US military aid. The United States also provided and oversaw the technical operations of the bombing campaign that was ever more capable of surgical strikes. The objective of this broadening of US cooperation was "to destroy definitively [FARC] terrorism."[37] As part of Operación Fénix, on 1 March 2008, a US-coordinated bombing raid 1.1 miles inside of Ecuador killed, for the first time, a member of the FARC leadership: Raúl Reyes, who was number two in the group's Secretariat. The US president and several senators (but not Ecuadorian president Rafael Correa) were informed beforehand.

This bombing and strafing of FARC encampments caused a shift in the calculus of the war: panic among the FARC ensued, with scores of fighters killed, captured, or deserted, and the group's internal communications were disrupted, isolating the Secretariat from its commanders, some for years. The FARC nonetheless managed to survive such constant Colombian military pressure by breaking into smaller mobile units, moving into rugged mountainous terrain with heavier cloud cover (returning to earlier guerrilla tactics), and with a steady flow of weapons, explosives training, and funding from drug trafficking. By 2008, one air force colonel at the US Embassy in Bogotá admitted ruefully, "We really underestimated how long this bombing campaign to bring the FARC to their knees would take. We thought it would be over by now."[38] In the end, Uribe never felt he would have to negotiate or be seen as "giving in to the narco-terrorists," but if another president came along and did negotiate, it would provide him with an opportunity to remain influential politically, as we will see with the referendum of October 2016.

Santos's Negotiating Strategy

A shift in strategy occurred with the election in 2010 of former defense minister Juan Manuel Santos. On 23 September 2010, the FARC's top military chief, Mono Jojoy (located by military intelligence after they managed to place a GPS chip in his specially designed new Adidas for his diabetes), along with twenty other guerrillas, was killed in another military air strike in the Macarena region, a FARC stronghold. But while Santos escalated the bombing campaign, reducing the seven-member military and political FARC Secretariat to two, and neutralizing numerous units by killing mid-level commanders and troops, he *remained open to negotiations*, marking a noteworthy change of direction from his predecessor. However, if the FARC refused, he insisted, "they can only await jail or the tomb." Overtures and letters to and from top FARC leader Alfonso Cano were made in 2010 and 2011, but when one of his generals phoned him after a bombing operation on 5 November 2011 to say that he "had Cano surrounded. Should we proceed?" Santos gave the order, and Cano was shot and killed.[39]

Unlike Uribe, Santos saw the FARC's ideological alliance with Venezuelan president Hugo Chávez's Bolivarian Movement as an entry point. Indeed, the very first week of his presidency, Santos directly approached President Chávez and asked him to intervene and speak with the new FARC leader Timochenko, who was then living in an isolated corner of Venezuela. Timochenko would later recall this meeting with Chávez:

> There was at this time so much fear, so much insecurity... and [Chávez] said to me, "Listen, I have all the certainty that through peace negotiations, one can attain something, but through war [you attain] nothing." I was certain that here was someone who would not put a knife in our back, that he wouldn't leave us hanging in the breach.... He provided us with the certainty that we needed [to go into these negotiations].[40]

Secret preparatory talks thus began in 2010–11, followed by secret exploratory talks with the peace commissioner, Sergio Jaramillo, and the president's brother, Enrique Santos, in Havana in early 2012; these progressed into formal, public negotiations later that year. In Havana, the FARC leadership understood they could not continue the fight much longer; they spoke in Havana of still being traumatized by the bombings. They realized they had only a limited margin of maneuverability, and thus, having taken the decision to transform the movement into a legal political party, came to the table having already decided they would disarm and demobilize. It then became a difficult matter of negotiating precisely how, when, and to whom they would hand over their weapons. The military, too, had its own concerns: the FARC's continued resilience in the face of devastating losses, and the terrible consequences for Colombian soldiers due to the FARC's increasing reliance on sharpshooters and explosives, meant that landmines were the leading cause of the high rate of military casualties. As General Flórez, the head of the Technical Sub-Commission, pointed out in 2016, "Our generation of officers of the armed forces and police were born in the conflict, we have lived the war. Even just three years ago, in 2013, there were 652 amputees and 200 deaths from combat."[41] In 2018, the commander of the armed forces confirmed that the armed conflict had "left 30,000 soldiers and police wounded, 12,000 amputees and 6000 dead."[42] Many elements of the air war, of combat casualties, and of the uncertainties over whether the conflict could in fact be ended were continually raised among the police and military officers in the *Conversatorios* during these years.

All of these elements led both the FARC and the Santos regime to view this moment in early 2012 as an opportunity. As the high commissioner for peace remarked, "we have before us the best opportunity in our history to end the conflict. I say this because I have been engaged with the FARC for more than a year in Havana and I am convinced that the opportunity is real."[43]

Divisions within Colombian Society

Divisions exist at all levels of Colombian society between civil society and the military, the rebels and the government, and the left and the right, creating barriers to the building of peace.[44] This was especially true with regard to the barrier between the armed forces, the political elite, and both former and current guerrillas.

For the military, the reluctance to cross boundaries is sometimes ideological, as General Tapias recounts: "One must dismantle many *tabús* [within the military]. When I was a young officer, there arose the opportunity to speak with a *guerrillero,* and that was almost a mortal sin!"[45] The fear was that by merely having a conversation, one would be seen as having been infiltrated by the FARC.[46] This *tabú* would arise a number of times in the *Conversatorios.*

But the reluctance is also social: military and police officers live in their own segregated communities, locked into a conflict that breeds its own form of exclusion and insider mentality.[47] It is extremely unlikely that Colombian military officers would have social ties, much less informal friendships, with journalists, academics, intellectuals, or political analysts. In the officers' universe, the "public sphere"—filled with politicians, ideologies, and everyday debates—is often viewed more as an intimidating social and political arena, and not as an arena of opportunity for deliberations about peace.

In parallel, social isolation is the norm for most political elites, including business leaders, intellectuals, journalists, and academics who keep to their own, with little access to members of the armed forces, whom they often hold in disdain. These sectors lack a forum that is generative of political debate, analysis, and reflection with officers.

Finally, there exists a critical mass of former guerrillas from the handful of revolutionary groups in Colombia who, as a result of the multiple peace negotiations in the late 1980s and '90s discussed earlier, disarmed, demobilized, and "reinserted" themselves back into civil society. Although often socially shunned by elites, these *reinsertados* have "crossed" a number of social boundaries to become politically active as governors, parliamentarians, and presidential candidates in the various political parties formed since 2004.[48]

How does one cross these boundaries between these military and civilian "subcultures," with their significant disparities and volatilities, "to dismantle these tabús" and embark on a series of conversations that, hopefully, help shape the makings of a negotiated peace?

The *Conversatorios*

Faced with these challenges, *Conversatorios* predicated on shifting the historical spoiler narratives were established. Their overriding purpose was to open a debate in which representatives from the political class, military officers, and ex-guerrillas would have the opportunity to entertain and analyze together important and current political issues in the midst of the conflict. Between 2002 and 2013, 665 active-duty colonels and navy captains from all four branches (army, air force, navy, and police) participated as part of their one-year promotional course (Curso de Altos Estudios Militares, or CAEM) at the War College. In addition, at the request of the police officers at CAEM, I organized two separate police *Conversatorios* for a number of generals in 2003 and 2004. Between 2007 and 2010, the entire corps of 68 generals and admirals participated in a number of *Conversatorios* specifically organized for them, and between

2010 and 2012, the 5 officers of two separate High Commands (some of whom had previously participated in the *Conversatorios* first as colonels and navy captains, and then as generals and admirals) participated in three separate *Conversatorios* organized specifically for them. In addition, hundreds of Colombian civilian presenters and a number of international experts participated. Finally, a series of courses on international humanitarian law and human rights were organized over a period of two years (2005–7) for 30 pilots as well as approximately 90 frontline combat troops at the request of two military schools (the Special Forces and the Cadets). Overall, at least 775 officers and noncommissioned officers participated in these dialogues and courses over the entire period of the project.

The *Conversatorios* encouraged a level playing field in which all participants had a chance to speak and to listen in an equal and respectful manner. Most significant for the officers was their low-profile nature; there was no media presence and all statements were unattributed in order to maintain the "Golden Rule" that everything said was off the record. These dialogues, then, were about instilling a process of dialogue within a society in which there is little dialogue or trust between sectors.

During this period, national security doctrine, refashioned primarily from the perspective of US counterinsurgency experience, remained the touchstone of the curriculum at the War College. Nonetheless, the majority of the school's directors during these years welcomed the *Conversatorios* into the curriculum in an attempt to introduce a peacebuilding perspective, and they were enthusiastic about attending the events as well.

I initially accepted the limits imposed by the directors of the school and the CAEM officers as to which participants they would and would not invite to the dialogue and what themes they would and would not discuss. Over the years, these limits were overcome (former guerrillas were invited, for example) and the dialogues sought to incrementally and gradually expand the officer, political elite, and ex-guerrilla dialogue horizons to move each sector outside their enclosed social circles and intellectual comfort zones to encourage dialogue about topics that were challenging and, at times, especially sensitive.

The method didn't demand doctrinaire agreement or assume ideological antagonism. Rather, a stream of conversation was encouraged that allowed participants to address the nature and roots of the political violence within Colombia. By removing conversation from the realm of the polemic—the norm in Colombia—and placing it in a more or less neutral forum in which all participants have equal time, some interesting concurrences of thinking and transformation of attitudes occurred. One former guerrilla expressed his views on social justice and poverty, while officers agreed that Colombia should address social inequality and poverty, especially in the countryside. At times, each side came to the realization that they may share similar ideas, even though such thinking may emanate from very different historical narratives.

A Modus Operandi of Gradualism

This range and variety of themes for the *Conversatorios* did not come about immediately or easily. Initially, officers did not easily forfeit their demonized image of the guerrilla-as-enemy (*bandidos*) and as *terroristas*; nor were they very open to members of civil society from "the left."[49] Hence, in the early *Conversatorios*, I at first felt it was too risky to introduce either themes or speakers who the officers considered "too progressive" and who were outside of their comfort zone. If officers suggested speakers, it was often more for the opportunity to make critical statements face to face than to have a respectful dialogue. Oddly, human rights NGOs mirrored this response. When I approached certain members of these groups, they were adamant in their unwillingness to meet with the military; they either offered a firm no or were only willing to participate if they could either confront or denounce the security forces. While a couple of NGOs dealing with forced displacement did enthusiastically participate in these dialogues, they remained an exception. And even with these NGOs, many officers believed they were "ELN guerrillas in disguise." It became clear that overcoming *tabús on both sides* was of paramount importance in the dialogues.

Thus, in the first series of *Conversatorios*, I organized a more academic discussion about the roots of the conflict, inviting Colombian academics and economists to discuss levels of impoverishment and the lack of land reform—points on which many of the officers agreed. Subsequently, I decided to involve increasingly progressive participants, including moderates from various political parties who held ideas about how to resolve the conflict that differed markedly from those of the officers. At each step, a careful calibration was made, after long discussions with my Colombian associates as well as with various potential participants, as to how far beyond their intellectual comfort zones each side could be taken. Occasionally, and only after careful deliberation, a former guerrilla would be invited to speak, intentionally attempting to break the *tabú* that General Tapias spoke of. This opened up space for discussion of the nature of the conflict, the actions of the insurgency, and the potential for future negotiations.

Before every event, I made an effort as director of the project to meet alone with each participant, both civilian and military, to help prepare them for an open, respectful discussion by suggesting ways to rephrase a question or comment to make it less antagonistic. This preparation, I would argue, was of significant help in furthering discussion and "calming the waters" between the parties.

By 2005 new political circumstances in Colombia made it possible to broaden the pool of discussants and the range of dialogue. With the initiation of paramilitary demobilization talks in 2003–4, the election of a number of congressional representatives from the new social democratic party, Polo Democrático Alternativo, together with a number of independent new mayors and governors in Medellín and Cali, I felt confident I could open up the political discussions by reaching out to these new, more progressive politicians. Interestingly, with each subsequent *Conversatorio* with a Polo or independent or ex-*guerrillero* representative, the officers insisted on having the opportunity to meet with similar representatives in the future. The increasing institutionalization and legalization of the Polo party, as well as the "multiplier effect" each *Conversatorio* had on the officers from one year to the next, made it easier to work with each new group of colonels and navy captains. Over time, I could touch on more "delicate" topics, inviting participants, for example, to discuss the government's demobilization talks with the paramilitaries under way at that time, as well as the potential for a humanitarian accord with the FARC, which the Uribe government was then considering.

By 2008, with my academic credibility, I took a leap of faith (and against the advice of one of my associates) and set up two rather historic events. At first the officers were reluctant to meet with former guerrillas, with whom there had been visible tension in the early conversations. Nonetheless, over time, each side came to value these discussions, surprised by the extent to which they could converse in a frank but respectful manner. Officers also came to learn that former guerrillas, who had been elected parliamentarians, mayors and governors, were, like themselves, not monolithic in their views but deeply divided, voicing strong disagreement, for example, with the FARC's violent agenda and drug-trafficking activities. This ideological friction among the former *guerrilleros* surprised the officers.

Yet *el tabú de la guerrilla* and "the left" in general was still very much present in officers' minds: in one special *Conversatorio* in 2004 organized for majors, I invited one of my associates, an ex-ELN guerrilla, to speak. At the end of his talk, one officer raised his hand and said "how very worried I am," as he found that he agreed with most of what this ex-guerrilla had said. Everyone drew in a breath, and then laughed. On another occasion, in 2006, the same associate spoke to a group of colonels and navy captains. One colonel remarked, "You know, I have been told by my colleagues from *Conversatorios* last year that I shouldn't listen to your talks, because I may be convinced by your ideas." Again, there was nervous laughter. The success of this gradual broadening of the discussion in the *Conversatorios* would generate a significant advance in a *Conversatorio* in 2008 when officers met with a former guerrilla commander who had just recently left the ELN.

Between 2010 and 2012, with the election of President Santos, I decided, in consultation with my associates, to focus on the bills that Congress was debating, one of which became the new Law on Victims and the Restitution of Land. I invited congressional representatives who wrote these laws and members of the United Nations Development Program (UNDP) team in Bogotá to discuss their report on land distribution in Colombia.[50]

By 2006, as the number of officers who participated in the three *Conversatorios* each year multiplied, we started to see a ripple effect: an *expectation* on the part of each new group that they would participate in these discussions, which allowed me to open each new year by asking them what they would like to discuss and with whom. There was a growing desire to have more engagement with a broader selection of participants and themes and to meet with those who held key positions in government— whom, they admitted, they normally would have little or no chance to meet in such small, off-the-record encounters, including over lunch and dinner during these two and a half days outside of Bogotá. By 2008, these dialogues had become an organic part of the curriculum for colonels who would soon be promoted to generals and admirals, playing a significant role in establishing durable contacts with different sectors of civil society. As they gradually progressed, there was a noticeable easing of officers' resistance to the perspectives of those they originally had believed to be fundamentally antagonistic to their own and their institution's interests. Veterans of past *Conversatorios* were able to converse fluently with members of different sectors, and they readily served as mediators between new, more nervous and standoffish officers and their similarly nervous civilian counterparts.[51]

Former guerrillas, leftist politicians, journalists, and human rights lawyers were subject to a similar ripple effect. They came to understand that their own negative prejudgments of the military had been erroneous. Having experienced a kind of ethnographic education, participants overcame their initial predispositions and caricatures of "the other."

Thus, the intention of these dialogues was to instil an openness to dialogue and comfort with and acceptance of difference within a military culture that had been fundamentally distrustful of and at odds with politicians and the elite as a whole, and with "the more progressive and leftist" civilians in particular.

This process of dialogue began to take on its own dynamic, such that if the formal talks broke down, the good relations and connections between parties were not necessarily damaged. This was the case in at least two instances. When President Pastrana called off peace talks in February 2002, a group of officers who were attending one of the first *Conversatorios* held long discussions into the night with the civilian commentators present about what this would mean in terms of the peace and in terms of the war. In the second instance, when talks with the ELN did not resume in late 2007, the *Conversatorio* with officers and an ex-ELN guerrilla not only continued unaffected, but indeed shifted more directly into the theme of negotiations and conflict resolution.

Illustrative Examples of *Conversatorios*

Concurrent with the political debates in Colombia, *Conversatorios* provided a forum in which different themes could be presented in some depth during two and half days of discussions with the participants at a hotel outside of Bogotá. These gatherings were intended to be generative of political debate, analysis, and reflection on a wide range of politically sensitive themes. The following selective descriptions of a number of *Conversatorios* are chosen from the thirteen years of work. They are organized into six themes: land tenure and economic inequities, negotiations with guerrillas, international models for peace, paramilitaries, the ELN peace talks, and negotiations with the FARC at el Caguán. I chose them to provide a sense of the range and depth of the discussions that unfolded over the years and the extent to which, at times, the armed forces and the other participants were introduced to new ideas and realities, and the extent to which there was more or less agreement. Overall, what I saw was a general expansion of the knowledge and horizons of the participants, which provided a better basis for the peace negotiations that would emerge.

Land Tenure and Economic Inequity

In one of the earliest *Conversatorios*, a leading Colombian social economist presented the social and economic disparities of the country. He laid out the costs of the conflict for Colombian society, particularly in terms of poverty, the need for social services, and the expanding military budget.[52] Although the officers were first taken aback by the speaker's long hair and attire ("He is a hippie!"), expecting to be hammered by "a leftist," they were surprised by how much they agreed with the analysis and arguments proffered by him and other speakers. They took copious notes, nodding their heads in agreement at the lack of social services and absence of the state in rural areas, and their discussions with the experts continued over lunch and dinner.

Another *Conversatorio* in 2005 dealt with the causes of the conflict, with an ex-M-19 guerrilla who was then serving as a Polo Democrático parliamentarian. He outlined the historical foundations of the conflict and the nature of agrarian "ruralism," detailing the expulsion of peasants and the concentration of land ownership, the impoverishment of the countryside, and the historical incapacity of the state to implement true agrarian reform. The next participant, an independent official of the mayor's office in Medellín, built on this history by describing how his office had played a decisive role in stopping the violence. He illustrated how the city's culture of illegality included the security forces in the 1980s, which called for "social cleansing": clandestine activities to assassinate petty criminals and delinquents associated with *bandas* in order to control the city. Based on these analyses and perspectives, discussion revolved around the dire poverty in the rural countryside, immigration of the poor to the cities, and the drug economy and its undermining of the capacity of job-creation to keep up with structured underemployment. As the parliamentarian remarked, "The next million dollars which is invested in the armed conflict should be earmarked not for security but for social investment." The officers, who had seen the poverty firsthand, commented on the need for the state to deliver social services to areas abandoned by the state, including poor *barrios* of the major cities, to undercut poverty and violence.

In one *Conversatorio* conducted in 2006 with the economic elite, entitled "The Role of the Private Sector in the Resolution of the Conflict and Post-Conflict," some of the officers voiced anger that this elite was only willing to pay a one-off war tax and little to nothing for social investment.[53] This *Conversatorio* was one of the more difficult in terms of facilitation, and reflected the historical tension between the political and economic elites and active-duty officers, which would manifest itself quite dramatically in 2016.

Conflict Issues: Negotiations with the Guerrillas

One *Conversatorio* in late 2005 centered on the humanitarian initiatives between the FARC and the Uribe government for the exchange of prisoners.[54] With peace and humanitarian initiatives between the Colombian government and the ELN as well as the FARC going on at the time, officers had the opportunity to speak with those involved in the mediation. This was a political period, toward the end of 2005, when the ELN, surprisingly, took the initiative to begin a dialogue in Havana with President Uribe during his reelection campaign. It was an attempt by the ELN to shift from a "military solution" toward the possibility of a negotiated accord, taking advantage of the promising success of the political left and independents with a governorship in Valle de Cauca and mayoralties in Bogotá, Medellín, Pasto, and Bucaramanga. President Uribe's inaugural address on 7 August 2006 took this initiative one step further. "Even at the risk of seeming to contradict his hardline Democratic Security Policy," he was willing to pursue a peace process with the ELN as well as meet with FARC commander Marulanda. He offered amnesties and pardons—all withdrawn when a car bomb attributed to the FARC exploded on the grounds of the Cantón Norte military base in Bogotá on 19 October 2006.[55]

Thus, this *Conversatorio* took place during "rumors" of potential negotiations with the ELN and humanitarian gestures for the recovery of the hostages held by the FARC—all of which starkly illustrated how the politics in Colombia do not fit into "black and white" categories, even under a hardline presidency. The participants in this *Conversatorio* included a Catholic bishop, an ex-minister with strong mediation experience with the FARC, a former M-19 guerrilla and now parliamentarian, a political analyst of security affairs, and the spokeswoman for the relatives of those kidnapped by (and who at the time remained in the hands of) the FARC. This *Conversatorio* entailed two parts. First, a discussion of a provision in the juridical framework of the special accords on humanitarian exchange in light of article 3 of the four Geneva Conventions. In these presentations, it was made clear that a humanitarian exchange has no juridical obstacles given that Colombia is a signatory of the Conventions and the Additional Protocols. Second, a discussion of the advantages and disadvantages in political and military terms for the state on the one hand, and the FARC guerrillas on the other, to enter into such an accord. There were presentations by the invited participants and a great deal of discussion, with two representatives in particular emphasizing the political nature of these initiatives and the need to reflect upon the armed forces' own constructive role in such processes.

Lessons Learned from International and National Peace Processes: El Salvador

Peace and post-conflict were the themes, selected by the CAEM officers themselves, to be discussed in the 2006 *Conversatorios*. They expressed the desire to base the discussions on several questions. How to make peace? What should be the social programs for peace? In what ways will the private sector support the post-conflict situation and overcome poverty? As such, one of the three *Conversatorios* focused on "Conflict, Negotiations and Post-Conflict in El Salvador: Lessons for Colombia" in an attempt to provide the officers with an opportunity to learn from other peace processes, with special attention paid to the participation of the armed forces in El Salvador.

Several high-level civilians participated: the former foreign minister of Colombia, who had served as director of the UN Mission in El Salvador, a Colombian social scientist and professor who had written on transitional justice and post-conflict scenarios, and a professor and ex-security consultant to President César Gaviria who had written on the Colombian armed forces and their role in the post-conflict situation. There was discussion about the challenges to a state of law posed by a transitional process that seeks reconciliation and a balance between peace negotiations and demands for justice. In addition, there was a discussion about the need for a major effort on the part of the armed forces to confront the challenge that peace negotiations and post-conflict settlements bring in terms of insecurity, especially with the demobilization of the *maras* in El Salvador.

It was suggested that the lessons from other peace processes could be applied to the ELN peace talks ongoing in Havana at the time, and a discussion ensued about negotiating peace in Colombia in the midst of the conflict without a ceasefire.[56] The conversation between the officers and the invited speakers focused on how the war in Colombia had been increasingly debilitating for all of the actors: for the guerrillas, for the paramilitaries, and for the armed forces. The professor suggested this was a conflict with a "horizontal characteristic": a confrontation of all actors with all others, in which there had been a surfeit of irregularities of war. This reality, another speaker suggested, had to be taken into account so as to apply the international standards of justice, but this did not imply total impunity. The debate about the characteristics of the conflict was quite animated, and the officers participated in a very active manner by bringing in examples from their own combat experience, arguing, questioning, and disputing the issues within an ambiance of trust.

Talks with Paramilitaries

In a 2007 *Conversatorio* entitled "Reflections about the Peace Processes in Colombia," two Colombian academics presented critical analyses of the partial demobilization process of paramilitaries adopted by the Uribe government.[57] Paramilitaries in Colombia, they explained, morphed from a punitive force of cattle ranchers and narcotraffickers to become part of the control mechanisms used by regional governments for territorial expansion over terrified populations. Their violent actions coexist with elected government in what has been called a "democratisation of violence."[58] Given this complexity, the presenters indicated the difficulties of dealing with such groups without a coherent state policy regarding disarmament and demobilization. They also identified the dangers represented in various areas of the country by the rearming of "new bands at the service of drug trafficking" with some of the same characteristics of the paramilitaries but "without the same attitude of counterinsurgency. It was unclear, they said, whether this was a "third generation" of paramilitaries or just drug traffickers. Several officers offered their own field experiences and worries, which coincided with the presenters' observations as to the relative "success" of these talks with paramilitaries and drug gangs, and the grave implications of these new "bands" for the escalation of conflict in their zones. As evidenced by their questions, the officers were deeply involved in trying to understand the complex implications of this analysis for the success of their military strategies against such an economic behemoth.

The ELN Peace Talks

While ex-guerrillas and officers in the *Conversatorios* made small but significant connections with regard to lessons learned in peace processes, there was still a sense among some officers that the guerrillas were unapproachable. Hence, in a 2008 *Conversatorio* entitled "Visions of Peace," I took a leap of faith and provided officers an opportunity to speak with a former high-ranking guerrilla who had recently voluntarily left the ELN. When the director of the War College learned who would be participating, he cancelled his other plans and flew with the group to the event for the full two and a half days at an *hacienda* near Medellín.

The evening began with a wine reception before dinner, and at my request this ex-guerrilla, with his long beard and glasses, reflected on his decision to leave the movement and his belief in the urgent necessity to conclude the Colombian conflict as quickly as possible through a negotiated political settlement. The officers were spellbound. In the morning, after breakfast, he spoke of the ineffectiveness and inappropriateness in the twenty-first century of armed struggle as a path for transforming Colombian society. Despite the military victories the armed forces were continuing to have against the guerrilleros—especially the FARC—without dialogues about a peaceful settlement, he averred, the country would begin to transition toward a new cycle of escalated violence. This would be fed by strategic alliances between the guerrilleros and narcos to protect drug transshipment routes and further monopolize the ownership of mega-projects for agrarian exploitation of energy, minerals, and water. Peace negotiations needed to be prioritized, he emphasized, if the necessary degree of economic justice and peace were to be realized.

A discussion ensued as to how both sides "constructed their views of the enemy." The former *guerrillero* asked the officers, "Who precisely is the enemy?" For the guerrillas in the rural countryside, there are two kinds of enemy: the rich (the landowners) and the security forces (police and military). But what you see as the enemy is not really the "enemy," only *los imaginarios del enemigo*—the imaginings of the enemy who you really don't ever know. These imaginings have led each side to place insurmountable barriers in the way of discussion and reconciliation, based not on material reality but on mental constructions.

Officers were extremely attentive throughout the *Conversatorio*, and especially when this ex-guerrilla raised the question toward the end of the two and half days, "If other countries have been able to negotiate an end to their conflicts, why not Colombia? If the old formulas to negotiate have failed, new approaches with both guerrilla groups could and should be undertaken to end the violence."

The urgency of these officers' questions indicated a desire on the part of many of these generals-to-be for a negotiated end to the conflict: "How does one negotiate with the ELN? With the FARC?" they asked him. "How does one end all this violence?" But what the officers expressed quietly to me during these two days was, "We *never* thought we would have this opportunity in our lifetime to meet with [such a prominent *guerrillero*] and meet with him, face to face. *Never, never!*" For the *guerrillero*, too, it was "very eye-opening" to speak with high-ranking officers on an informal, *non-confrontational* basis about the different possibilities for negotiating peace. Each side expressed surprise at how open the other side was to negotiations.

Yet when it came time to take photos with this guerrilla, a number of officers backed away. For some, *el tabú*, especially over the Internet, still prevailed, and they feared how this might affect their careers. Nonetheless, others were enthusiastically open: one colonel, whom I would visit in the field two years later, told me that based on this "extraordinary meeting," he had attempted to organize his own *Conversatorios* with cattle ranchers and members of civil society about local problems, with very mixed results.

The Talks with the FARC at San Vicente del Caguán: A View from the Peace Commissioner

In early 2012, a *Conversatorio* was organized under the title "Towards a Negotiation: Lessons from the Process at el Caguán." The intention was to gain insight into the lessons learned from past peace talks. To this end I encouraged Peace Commissioner Camilo Gomez to participate in a critical discussion with the officers to address a series of questions: How does one negotiate? What is negotiated? What are the conditions, strategies, and political/military/international climate for negotiating? Should one negotiate a bilateral ceasefire? What type and for how long? Should it be at various locations or a concentration of forces for which one would need a *zona*? Do you utilize a third party for verification? Must a ceasefire preempt talks? Does a ceasefire imply military defeat?

At the beginning, officers readily admitted they had felt "deceived" by the FARC and had had little faith in the government negotiations during President Pastrana's tenure. But towards the end of the two and a half days of discussion, they said they came to appreciate, by trying to answer these questions, how very difficult negotiations are.

A Shift in Mindset

Over time, one could sense a shift in the *Conversatorios*. The more moderate officers were more questioning and, as General Tapias had hoped, increasingly open to negotiations with the FARC as the way to end the conflict. Over the years, one sensed this silent minority becoming more of a vocal majority. However, it is also clear that there remained, and remain today, officers—mostly older colonels from the more hardline *tendencia* primarily but not only from army intelligence—who still hold to the Cold War ideas that negotiations are equivalent to military defeat, who still refuse to consider the possibility of dialogue with *la guerrilla*, and who still harbor deep suspicions and *tabús* about "the left." My later work on more than twenty Ceasefire Seminars-Workshops with the Technical Sub-Commission and the new Comando Estratégico de Transición between 2013 and 2016 provided me the opportunity to gain a better sense of the new and younger generation of navy, police, army, and air force intelligence officers who would work with the FARC in Havana on the architecture and implementation of the ceasefire, and who are slowly replacing these hardliners and their *tabús*.

Conversatorios with Generals, 2009–12

As the CAEM colonels who had participated in the *Conversatorios* were being promoted over the years to brigade and division generals, and then moved up into the High Command, a new threshold for the Skilling for Peace Project was reached when, in 2009, the chief of the armed forces (who had participated in the first *Conversatorios* in 2002) requested I provide *Conversatorios* for "my sixty-eight generals and admirals as well as the High Command." I suggested that the first two *Conversatorios* for the sixty-eight officers (who were divided into two smaller groups of thirty-four for easier discussion) could serve as a venue in which the officers could meet with high-profile presidential candidates regarding their visions of "Security, Human Rights and Peace." This was the first time dialogues had been held between the security forces and presidential candidates, among whom were several congressional representatives of left-wing and liberal parties. In a country so long afflicted by armed conflict, the relationship between these parties and the armed forces has been characterized by serious mutual recrimination and distrust. The left and liberal parties have viewed "la Fuerza Publica"[59] as a source of human rights violations and political crimes—as well as a major obstacle to their coming to power. For the military and police, the left/liberals have been allied or even complicit with *la guerrilla*, directing a juridical and political war internationally against Colombia and against the armed forces.

This frank dialogue included critical discussions of human rights violations, the successes and failures of President Uribe's democratic security policy, and the urgent need to negotiate with the guerrillas. At one point, a left candidate asked the generals and admirals whether the armed forces would respect and comply with a democratically elected left government; a number of the officers asked in turn if the left "considered the current military and police class as legitimate"? Based on affirmative responses from each side, an interesting exchange of viewpoints occurred later as to how to resolve the conflict. There were also very frank criticisms by a number of the candidates regarding human rights violations by the security forces and the need to follow international humanitarian law in military operations.

This *Conversatorio* indicated how much trust and access had been developed with high-ranking officers, and how important it was to maintain this trust. With direct access to the entire corps of sixty-eight generals and admirals stationed throughout the country, this remained the only dialogue space where officers could express their concerns with other members of Colombian society.

Moreover, at the request of the admiral (the first to be appointed chief of the armed forces and who had served as a fellow cadet with the now President Santos), three more *Conversatorios* were organized strictly for the five-member High Command: one with the authors of the new UNDP report on the Law of Restitution of Land; another with ten directors of the media concerning "Debates on the Current Reality of the Country"; and one for the High Command to explain to these same directors the Strategy for Security and Peace then being drawn up under President Santos.

Taking the Project in a New Direction, 2012–17

In my discussions about a new series of *Conversatorios* in early 2012, the new director of the War College urgently requested seminars on conflict resolution and international examples of how other militaries were engaged in peace processes. This request was clearly the result of discussions among high-ranking officers about the secret talks with the FARC underway in Havana since February. In March, moreover, representatives from three different sectors—military officers, former guerrillas, and parliamentarians—raised concerns with me about the role of the armed forces in potential negotiations. It became increasingly clear that trust-building dialogues between the armed forces and different sectors of Colombian society to discuss current political issues needed to be broadened to prepare officers for such an eventuality. By August 2012 when the talks became public, even the FARC were demanding active-duty officers be seated at the table in Havana.

Hence, toward the end of 2012 and throughout 2013, my discussions with members of the High Command and several *plenipotenciarios* (negotiators) of the Colombian government delegation led me to take the decision to shift the focus of the *Conversatorios*. At the request of the newly appointed director of the War College, I invited a number of international experts to the *Conversatorio* of 4–6 April 2013, to discuss "International and National Experiences with DDR" in the disarming and demobilizing of insurgent groups in Northern Ireland, Mozambique, and Aceh (Indonesia). It was at this event that colonels were first introduced to the idea of a "dignified exit" for insurgents coupled with the paramount need for a respectful and solemn handing over of weapons to a third party to help ensure the combatants did not feel humiliated and return to war.

In addition, with increasing demands from the Joint Command and the Office of the High Commissioner for Peace to prepare their advisors on ceasefire typologies and the different modalities of monitoring and verification, *Conversatorios* began to parallel Seminars-Workshops that focused increasingly on the empirical and technical elements of a Colombian ceasefire and DDR program that would directly engage the military, police, and civilian advisors. The demand was so great that an intensive four-day course on ceasefires was requested for January 2014 by the director of the War College for the twenty-two CAEM colonels (one police colonel would later join us as a general on the Technical Sub-Commission). Given the advances at the negotiating table, and the demand for more training, the Seminars were able to build on the trust the *Conversatorios* had engendered over the thirteen years; eventually, due to time and funding constraints, the *Conversatorios* were entirely replaced by the Seminars. My decision to shift the focus for these next four years of the peace process proved to be prescient.

FARC-Government Talks, August 2012

With President Santos's official announcement on 29 August 2012 that formal, public negotiations were indeed in progress, with a negotiating team focused on "Six Points on the Route to Peace,"[60] he made it a point to meet with active-duty officers at the Special Forces air base in Tolemaida, as well as with the retired officers associations, to try and head off any forms of resistance (unlike President Pastrana in 2000). He and his defense minister insisted that, contrary to what had occurred at el Caguán, there would be no *despeje,* and that military actions would continue throughout the country during the talks. Santos also appointed two retired officers to the delegation: a former chief of the army, General Mora, and former chief of the National Police, General Naranjo,[61] to provide a voice for *La Fuerza Pública* at the negotiating table. The president emphasized that "we are learning from the errors of the past in order not to repeat them."[62]

High Command Special *Conversatorio*

With this official pronouncement, I was summoned in early September by the newly appointed commander of the armed forces to a meeting with the High Command. He requested that I organize a Special *Conversatorio* in October for his five-member High Command (almost all of whom had participated in the *Conversatorios* as colonels and navy captains), as well as forty officers, entitled "International Experiences of Peace Processes." At this meeting, participants insisted they wanted to learn what roles the military had taken on in these processes, and what this would mean for their institution in the long run. "We know nothing about peace, we are only trained in combat," the general stated frankly to me. I accepted wholeheartedly, but suggested it would be opportune not only to focus on two peace processes in Nepal and El Salvador but also to invite both sides of each process to gain the perspectives of insurgent and military commanders, and what challenges both faced. This idea of inviting insurgent commanders was acceptable to some, but not all, of the High Command at this time.[63]

At the Special *Conversatorio* in October 2012, the Salvadoran and Nepali generals explained that they had each been summoned by their respective governments to arrive directly by helicopter from combat to the negotiation table *without any preparation.* "It took a great deal of time for me to adjust from seeing the Maoists as my hated enemies to my partners in negotiations," remarked the Nepali general. This lack of preparation astonished the Colombian officers, and in many ways facilitated the next steps in preparing themselves, their officers, troops, and their institution in general for the talks, as well as for the implementation of what was finally decided in Havana. It was a complicated period for the armed forces, which had to maintain combat offensives while also preparing for peace.

Ceasefire Seminars-Workshops, 2013–16

Learning of this Special *Conversatorio* for the High Command, General Mora, whom I had met with in 2002, and who now served as part of the government delegation in Havana, suggested he and I organize a breakfast for all of the government negotiators and the international invitees to briefly discuss each of their experiences. Based on this breakfast, and the positive reputation the *Conversatorio* project had long enjoyed at the War College and at the High Command, the negotiators requested that I provide a series of seminars for themselves and their advisory teams on a number of themes in relation to the points of the peace accords in Havana.[64] In particular, they wanted to discuss Point 3, "El Fin del Conflicto": the international options and experiences with ceasefire agreements, with monitoring and verification, as well as how to design a DDR program.

Between early 2013 and mid-2015, fourteen Ceasefire Seminars-Workshops were then organized by me in Bogotá in close collaboration with a Swiss senior mediator for each of the advisory committees of the Joint Command and the Peace Commissioner's Office.[65] International experts were invited to speak about how the Independent International Commission on Decommissioning of the IRA had functioned, the possible modalities for disarmament (referred to as *dejación de armas* by the FARC, based on past Colombian peace processes), arms containment, the different typologies of ceasefires and their protocols, the different structures for monitoring and verification, as well as forms of insurgent-disciplined demobilization, among many other topics. We drew examples from Aceh, Mozambique, Nepal, El Salvador, and Northern Ireland, among many others, but the focus always remained on the nature of the conflict and how to end the war in Colombia. We made it clear there was no "magic" international formula for a successful process; we were presenting "options" to help the Colombians fashion their own ceasefire and DDR to fit the particularities of the Colombian conflict.

An important element included was the concept of DDR-in-peace, which places at the center of its focus preventing the demobilized combatant from once again picking up a gun and joining criminal bands or other guerrilla groups still operating. This "end of the state of war" profile demands a DDR program that provides a dignified exit from the life of combat, and an accompaniment during the most difficult stage when a combatant hands over his or her weapon to a third party, and gradually leaves the structured environment of a chain of command for an individualized new life of constructive employment and family. *Negotiations are not about a humiliating surrender*, we would emphasize.[66] This "exit with dignity" meant that in late 2016 and early 2017, when over eight thousand FARC combatants were moving from their encampments to the twenty-six zones in which to disarm, overseen along the way by police and military, who formed rings of security, they would be treated with respect, and provided medical treatment, food, and housing. This element first met with some resistance among officers and civilian advisors in the Ceasefire Seminars, who were more familiar with the DDR-in-war model, but over time, it was assiduously incorporated into the training, and would impress two Salvadoran monitors of the ceasefire later on.[67]

In August 2014, the two advisory teams were collapsed into one, with President Santos appointing Major General Flórez head of the new Comando Estratégico de Transición, within which the SubComisión Técnica, with nineteen officers and civilians, functioned. Major General Flórez was later accompanied by a coterie of three other generals and one admiral (all of whom had participated in the *Conversatorios* of 2007, 2008, and 2014 as coronels and navy captains). The Sub-Commission was slated to finalize Point 3 with the FARC in Havana.

Between April 2013 and December 2014, an intensification of our work focused on helping the group design a carefully calibrated Colombian bilateral and definitive ceasefire, and a timetable and architecture for zones of disarmament and a modality for demobilization. The model went through at least twenty-eight drafts over an intense several months. These were then presented by the Sub-Commission to the High Command and the presidency, both of which would pass on their edits. Once the Seminar preparation was complete in early 2015, the Sub-Commission arrived in Havana to meet with the FARC commanders.

At the first meeting on 5 March 2015, there was a stiff formality, uneasiness, and much distrust. With a series of confidence-building measures, however, more cordial relations developed, and a bilateral and definitive ceasefire was worked out and signed on 23 June 2016. During this same period—throughout 2015 and into early 2016—Major General Flórez requested that I undertake another series of Seminars to train other military advisors in his Comando Estratégico de Transición (COET) in Bogotá in ceasefire and its implementation.

The Referendum Vote of 2 October 2016

Despite this careful crafting of the ceasefire at the negotiating table, one particular decision imposed by the political elite could have resulted in a terrible failure. When President Santos unilaterally imposed a referendum for 2 October 2016 onto the timetable (apparently on the advice of personal international advisors), the FARC feared disarming beforehand, as had been scheduled; they worried that a negative vote could have left them vulnerable to a new US president's policy towards Colombia, and the possibility of a *santista* government's willingness or incapability to pursue authentic implementation—or worse, a renewed bombing campaign. "They would be rabbits trapped in the headlights," one advisor remarked. Indeed, at that moment, there were several columns of FARC combatants outside their enclaves under the protection of the army. While President

Santos was considering resigning after such a defeat, Timochenko sent a text message to the peace commissioner that "the FARC continue to be willing to proceed towards peace."[68]

With the No vote prevailing, the now Senator Uribe began making hundreds of demands for changes to the original accord, of which President Santos accepted some forty. It was fortuitous that the structures of the ceasefire, signed only four months earlier and of which there were no violations over the subsequent period of thirteen months, could underpin the negotiations while there ensued, as one Colombian advisor surmised, "a battle between the elites." (That same advisor asked, "Who are the spoilers now?") Although they had fought against the referendum in Havana, it was extremely fortuitous that the FARC were willing to accept any changes to the accord, and the final agreement was signed on 24 November 2016.

From War to Peace?

It is no small achievement that the traditional adversaries in this conflict—military officers and guerrillas who had felt the brunt of the combat with high casualty rates, and both of whom had been serious spoilers over the past thirty-two years, especially during the presidency of Pastrana—sat down and jointly wrote a bilateral, definitive ceasefire; traveled together by helicopter to the twenty-six zones to delineate the coordinates and protocols for disarmament and demobilization; coordinated rings of security by the police and military around these zones; maintained radio contact during the movement of eight thousand combatants to these zones, who then handed over their weapons; and established a joint Monitoring and Verification Mission with the United Nations. Right-wing politicians, led by two past presidents who had failed at peace, Pastrana and Uribe, served as spoilers with the No campaign and an attempt to legislatively block implementation of the accord. The security forces' and the FARC's carefully and jointly crafted ceasefire effectively saved Colombia from another peace failure.

In an interview in September 2016, General Flórez summed up his thoughts about being part of this peace process as a soldier:

INTERVIEWER: When President Santos named you the head of the Technical Sub-Commission [in August 2014], what went through your mind?

GEN. FLÓREZ: I thought: would peace be positive for my career, for my life as a military officer? To make peace with a Sub-Commission with a guerrilla I have fought personally? . . . I thought that for me, as a Colombian soldier, and my family, absolutely nothing good would come of it. But for the country, yes. . . . You know that in the past three [peace] processes, combat continued with the FARC. In this process, I didn't have to fire one single shot. With such differences of visions, we of the Sub-Commission achieved consensus, which had seemed impossible. We achieved this with dialogue, we reached an agreement, an understanding between us to construct a bilateral, definitive ceasefire. It represents a commitment to compliance. . . . We must end this war and enter into reconciliation.

INTERVIEWER: How do you respond in one word when I mention the word "guerrilla"?

GEN. FLÓREZ: Colombiano.[69]

Constructively engaging the military and police with civil society in trust-building *Conversatorios* and providing Ceasefire Seminars for advisors for close to seventeen years, I would argue, helped officers deal with the contradiction of waging a war while negotiating a peace, and with moving from annihilation of the enemy to negotiating a structure, timetable, and protocols for a bilateral ceasefire and definitive peace. By initiating colonels and generals into the language of "operational negotiations" in these Ceasefire Seminars, a clear commitment was generated on their part to begin to accept a peace settlement, and to begin to visualize negotiations with the other side.

The hope for the Skilling for Peace Project was, from the beginning, to prevent spoilers from once again stymieing efforts at peace, to generate dialogue with civil society, to end the *tabú* against speaking with ex-guerrillas as well as progressives, and to initiate changes of *mentalité* that would allow for negotiations and put an end to the war. But events suggest much more was accomplished—namely a direct engagement with and commitment to peace by high-ranking, active-duty officers and their military advisors in conjunction with civilian advisors from the Peace Commissioner's Office. This Technical Sub-Commission drafted a Colombian ceasefire and negotiated its details and coordinates with the FARC in Havana, with both sides working on a pedagogy of peace for their own troops. And when the No victory in the 2016 referendum threatened the peace talks with collapse, both sides worked together to make certain that the ceasefire held, with no violations. By virtue of these commitments, it is my firm belief that these *Conversatorios* and Ceasefire Seminars accomplished what I had hoped they would. And they underscore two important elements that are too often ignored in these processes: how central ceasefires and DDR programs are to the success of peace processes; and the need to prepare the armed forces for a ceasefire by shifting them away from a demand for a humiliating surrender to a faith in the value of working together with the insurgency.

More recent attempts at peace negotiations with the ELN provide interesting insights into the possibility of further gains. In January 2017, the same general who headed COET and the Technical Sub-Commission requested that I urgently organize new Ceasefire Seminars to parallel the peace talks with the ELN in Quito, Ecuador. Four Seminars were undertaken between January and August 2017 to complement the work of the government delegation, which included two retired army generals. There was also an effort to acquaint the ELN delegation with potential ceasefire models and protocols, which had to be, in their minds, "very different from that of the FARC." A three-month bilateral ceasefire was negotiated in September 2017, but because of violence on the part of two ELN commanders, this was suspended after January 2018.

In the lead-up to the presidential elections of May 2018, President Santos tried to accelerate the talks, calling in three "advisors" in November 2017, which unfortunately led to the resignation of the peace commissioner and many in his original delegation, further stalling the process. With a new delegation, talks in Havana continued to the end of Santos's tenure.

Despite these procedural difficulties, the urgency with which the military sought to continue its preparations for the talks with this second guerrilla group indicates the continuation of a strong commitment to the peace effort on the part of the armed forces. As one officer who had been part of the earlier Technical Sub-Commission commented to me in late 2017, "If we can bring the ELN on board, then we would be able to put an end to the guerrilla epoch in Colombia!"

The 2018 Presidential Election

As this chapter goes to press, Iván Duque, the *uribista* candidate for Centro Democrático, has won the second round of the 2018 presidential elections against Bogotá mayor and ex-M-19 member Gustavo Petro, with Duque securing 50.87 percent of the vote and Petro 46.42. Despite a victory for anti-peace *uribistas* under Duque, many analysts are hailing this election as the largest vote for a leftist candidate in Colombian history, with more voters choosing pro-peace candidates than those critical of the accords.[70]

Nonetheless, Duque is a fierce critic of the peace accords. It is likely he will seek changes in details of the accord and withdraw funding for its implementation. Instead of the promised restitution of land and reparations for victims, it is believed he will likely promote rural development for extractive industry and favor large landowners. He may even prohibit the FARC from taking their seats in Congress, even though this was an essential part of the negotiated accords, once they had disarmed. Moreover, it is unclear if he will continue the peace talks with the ELN guerrilla group in Havana, or what his presidency means for the security forces, especially those officers whose openness to dialogue with the FARC was essential for a successful end to the conflict.[71] It is expected this new government will bring in an entirely new High Command with promotions of more hardline officers, who would be very different from those promoted by President Santos.

Narco-paramilitary spoilers are increasing their dirty war in the first weeks of the Duque presidency, with five systematic assassinations of rural social leaders and demobilized FARC guerrillas in the demilitarized zones—a situation that has grown increasingly grave since 1 January 2016, with a total of 311 leaders assassinated.[72] Is this escalation of violence an indication narco-paramilitaries will continue to serve as serious spoilers, as in every other process in the past?

Notwithstanding all that may happen, what this small, low-profile project illustrates is that with the appropriate venue and form, it is possible to create dialogues that can help to shift spoiler narratives. Such *Conversatorios* and Seminars have led, and may continue to lead, to the discovery that quite a significant number of military officers, political representatives, and former guerrillas are more than willing to engage in meaningful dialogue on how to build peace together and to potentially change the historical narratives, *mentalités*, and institutions of which they are a part. But more than that, they are also willing to go further—to put their careers on the line, if necessary, to bring about an agreement with the other side. What this account demonstrates is that over the long term, the very possibility of the military and the guerrillas dismantling *tabús* and working together to make certain a ceasefire is carefully crafted and fully implemented—indeed, rescuing the process at a time of crisis and potential failure—roundly refutes the image of Colombia, and of Latin America in general, as inexorably and intractably violent.

Notes

1. Carlo Nasi, "Spoilers in Colombia: Actors and Strategies," in *Challenges to Peacebuilding: Managing Spoilers during Conflict Resolution*, ed. Edward Newman and Oliver Richmond (Tokyo: UN University Press, 2006), 219.

2. Stephen Steadman, "Spoiler problems in peace processes," *International Security* 22, no. 2 (1997): 5.

3. Nasi, "Spoilers in Colombia," 227 and 237.

4. Demobilizations of M-19, EPL, CRS, PRT, and MAQL rebels.

5. Col. (retired) Carlos Velázquez, "Las fuerzas militares en la búsqueda de la paz con las FARC," Working Paper No. 7, Fundación Ideas para la Paz (June 2011): 16.

6. Nasi, "Spoilers in Colombia," 227 and 237.

7. Nasi, "Spoilers in Colombia," 237.

8. Velásquez's analysis of the armed forces in the peace process implemented by Barco differs quite decidedly from Nasi's. See Nasi, "Spoilers in Colombia," 17.

9. Velásquez, *Las fuerzas militares*, 22.

10 Ironically, Bedoya included at this time the new term "narco-guerrilla" to describe the FARC and the *cocaleros*, reflecting the "hyper-narcoticized" language of the DEA, while the military served a government that had received drug monies from the Cali Cartel for its political campaign, as Velasquez points out. See Velasquez, *Las fuerzas militares*, 23.

11 León Valencia, cited in Nasi, "Spoilers in Colombia," n45.

12 General Fernando Tapias, interview by Cecilia Orozco, *Y Ahora Que?*, 2002, 38; General Fernando Tapias, interview with author, 2 March 2009.

13 The 18,000-member FARC demanded a demilitarized zone the size of Switzerland within which to hold talks. Within this zone, the FARC were holding hundreds of captured military and police officers, together with kidnapped civilians and politicians. Andrés Pastrana, *La Palabra Bajo Fuego* (Bogotá: Planeta, 2005), 92; General Fernando Tapias, interview with author, 2 March 2009.

14 Col. (retired) Carlos Velázquez, interview with author, 24 November 2008. Nasi's data from the Defense Ministry shows that during Pastrana's administration, the armed forces fought against the guerrilla far more intensely than against paramilitary groups. See Nasi, "Spoilers in Colombia," 235.

15 Velázquez, *Las fuerzas militares*, 20.

16 Personal communication with Camilo Gómez, 22 September 2011, as well as several other conversations in 2012. Gómez complained that "the High Command did not allow me to meet with the generals at the time"; author's conversations with staff at the presidency in late 2001 and early 2002. The concern over preparing and calming the anxieties of the armed forces with briefings arose several times in meetings between generals and President Pastrana, one of whom noted that the president had met more often with FARC leader Marulanda than with his own generals. See Tellez and Sanchez, *Ruido de Sables*, 317, and 292–329. For more general background on the Colombian armed forces, see Francisco Leal, *El Oficio de la Guerra* (Bogotá: IEPRI, 1994), and Andrés Dávila, *El Juego del Poder* (Bogotá: Uniandes/CEREC, 1998).

17 Téllez and Sánchez, *Ruido de Sables*, 337. This incident occurred during one of the first *Conversatorios*, referred to later on.

18 See Gustavo Duncan, *Los señores de la guerra* (Bogotá: Planeta, 2006), and Mauricio Romero, *Paramilitares y autodefensaas 1982–2003* (Bogotá: IEPRI, 2003).

19 León Valencia, "The ELN's Halting Moves Toward Peace," in *Colombia: Building Peace in a Time of War,* ed. Virginia Bouvier (Washington, DC: USIP, 2009), 108. There were also differences between 2 generals, the president, and the peace commissioner when the ELN kidnapped 60 persons in September 2000, and in response, FUDRA (Fuerza de Despliegue Rápida) troops killed 17 guerrillas and held territory so that the hostages were deprived of medical treatment. In the end, the hostages were released, and one general was sacked. See Téllez and Sánchez, *Ruido de Sables,* 325–6.

20 Nasi, "Spoilers in Colombia," 235.

21 General Tapias, interview with author, 2 March 2009.

22 Col. (retired) Carlos Velásquez's excellent historical overview of the armed forces' very unstable collaboration with civilian presidents' attempts at peace in Colombia suggests a number of these questions. See *Las fuerzas militares*, 16.

23 Velásquez, *Las fuerzas militares*, 21.

24 Tapias, interview with author, 2 March 2009.

25 The FARC had demanded the total withdrawal of troops from the barracks at the Batallón de Cazadores in San Vicente del Cagúan, as well as the withdrawal of the staff at the Public Prosecutor's Office in this *zona de distension*. The guerrillas' insistence on territorial use during talks is not new in the history of Colombia. See León Valencia, *Adiós a la Politica, Bienvenidos a la Guerra* (Bogotá: Intermedio Editores, 2002), 35 and 38.

26 Comment by army general to author, anonymous, 18 February 2012

27 Velásquez, *Las fuerzas militares*, 22.

28 See Valencia, "The ELN's Halting Moves," 108.

29 "Declaraciones de Alfonso Cano," 30 July 2012; Marc Chernick, "The FARC at the Negotiating Table," in *Building Peace in a Time of War*, ed. V. Bouvier (Washington, DC: USIP, 2009).

30 Comment by army colonel, anonymous, 22 February 2002. Emphasis is his, indicating a lack of distrust in everyone, including the political elite.

31 León Valencia, Luis Eduardo Celis, Joe Broderick, Fernando Hernandez, and Antonio Sanguino, *El regreso de los rebeldes: De la Furia de las armas a los pactos, la crítica y la esperanza* (Bogotá: Corporación Nuevo Arco Iris, 2005), 20. Curiously, given the ELN's closer connections to social movements and trade unions, the officers believed a loss of political legitimacy would be very much less costly for this insurgency group than for the FARC.

32 Comment by army colonel, anonymous, 12 September 2008.

33 León Valencia is a former ELN guerrilla who led the dissident group Corriente de Renovación Socialista (CRS) in taking the decision to demobilize under President Gaviria, a novelist, and former *Semana* columnist. Alberto Lara is a human rights lawyer.

34 All *Conversatorios* over thirteen years were generously funded by the Norwegian Foreign Ministry, with the exception of the High Command Special *Conversatorio* in October 2012, whose costs were shared with the Swiss Embassy in Bogotá. In addition, the Swedish Embassy in Bogotá generously funded numerous Seminars on Human Rights and International Humanitarian Law between 2004 and 2006 as well as four Ceasefire Seminars in 2017. Finally, the Swiss Embassy and Swiss Federal Department of Foreign Affairs very generously funded part of the 2012 Special *Conversatorio*, as well as over twenty Ceasefire Seminars between 2013 and 2016.

35 Velásquez, *"Las fuerzas militares*, 29.

36 Army general, anonymous interview with author, 18 February 2008.

37 Velásquez, *"Las fuerzas militares*, 30.

38 US air force colonel, interview with author, Bogotá, 21 November 2008.

39 At a talk at Harvard on 20 September 2017, Santos explained his decision by saying that he had been informed that Cano was not interested in peace talks. In an earlier interview with Jon Lee Anderson, he stated, according to Anderson's paraphrase, " 'We had begun our talks with the FARC and I didn't want to ruin them. . . . And it worked out.' If the FARC commanders were talking, it must be because they were weakened by the strikes, and Cano's death wouldn't change that; it could even help." See Jon Lee Anderson, "Colombian guerrillas come out of the jungle," *New Yorker*, 1 May 2017.

40 "Démosle una oportunidad a la paz: Timochenko" *Semana* (Bogotá), 30 January 2016.

41 "Pregunta Yamid," *Semana TV*, 7 September 2017.

42 General Mejía, "Panel de Paz: Colombia 2040," Colombian Student Conference, Harvard University and MIT, 2 May 2018. Comparative figures for the FARC are difficult to obtain.

43 Sergio Jaramillo, "Transition in Colombia" (lecture at Externado Universidad, 9 May 2013).

44 See Marco Palacios and Frank Safford, *Colombia: País Fragmentado, sociedad dividida* (Bogotá: Norma, 2002).

45 General Tapias, interview with author, 2 March 2009.

46 Army colonel, comment to author, anonymous, 6 April 2005. Such infiltration (posing, for example, as soldiers) and buying information was known by the military to be an integral part of the FARC's strategy at least since 1982. See Juan Estéban Ugarriza and Nathalie Pabón Ayala, *Militares y guerrillas: la memoria histórica del conflicto armado en Colombia desde los archivos militares, 1958-2016* (Bogotá: Editorial Universidad del Rosario, 2017), 134, passim.

47 This social distance also holds between the police and the military, with only a handful of "cross force" couples.

48 For example, *los indignados* was a new political movement of greens, progressives, liberals, and ex-Polo Democrático Alternativo (the first new left-center political party formed in 2003), that arose in August 2012, among whose members included an ex-M-19 guerrilla. See "Los 'indignados' que se dieron cita en Ríonegro," *Semana* (Bogotá), 12 August 2012.

49 Indeed, while the term "former guerrilla" is used in this chapter to describe those guerrillas who recently left the movement as well as those who left as a result of the accords worked out with the Barco and Gaviria governments in order to recognize differences of views internal to the insurgency movements, military officers as a general rule did not make this distinction. Their mindset is that once a guerrilla, always a guerrilla, even if she/he "claims" to have left the movement due to ideological differences.

50 See *Quinto Informe Nacional de Desarrollo Humano de la Tierra al Territorio: Hacia el Desarrollo Humano Rural en Colombia*, PNUD, 16 September 2010.

51 It was usual for generals in whose jurisdiction a *Conversatorio* was being held, to be invited to the reception and dinner the first night of the event. They often participated in long discussions with both military and civilian participants.

52 For background, see Luis Jorge Garay, ed., *Repensar a Colombia: Hacia un Nuevo Contrato Social* (Bogotá: Agenda Colombiana de Cooperación Internacional y PNUD, 2002).

53 The first and one-off "security tax" was levied from a small number of wealthy individuals and large corporations shortly after President Uribe took office in 2002. At a meeting in Cartagena with Bill Clinton in the late 2000s, the elites were told that if they wanted to win the war, they had to pay with money and blood. That is, pay more taxes and go to the front in combat. "And as the rich don't want to pay taxes and don't want to fight, they are trying to resolve the war with professional soldiers." See "La Guerra se puede acabar: Entrevista con Marco Palacios," *Semana* (Bogotá), 12 August 2012.

54 For a chronology of humanitarian agreements and prisoner exchanges between 2002 and 2007, see "Boletines de Paz: El acuerdo humanitario y las posibilidades de un proceso de paz," Fundación Ideas para la Paz.

55 Valencia, "The ELN's Halting Moves," 95.

56 Several authors have raised this issue, presuming that one must come before the other. However, as Luc Chounet-Cambas's study points out, the Salvadoran *guerrilleros* held out until the last meeting for such a ceasefire, once their demands for political reforms were met. See Luc Chounet-Cambas, "La negociación del alto el fuego. Problemas y opciones para los mediadores," *Serie Prácticas de Mediación #3* (Geneva: Centro para el Diálogo Humanitario, March 2011).

57 Between 1998 and 1999 alone, massacres by the paramilitaries in different areas of the country increased by 71 percent, with the number of victims increasing 36 percent; see Velásquez, "*Las fuerzas militares*, 171. On paramilitarism, see Mauricio Aranguren Molina, *Mi Confesión. Carlos Castano revela sus secretos* (Bogotá: Editorial Oveja Negra, 2001).

58 Francisco Gutiérrez y Mauricio Barón, "Re-Stating the State: Paramilitary Territorial Control and Political Order in Colombia (1978–2004)," *LSE Working Paper No. 66*, Crisis States Programme, September 2005.

59 The term "la Fuerza Pública" (public force) includes both the armed forces and the police.

60 "Los seis puntos de la 'hoja de ruta' de la paz," *Semana* (Bogotá), 29 August 2012.

61 General Mora had authorized and supported the participation of twenty-two colonels in the first *Conversatorio* in February 2002; the chief of police had participated in one *Conversatorio* in 2002.

62 "Acercamientos Gobierno-FARC: por qué no es el Caguán," *Semana* (Bogotá), 1 September 2012.

63 Funding for half of the Special *Conversatorio* in 2012 as well as for all fourteen Ceasefire Seminars for the SubComisión Técnica between 2013 and 2015, in addition to another series of seminars for the Comando Estratégico de Transición in 2015–16 was

64 generously provided by the Swiss Embassy in Bogotá and the Swiss Federal Department of Foreign Affairs.

64 Ultimately, the Norwegian Special Envoy to Colombia rejected the government delegation's request to hold the Seminars in Havana; he also declined to share the costs. Subsequently, Seminars-Workshops for the delegation's advisors were organized in Bogotá, entirely funded by the Swiss Federal Department of Foreign Affairs.

65 Julian Thomas Hottinger, a senior mediator at the Swiss Federal Department of Foreign Affairs, has been involved in the negotiations of various ceasefires throughout the world.

66 This is in contrast to DDR-in-war, one of the central elements of counterinsurgency programs used by armed forces around the world since the US war in Vietnam. In Colombia, it had been set up as a campaign (through radio advertising, among other methods) to encourage the desertion and surrender referred to as the "demobilization and reinsertion" of guerrillas. Its major purpose was to provide military intelligence with access to the internal workings of the FARC and ELN and their leaders for combat and bombing purposes.

67 Salvadoran ambassador to Colombia, personal communication, 23 May 2017.

68 María Jimena Duzán, "La noche de las lágrimas: un capítulo del nuevo libro de María Jimena Duzán," *Semana* (Bogotá), 14 July 2018.

69 "Pregunta Yamid" *Semana TV*, 7 September 2017.

70 The independent former mayor of Medellín and governor of Antioquia, Sergio Fajardo, matched Petro in the first round, with 24 percent, and former negotiator Humberto de la Calle brought in 2 percent of the vote.

71 ACORE, the Colombian Association Retired Officers, which supported Duque's candidacy and has always opposed the peace process with the FARC, was publicly very critical of the active-duty officers negotiating in Havana, especially General Flórez.

72 Defensoría del Pueblo report, cited in "Imelda Daza considera volver al exilio ante ola de violencia contra líderes sociales," *El Espectador* (Bogotá), 6 July 2018; see Nasi, "Spoilers in Colombia," 235.

CONTRIBUTORS

MICHELLE D. BONNER is professor of political science at the University of Victoria. Among other books, she is the author of *Policing Protest in Argentina and Chile* (2014), which was awarded the Canadian Political Science Association's 2015–16 Comparative Politics Book Prize, and is now available in Spanish. She is also the coeditor of *Police Abuse in Contemporary Democracies* (2018), as well as the author of many articles. She is currently working on a book manuscript on the role of media in punitive populism. She has been publishing on issues pertaining to democracy and police violence for many years, which she views through the lens of protest policing, punitive populism, media, transitional justice, and discourse.

ANDREAS E. FELDMANN is associate professor in the Latin American and Latino Studies Program and Department of Political Science and principal investigator of the Global Immigration Cluster Initiative at the University of Illinois at Chicago. He investigates topics in the intersection of comparative politics and international relations with a focus on Latin America. His research interests include forced migration, political violence and terrorism, human rights, and South-South cooperation. He is the author of *New Migration Patterns in the Americas: Challenges for the 21st Century* (2018) and has published articles in various journals, including *Politics and Society, Terrorism and Political Violence, Studies in Conflict and Terrorism, Third World Quarterly, Forced Migration Review*, and *Latin American Politics and Society*, among others. Dr. Feldmann has worked as a consultant of the International Development Research Centre, the Carnegie Endowment for International Peace, the United Nations High Commissioner for Refugees, and has served as assistant to the Special Rapporteur on Migrant Workers and Members of their Families of the Inter-American Commission of Human Rights (2000-6). He previously worked at the Instituto de Ciencia Política of the Universidad Católica de Chile (2005-14) and the Human Rights Program of the University of Chicago (2003-5). He earned a PhD in political science at the University of Notre Dame.

FRANCISCO GUTIÉRREZ SANÍN is one of the leading experts on the intersections between politics and violence in Latin America. He studied anthropology at the Universidad de los Andes in Colombia and earned a PhD in political science from the University of Warsaw. He is a researcher at the prestigious Institute of Political Studies and International Relations at the Universidad Nacional de Colombia. He is also currently a columnist for *El Espectador* (Bogotá) and heads the Observatory on Land Restitution, created to monitor the process of returning land to farmers. Some of his recent publications include "What Should We Mean by 'Pattern of Political Violence'? Repertoire, Targeting, Frequency, and Technique," *Perspectives on Politics* 15, no. 1 (2017): 20–41 (coauthored with Elizabeth Wood); "Agrarian Elite Participation in Colombia's Civil War," *Journal of Agrarian Change* 17, no. 4 (2017): 739–48 (coauthored with Jennifer Vargas); and "The FARC's Militaristic Blueprint," *Small Wars and Insurgencies* 29, no. 4 (2018): 629–53.

J. PATRICE MCSHERRY is a professor and researcher currently associated with the Instituto de Estudios Avanzados (Institute for Advanced Studies) of the University of Santiago, Chile, and Long Island University. She holds a PhD in political science from the CUNY Graduate School. A three-time Fulbright Award recipient, she has won various academic honors and grants, including the David Newton Award for Excellence in Teaching, Long Island University (2008) and the Distinguished Alumni Award from the Political Science MA-PhD Program of the Graduate Center, City University of New York (2009). She is the author of *Chilean New Song: The Political Power of Music, 1960s–1973* (2015); *Predatory States: Operation Condor and Covert War in Latin America* (2005), named a Choice Outstanding Academic Title in 2006; *Incomplete Transition: Military Power and Democracy in Argentina* (1997; reissued 2008); and the coeditor (with John Ehrenberg, José Ramón Sánchez, and Caroleen Marji Sayer) of *The Iraq Papers* (2010). She has written numerous articles on the New Song movement, military regimes in Latin America, Operation Condor, the Cold War, and US foreign policy in Latin America. Dr. McSherry has taught courses on these themes as well as on human rights, transitions to democracy, and Latin American politics.

ANTHONY W. PEREIRA is a professor and director of the Brazil Institute at King's College London. He has a BA in politics from Sussex University and an MA and PhD in government from Harvard University. He has held positions at the New School for Social Research, the Fletcher School of Law and Diplomacy, Tulane University, and the University of East Anglia. His books include *Ditadura e Repressão* (2010); (with Lauro Mattei) *The Brazilian Economy Today: Towards a New Socio-Economic Model?* (2015); and (with Jeff Garmany) *Understanding Contemporary Brazil* (2019). Dr. Pereira is currently working on a book on the formation of the Brazilian state. He can be reached at anthony.pereira@kcl.ac.uk.

PABLO PICCATO (BA, Universidad Nacional Autónoma de México, 1989; PhD, University of Texas at Austin, 1997) is professor in the Department of History, Columbia University. His research and teaching focus on modern Mexico, particularly on crime, politics, and culture. He has taught as visiting faculty in universities in Mexico, Argentina, Brazil, and France, and has been director of Columbia's Institute of Latin American Studies, vice chair of the Department of History, and university senator. His books include *City of Suspects: Crime in Mexico City, 1900–1931* (2001), *The Tyranny of Opinion: Honor in the Construction of the Mexican Public Sphere* (2010), and *A History of Infamy: Crime, Truth, and Justice in Mexico* (2017).

PABLO POLICZER is an associate professor of political science and the director of the Latin American Research Centre at the University of Calgary. A specialist in comparative politics, his research focuses on the evolution of violent conflict—especially among armed actors such as militaries, police forces, and nonstate armed groups—in authoritarian and democratic regimes. He held the Canada Research Chair in Latin American Politics (2005–15), at the University of Calgary, and was also an active fellow at the Latin American Research Centre before being appointed director in 2015. His book *The Rise and Fall of Repression in Chile* (2009) was named a *Choice* Outstanding Academic Title by the Association of College and Research Libraries, and won the 2010 award for best book in comparative politics from the Canadian Political Science Association. Dr. Policzer obtained his PhD in political science from the Massachusetts Institute of Technology, and his BA (honours, first class) in political science from the University of British Columbia.

JENNIFER SCHIRMER holds a PhD in political anthropology. She is currently a 2018–21 visiting fellow at the Latin America and Caribbean Centre at the London School of Economics, and an affiliate at the David Rockefeller Center for Latin American Studies at Harvard University. Between 2000 and 2013, she directed a dialogue project that served as a precursor to the peace talks under Colombian president Juan Manuel Santos. In addition, between 2013 and 2016, she organized over twenty-five Seminars to help skill the Technical Sub-Commission for the drafting of a bilateral ceasefire and disarmament and demobilization program for the negotiations in Havana with the FARC. In 2017, she served as an independent consultant to the ELN process. She is currently writing a book on the Colombian peace process. Her book *The Guatemalan Military Project: A Violence Called Democracy* won a PIOOM Human Rights Award. She is the recipient of two John D. and Catherine T. MacArthur Foundation Research and Writing Grants for her research on the insurgency in Guatemala and the relatives of the disappeared in Argentina and Chile.

INDEX

A

Accord among Parties for Democracy. *See Concertación*
acuerdo humanitario, 179. *See also* Chávez, Hugo
Acuña, Jorge, 130. *See also* Carabineros de Chile
Agee, Philip, 55. *See also* CIA
Alarma!, 97. *See also nota roja*
Allende, Salvador, 59, 65
Álvarez Vargas, Víctor Julio, 191
Alvear, Soledad, 125
Amnesty International, 119
anemic states, 30
anticommunism, 54, 58, 79
Anti-Terrorist Statute. *See* Decree 180
Arancibia Clavel, Enrique, 70. *See also* DINA
Árbenz, Jacobo, 59, 62
Archives of Terror, 69
Arellano Félix clan, 95. *See also* drug trafficking
Aristide, Jean-Bertrand, 22–25, 33, 38–39, 41. *See also Chimères*; Fanmi Lavalas
Armée du Nord, 25. *See also* Phillippe, Guy
Attorney's syndrome. *See síndrome de la procuraduría*
AUC (Autodefensas Unidas de Colombia), 204. *See also* paramilitaries
Aylwin, Patricio, 133. *See also* Christian Democratic Party (Chile); *Concertación*

B

Bachelet, Michelle, 10, 122, 124, 127, 130, 134
Barco, Virgilio, 176, 201
Bernales Ramírez, José Alejandro, 128, 131. *See also* Carabineros de Chile
Betancourt, Íngrid, 178–79, 181. *See also* kidnapping in Colombia
Betancur, Belisario, 176
Bolaño, Roberto, 89, 103, 105
Bolivarian Movement, 212. *See also* Chávez, Hugo
Bordaberry, Juan María, 68
Brazilian police, 11, 145; and the 1964–85 military dictatorship, 151; during the first presidency of Getúlio Vargas, 150; in the Old Republic, 150; main historical functions, 150

C

CAEM (Curso de Altos Estudios Militares), 208, 214–15, 222, 227, 230
Cali Cartel, 202, 239n10. *See also* drug trafficking
Candido Mendes University, 151
Cannibal Army, 25
Cano, Alfonso, 211. *See also* FARC
Carabineros de Chile, 10, 84n48, 113, 117; and land disputes, 119; and repression of social protest, 118-120; and social accountability, 122, 124-129, 130-133; and the Interior Ministry (*see* Interior Ministry [Chile]); during the Pinochet regime, 119

249

Cardemil, Alberto, 128. *See also* National Renewal Party (Chile)
Carter administration, 60
Castaño, Carlos, 204. *See also* AUC; paramilitaries
Ceasefire Seminars-Workshops, 200–201, 227, 231
CEDPH (Conselho Estadual de Defesa de Pessoa Humana), 156
Cedras, Raoul, 22, 24, 39
Centre for Studies of Criminality and Public Security. *See* CRISP
Centre for Studies of Security and Citizenship. *See* CESeC
Centre for the Study of Coercive Institutions. *See* NIC
Centre for the Study of Violence. *See* NEV
Centro Democrático, 237. *See also* Duque, Iván; Uribe, Álvaro
Cepeda, Fernando, 187
CESeC (Centro de Estudos de Segurança e Cidadania), 151
Chamblain, Louis-Jodel, 25. *See also* Phillippe, Guy
Chávez, Hugo, 76, 179, 212
chefs de section, 25, 31
Chicago Boys, 117. *See also* Pinochet regime
Chilean coup of 1973, 54, 65, 114, 117, 119, 133, 187. *See also* Allende, Salvador; Pinochet regime
Chilean Criminal Code, 123
Chilean National Police. *See* Carabineros de Chile
Chimères, 24. *See also* Aristide, Jean-Bertrand; Fanmi Lavalas
Christian Democratic Party (Chile), 125
CIA (Central Intelligence Agency), 55, 62–66, 72–73
Clopatofsky, Jairo, 188
COET (Comando Estratégico de Transición), 233, 236
College of Journalists (Chile), 131–32. *See also* Guillier, Alejandro

Colombian Constitution of 1991, 176, 185, 189
Colombian Constitutional Court, 186
Colombian drug cartels, 39. *See also* Cali Cartel; drug trafficking
Colombian kidnappings. *See* kidnapping in Colombia
Colombian peace referendum, 236
Colosio, Luis Donaldo, 102, 110n33. *See also* murder in Mexico
communiqué 002, 181. *See also* FARC
Concertación, 134. *See also* Christian Democratic Party (Chile); Socialist Party of Chile; Party for Democracy (Chile)
Conference of American Armies, 67
Conference of Intelligence Commanders, 68
contempt-for-authority legislation in Chile, 122–23. *See also* Chilean Criminal Code; Law of State Security (Chile)
contingency, 4–5, 7, 9, 19, 27, 35, 80, 147
contingent factors for violence: globalization, 7–8, 21–22, 35–38, 41–42; influencing factors, 37
Contreras, Manuel, 66, 68. *See also* DINA
Convivir, 190–192, 197n54. *See also* Superintendencia de Vigilancia y Seguridad Privada
Coordinating Assembly of Secondary Students (Chile), 122. *See also* Sanhueza, María Jesús
Correa, Rafael, 211
corregedoria, 153, 157–60, 168n55, 169n65. *See also* Brazilian police; Police Ombudsmen
corruption in Haiti, perceptions of, 39
corveé, 30
counterhegemony, 56, 76, 78
counterinsurgency regime, 54–55, 58, 73, 75, 80
Covas, Mario, 157
criminal violence, 1, 3, 5, 89, 96, 104, 171

CRISP (Centro de Estudos de Criminalidade e Segurança Pública), 151
Cuban Revolution, 53, 58, 61. *See also* Guevara, Ernesto (Che)
Curso de Altos Estudios Estratégicos, 200

D

DAS (Departamento Administrativo de Seguridad), 191–92
DDR (disarmament and demobilization programs), 206, 229, 231–32, 236, 243n66
De Quincey, Thomas, 90
DEA (Drug Enforcement Administration), 210, 239n10. *See also* drug trafficking
Decree 180, 176
demilitarized zone, 203, 207, 239n13. *See also* San Vicente del Caguán; *zona de despeje*
democratic security policy, 210, 222, 228
democratization in Haiti, 38
democratization of violence, 224
Dessalines, Jean-Jacques, 30
DIA (Defense Intelligence Agency), 71. *See also* CIA
DINA (Dirección de Inteligencia Nacional, Chile), 66, 68, 70, 84n48, 119. *See also* Contreras, Manuel; DNII; SIDE
DNII (Dirección Nacional de Información e Inteligencia, Uruguay), 63–64. *See also* DINA; SIDE
Document NSC-141, 61
drug trafficking, 76, 89, 91, 102–3, 210–11, 224. *See also* Arellano Félix clan; Cali Cartel; Colombian drug cartels; DEA; Gulf Cartel; Los Zetas
Duque, Iván, 237, 243n71
Duro y directo, 102. *See also nota roja*
Duvalier regime, 21–22, 35, 38–39, 41

E

Echeverri Mejía, Gilberto, 191
economic explanations of violence in Haiti, 33–35
Edwards, Agustín, 123. *See also El Mercurio* (Chile); Fundación Paz Ciudadana
El Mercurio (Chile): as a media conglomerate, 117; as agenda-setting news source, 116; during the Pinochet dictatorship, 117
El Tiempo (Bogotá), 184, 188
ELN (Ejército de Liberación Nacional), 174, 176, 178, 180, 200, 202–4, 207, 216, 218–25, 236–37, 239n19, 240n31, 240n33, 243n66
emancipation in Haiti, 30–31
Embassy of the Dominican Republic, takeover of, 174. *See also* M-19
encapuchados, 126. *See also* Carabineros de Chile; *El Mercurio* (Chile)
EPL (Ejército Popular de Liberación), 176, 202, 238n4
Escalona, Camilo, 125, 132–33. *See also* Socialist Party of Chile
Escuela Superior de Guerra (Colombia). *See* War College
ESMA (Escuela de Mecánica de la Armada), 67. *See also* Orletti Motors; SIDE
Espina, Alberto, 130. *See also* National Renewal Party (Chile)

F

Falklands War, 60
Fanmi Lavalas, 24. *See also* Aristide, Jean-Bertrand; *Chimères*
FARC (Fuerzas Armadas Revolucionarias de Colombia), 13, 174, 176–79, 181, 183, 194n1, 194n15, 200, 202–5, 207–8, 210–13, 217–18, 220–22, 225–27, 229–30, 232–43
Federal University of Minas Gerais, 151
Federal University of Pernambuco, 151
Fifth Summit of the Americas, 146

Index *251*

Ford administration, 71
Foreign Terrorist Organizations (FTOs) list, 210. *See also* FARC; US State Department
Fort Gulick, 63. *See also* Panama Canal Zone; School of the Americas; Special Forces
François, Michel, 22. *See also* Cedras, Raoul
FRAPH (Front Révolutionnaire pour l'Avancement et le Progrès Haïtien), 24
Frente Amplio (Uruguay), 59
Frente Nacional (Colombia), 174
Front de Reconstruction Nationale, 25. *See also* Metayer, Buteur
Front de Resistance du Sud, 25. *See also* chefs de section
Fuentes Alarcón, Jorge Isaac, 72, 84n48. *See also* Rettig Commission (Chile)
Fundación Paz Ciudadana, 123. *See also* Edwards, Agustín

G

Galeano, Eduardo, 146
García Núñez, Sergio, 101
Gavazzo, José, 69–70, 72. *See also* Orletti Motors
Gaviria, César, 177, 190, 201–2, 223, 240n33, 241n49
George W. Bush administration, 77. *See also* War on Terror
Giardi, Guido, 131–32. *See also* Party for Democracy (Chile)
Gómez, Camilo, 204, 209, 226, 239n16. *See also* Office of the High Commissioner for Peace
González Rodríguez, Sergio, 105. *See also* Bolaño, Roberto
Goulart, João, 59
Green Berets, 63. *See also* Special Forces
Guevara, Ernesto (Che), 63. *See also* Cuban Revolution

Guillier, Alejandro, 132–33. *See also* College of Journalists (Chile)
Gulf Cartel, 95. *See also* drug trafficking; Los Zetas

H

Haiti earthquake of 2010, 19, 26
Havana peace talks, 200, 208, 212–13, 221, 223, 227, 229, 231, 233–34, 236–37. *See also* FARC
Henríquez, Héctor, 130–131. *See also* Carabineros de Chile
Huesos en el desierto, 105. *See also* González Rodríguez, Sergio
Human Rights Commission (Chile), 129, 131
Human Rights Watch, 119

I

Ibáñez del Campo, Carlos, 118. *See also* Interior Ministry (Chile)
ICC (International Criminal Court), 77
IMF (International Monetary Fund), 59, 76
Independent Democrat Union (Chile), 130
Independent International Commission on Decommissioning of the IRA, 232
inquérito policial, 151
Instituto São Paulo Contra Violência, 151
Intelligence Advisory Committee (Operation Condor), 72. *See also* CIA; DIA
Inter-American System, 54, 64, 74; Cold War Inter-American Security System, 61; Inter-American Defense Board, 61
intercambio humanitario, 178. *See also* Betancourt, Íngrid
Interior Ministry (Chile), 132–33
internal enemies' doctrine, 54, 61, 64

J

Jara, Osvaldo Ezequiel, 130–31. *See also* Carabineros de Chile
Johnson, Lyndon, 63. *See also* Rostow, Walt

K

kidnapping in Colombia: and the death penalty, 186–88, 196n51; as a political tool against the system, 174; as policing mechanism, 181; by common criminals, 177; formal institutional responses to, 183; in the 1960s, 174; in the 1990s, 176; industrialization of, 174, 180, 183

Kissinger, Henry, 65. See also Nixon, Richard

Krassnoff, Miguel, 72. See also DINA; School of the Americas (SOA)

L

L'Ouverture, Toussaint, 30
La Moneda (palace), 126, 128
La Nación (Buenos Aires), 120
La Prensa (Mexico), 99
La Técnica (Dirección Nacional de Asuntos Técnicos, Paraguay), 63. See also DINA, DNII, SIDE
La Tercera (Santiago), 117
La Violencia, 174
Law 733 (Colombia), 186, 189, 196n42
Law of State Security (Chile), 118, 123
Ley Antisecuestro 40 (Colombia), 185
López Obrador, Andrés Manuel, 105
Los Zetas, 95. See also drug trafficking

M

M-19 (Movimiento 19 de abril), 174–76, 180, 182, 220, 222, 237
Malvinas War. See Falklands War
maras, 223
Margolles, Teresa, 96
Martelly, Michele, 26
Marulanda, Manuel, 222, 239n16. See also FARC
MAS (Muerte a Secuestradores), 175. See also kidnapping in Colombia; M-19

mechanisms, 6–7, 9, 12–14, 21–22, 28, 30, 36, 41, 43, 57, 80, 94, 115, 121–22, 127, 130, 135–36, 145, 147–48, 151–52, 163, 185, 224

Médici, Emílio Garrastazu, 65
Mendoza, Élmer, 103. See also murder in Mexico
Mercado, José Raquel, 174
Metayer, Buteur, 25
Metinides, Enrique, 96
Michelsen, Camila, 180, 182. See also kidnapping in Colombia
Military Code of Justice (Chile), 123
Ministry of Defense (Chile), 132–33, 141n81
Moïse, Jovenel, 26
Montenegro, Luis Enrique, 191–92. See also DAS
murder in Mexico: as public discourse, 89, 91, 96, 100, 102, 104; political meaning of, 100; practices of, 91

N

narcomantas, 103. See also drug trafficking; murder in Mexico
narratives, 96–97, 99, 101, 104, 208, 214, 216, 238
National Renewal Party (Chile), 128
National Security Law (Brazil), 154
NEV (Núcleo de Estudos da Violência), 151, 169
NIC (Núcleo de Estudo das Instituições Coercitivas), 151
Nixon, Richard, 65, 71, 83
nota roja, 9–10, 96–97, 99–100, 102, 104. See also murder in Mexico
Nueva Fuerza Democrática, 202. See also Pastrana, Andrés

O

OAS Resolution 837 of 2003, 188. *See also* kidnapping in Colombia
Obama, Barack, 146
Ochoa, Marta Nieves, 175. *See also* MAS; M-19
Office of the High Commissioner for Peace (Colombia), 229. *See also* Gómez, Camilo
Operación Fénix, 210
Orletti Motors, 67. *See also* ESMA; Krassnoff, Miguel

P

País Libre (foundation), 185, 194n7. *See also* kidnapping in Colombia
Panama Canal Zone, 63, 73. *See also* School of the Americas
Paramilitaries: and American covert operations, 62–63; and kidnapping in Colombia, 12, 172–73, 175–76, 178, 181, 190–93, 196n49, 197n54; and Operation Condor, 66, 71; and the Colombian peace process, 201–4, 209, 217, 220, 223–24, 237–38, 239n14, 242n57; in Haiti, 22, 25, 27, 35, 39, 42; in Mexico, 105
Party for Democracy (Chile), 130–31
Pastrana, Andrés, 177–79, 202–5, 207–10, 219, 226, 230, 234
Perón, Juan, 55, 66
pescas milagrosas, 177, 195n28. *See also* kidnapping in Colombia
Petro, Gustavo, 237, 243n70
Phillippe, Guy, 25
Pinochet regime, 117–19, 141n83
Pinochet, Augusto, 77
pistoleros, 95, 101. *See also* sicarios
Plan Colombia, 203–5
Police Ombudsmen, 146, 150, 160, 168n59
Polo Democrático Alternativo, 217, 220, 241n48

Préval, René, 24, 26
PRI (Partido Revolucionario Institucional), 102
Proyecto de Ley No. 46 (Colombia), 185
Public Security and Information Office (Chile). *See* Public Security Council (Chile)
Public Security Council (Chile), 133
PVP (Partido de la Victoria del Pueblo, Uruguay), 72

Q

Queirolo, Luis, 67. *See also* Conference of American Armies
Quito peace talks, 236. *See also* ELN

R

Ravix, Remissanthe, 25
rentier state, 30, 34
Rettig Commission (Chile), 72
Reyes, Raúl, 211. *See also* FARC
right to self-defense, 191
Rio Pact of 1947 (Inter-American Treaty of Reciprocal Assistance), 61. *See also* Inter-American System
Riveros, Santiago, 73, 84n50
Rodríguez, Félix, 63. *See also* CIA; paramilitaries
Rostow, Walt, 63

S

Samper, Ernesto, 177, 187, 190–91, 202
San Vicente del Caguán, 205, 220, 226, 230, 240n25. *See also zona de despeje*
Sánchez Reisse, Leandro, 72
Sanhueza, María Jesús, 122, 125, 128. *See also* Coordinating Assembly of Secondary Students
Santos, Juan Manuel, 200, 205–6, 211–13, 218, 228, 230, 232–37, 241n39
São Paulo Institute against Violence. *See* Instituto São Paulo Contra Violência

School of the Americas (SOA), 61, 78. *See also* Panama Canal Zone
Second World War, 53, 61–62
Secretariat of Social Defense (Brazil), 157, 168
security dilemma, 29
security doctrine, 8, 55, 58, 60, 68, 78, 81, 215
self-censorship, 116, 122–25, 135
SEMEFO (art project), 96. *See also nota roja*
SENASP (Secretaria Nacional de Segurança Pública), 154
Serviço Nacional de Informações, 63. *See also* DINA; DNII; La Técnica; SIDE
sicarios, 95. *See also pistoleros*
SIDE (Secretaría de Inteligencia del Estado, Argentina), 67. *See also* DINA; DNII; ESMA; La Técnica; Orletti Motors; SIDE
síndrome de la procuraduría, 188–89
Skilling for Peace Project, 199, 201, 205, 227, 235
sleeper institutions, 162
Socialist Party of Chile, 125, 132. *See also* Escalona, Camilo
Special Forces, 62–63, 71, 84, 109, 126, 130, 215, 230. *See also* Green Berets
State Council for the Defense of the Human Person. *See* CEDPH
state terror, 53, 55
Statute for the Defense of Democracy. *See* Decree 180
structural explanations of violence: and kidnapping in Colombia, 173, 182, 193; and Operation Condor, 53, 56–60, 74–79; and student protests in Chile, 114, 116, 133–34, 136; and violence in Brazil, 143, 145–46; applied to Haiti, 20–22, 26–28, 31–32, 35–36, 40–42; theoretical framework, 2–14
Superintendencia de Vigilancia y Seguridad Privada, 190. *See also Convivir*

T

Teachers' College of Puente Alto, 131
Timochenko, 212, 234, 241. *See also* FARC
Transparency International, 40, 52
Trujillo, Carlos Holmes, 191

U

Unión Patriótica, 202
United Nations: MINUSTAH (United Nations Stabilization Mission in Haiti), 25–26; UNDP (United Nations Development Programme), 50, 218, 228; UNHRC (UN Human Rights Council), 70; United Nations Mission in El Salvador, 223
United States: Cold War foreign and economic policy towards Latin America, 58–59; hegemony, 8, 53, 59, 74, 77; involvement in Operation Condor, 71–74; military base in Manta, 78; Mobile Training Teams, 55, 62; occupation of Haiti, 31; US Army Caribbean School (*see* School of the Americas); US Southern Command, 73; US State Department, 45, 83, 119, 203, 210
University of São Paulo, 151, 167–68
Uribe, Álvaro, 178–79, 189, 191–92, 194, 197, 207–8, 210–12, 217, 221–22, 224, 228, 234, 242
USSR, collapse of the, 77

V

Vadora, Julio, 68. *See also* Conference of American Armies
Vargas, Getúlio, 151
Violence and Social Orders, 148–49, 166
violence in Haiti, patterns of, 22, 35
violent pluralism, 2
Viva Rio (foundation), 151

W

War College, 200, 209, 214–15, 224, 229–31
war on terror, 77–78, 82
Washington consensus, 76
weak states, 2, 28, 38, 49
White, Robert, 73
World Bank, 59, 76

Z

Zaldívar, Andrés, 125–26, 139–40. *See also* Interior Ministry (Chile)
Zedillo, Ernesto, 102
zona de despeje, 203–4. *See also* San Vicente del Caguán

Shakespeare
The Natural World
A Reference Guide

Professor
Robert S. Ely